INTERIOR RENOVATION AND RESTORATION OF PRIVATE DWELLINGS

INTERIOR RENOVATION AND RESTORATION OF PRIVATE DWELLINGS

Byron W. Maguire

P T R Prentice Hall, Englewood Cliffs, New Jersey 07632

Library of Congress Cataloging–in–Publication Data

Maguire, Byron W.
    Interior renovation and restoration of private dwellings /
by Byron W. Maguire.
      p. cm.
    Includes index.
    ISBN 0–13–474537–X
    1. Dwellings—Maintenance and repair. I. Title.
TH4817.M338   1994
643'.7—dc20   93–37227
                                                 CIP

Editorial/production
  and interior design: *bookworks*
Artist: *Russ Duckworth*
Cover designer: *Wanda Lubelska*
Copy editor: *Zeiders and Associates*
Manufacturing manager: *Alexis R. Heydt*

© 1994 by P T R Prentice Hall
Prentice-Hall, Inc.
A Paramount Communications Company
Englewood Cliffs, NJ 07632

The publisher offers discounts on this book when ordered
in bulk quantities. For more information, contact:

  Corporate Sales Department
  P T R Prentice Hall
  113 Sylvan Avenue
  Englewood Cliffs, NJ 07632

  Phone: (201) 592–2863
  FAX: (201) 592–2249

Printed in the United States of America

10 9 8 7 6 5 4 3 2 1

ISBN 0-13-474537-X

Prentice-Hall International (UK) Limited, *London*
Prentice-Hall of Australia Pty. Limited, *Sydney*
Prentice-Hall Canada Inc., *Toronto*
Prentice-Hall Hispanoamericana, S.A., *Mexico*
Prentice-Hall of India Private Limited, *New Delhi*
Prentice-Hall of Japan, Inc., *Tokyo*
Simon & Schuster Asia Pte. Ltd., *Singapore*
Editora Prentice-Hall do Brasil, Ltda., *Rio de Janeiro*

CONTENTS

10   ENVIRONMENTAL SYSTEMS (AIR-CONDITIONING AND HEATING SYSTEMS)   289

PREFACE

This book on the interior renovation and restoration of private dwellings has been prepared for both the homeowner and the contractor who must work out renovation or restoration problems with an owner's home. Many jobs are seemingly simple and can be performed by the owner with modest trade skills and knowledge. Other jobs, also seemingly simple, are well beyond the capabilities of the semiskilled homeowner. They require the skill and knowledge of experts to restore the interior to its original condition.

The key to deciding what to do about a problem and how to ensure that the job is done with quality is contained in this book. The information is written in common language rather than technical jargon. The details are varied and informative and provide a basis for intelligent discussion between a contractor and a homeowner. On the other hand, the details may be sufficient for the owner to attempt to perform the jobs. Some of the details include definitions of the problem as seen by an experienced contractor. Following these discussions are alternative solutions that provide the owner with several options, which can be performed for various costs.

It is important to understand what constitutes a contract for restoration. Each project contains information pertaining to contracting for the work. *Statements of work* describe the specifications that form the foundation of a good-quality contract. Sample contract descriptions and contents are provided. Some are fixed-price types and others are various time-and-materials types. Reasons for their selection are provided in relation to fairness to both parties.

Scoping the work effort is often a major problem for an owner. Trying to determine how much materials and labor will be required, what types of materials and skills will be needed to make the restoration, and other concerns are satisfied in the *Material Assessment and Activities Planning Chart* for the number of days to complete each phase of the work sections in each Project.

Beyond these details, we give descriptions as to how the work will progress which provide a sense of how much normal living will be interrupted. They are also important in understanding why high-quality workmanship takes time.

For the contractor, we have provided a structure of understanding how to approach the homeowner, who may be unsure and wary. Winning their confidence that your work is first quality and that their satisfaction is paramount can be a demanding undertaking. Many ideas regarding integrity and interaction are expressed in the text.

Being honest with the owner is important. The contractor is in business to provide a high-quality service and product but to stay in business, must also make a profit. To this end, the owner of this book will understand the need for adding overhead and profit to the costs of direct labor and materials. Sometimes we address these items as variable costs and fixed costs. We know that no profit can be made until all fixed costs for the year have been covered by funds received from completed contracts. We know that variable costs such as insurance and travel must be accounted for, for every job; yet they are not materials, nor are they labor. We have provided the owner with clear facts about these requirements so that he or she can understand what a fair price is and how it is established. The contract need not specify these items, but the work-up sheet in the office will indicate them clearly.

There are ten chapters in the book. Each is focused on a specific part of the interior of a private dwelling. Within each chapter there are specific projects, as outlined in the contents. These were chosen specifically to be broad in scope so that many aspects could be discussed. However, I felt that although they needed to be broad for study purposes, the contractor or owner also needed a quick reference list that could pinpoint a problem. Therefore, I have included an appendix with this detail. The list identifies some 149 different problems and directs the reader where to find details corresponding to them.

Chapter 1 covers a wide range of problems related to walls and ceilings. These parts of the house take a severe beating from everyday living and from physical damage due to storms, fire, and the like. A multitude of things can go wrong, and most of them are explained and fixed. Discussions range from damaged drywall and plaster to restoring paneling and wainscot and replacing wallpaper.

Chapter 2 continues the discussion on ceilings. In this chapter we describe a variety of textured, plastered, tile, and drop ceilings. There are many solutions and these are explained.

Chapter 3 deals with floors. We deal with strip and block wood flooring, resilient (vinyl and others) flooring over a wood base and over a concrete base, replacing carpeting, and how to restore terrazzo, marble, ceramic and clay tiles, and brick. Because there is such a wide variety of materials from which to choose, there are problems unique to each and we discuss these. We provide ample details on how to solve problems with squeaky floors, problems with failed cements, damaged surfaces and solutions for all the problems.

In Chapter 4 we spend a lot of time explaining how damaged interior doors and their frames are repaired and replaced. Both the unit door and on-site door installations are covered in detail. Doors are a problem over time. Every imaginable problem that can go wrong is covered in this chapter. We provide details on how to make the door fit better and close snugly. We also describe problems with closet bifold doors and pocket doors. Solutions to these kinds of problems are included.

In Chapter 5 we find solutions to problems concerning interior trim. Because millions of homeowners have homes over thirty years old, we provide details on how to restore their baseboard, door and window trim, chair rails, and ceiling molding. We also discuss how to restore moldings in more modern homes, which use less molding and trim and much simpler designs.

Chapter 6 shifts from the parts of the home that require carpentry skills to electrical service. A wide variety of problems are identified and alternative solutions are provided. Some include restoring the quality and service of switches, outlets, and lighting fixtures and replacing fuses and circuit breakers. We even have a project to restore serviceability to an entry bell or chimes.

Chapter 7 shifts from carpentry and electrical skills to plumbing. These problems deal with damaged or inoperable commodes and water closets, repairing and replacing water faucets and valves, refurbishing the hot-water heater, and removing and replacing appliances that use plumbing. We discuss the need to clean waste lines and to make sure that all connections have the proper parts and are made leak-proof. We discuss the old water systems and how today's products can be substituted.

Chapter 8 focuses on staircases. Several types of construction are used to create a staircase and each is illustrated. We also provide descriptions of each and identify the problems that can happen. Details on correcting the problems are clear and show how difficult the work is. Some of the areas covered include damaged stringers, treads and risers, bullnose and other moldings, integrating the staircase trim with the room baseboard, and problems with newel posts and banisters. Another important feature is the project on refinishing the staircase. In one project we fully examine transparent finishes, and in the next we discuss recarpeting the treads and risers. Most of these jobs require extensive skill and experience to perform; however, refinishing the staircase, for example, can be done by the homeowner.

Chapter 9 provides solutions to all the problems that can happen to interior cabinets. Except for the catastrophic damage caused by natural or other causes, most problems with interior cabinets happens gradually. When the time to react occurs, usually more than one problem needs work. The chapter is organized to solve problems with doors first. Then we describe the tasks needed to restore the interior parts of the cabinets, which include drawers, roll-out shelves, and adjustable shelves. The next project covers countertops made from ceramic and plastic and the ways they are constructed. The final project describes the work and products needed to restore the exterior of the cabinets.

Chapter 10 provides solutions to many problems that owners have with heating and air-conditioning systems. First, we examine all the maintenance tasks needed to keep the system and subsystems operating properly. Many of these can be done simply by owners, thus avoiding maintenance expenses. Some are best done by experts. We also discuss the subject of annual and as-required contracts for maintenance that sometimes result in a reasonable contract price. The remainder of the chapter is divided into projects that aid us in understanding forced-air systems, refrigerated air-conditioning systems, heat pump systems, and hot-water and steam heating systems. These subjects provide considerable insight into the complexities and dangers of making restorations.

Problems, suggested solutions, materials and labor details, contract definitions, and descriptions and studies are given in the sequence in which work must be done. This is a handy book to have in your reference file in your home or office. Homeowners can readily locate a problem discussion and read about the options for corrective action. Contractors can use it for quick reference on how to approach a job and an owner, and may also use it as a reminder of how to develop fair and equitable contracts.

Good luck with the efforts you make to maintain the quality of a home regardless of its age.

Byron W. Maguire

INTERIOR RENOVATION AND RESTORATION OF PRIVATE DWELLINGS

1

WALLS AND CEILINGS

OBJECTIVES

To review the elements of a construction contract
To restore damaged drywall or ceiling
To reinstall loosened paneling
To strip and refinish wainscot
To repaint walls and ceilings
To replace wallpaper
To repair damaged lath and plaster walls and ceilings

OPENING COMMENTS

Conditions or circumstances that necessitate corrective action. Let's begin with conditions on walls and in some cases ceilings caused by family members. (Several special treatments of ceilings are covered in Chapter 2.) Scars made from toys banging into walls, smoke from cigarettes, pipes, and cigars, furniture being moved and striking the walls, horseplay that causes dents and breakthrough in drywall materials, falling through the ceiling from the attic, and failed attempts to make patches on walls and ceilings round out most of the causes.

Natural conditions also cause damage to one degree or another. Storm damage that blows rain through a broken window and soaks drywall or paneling is one cause. Others are a broken water pipe, damaged wastewater connections, a leaking commode or an overflow from the evaporator coils in an air-conditioning system, and damaged ceilings due to roof leaks. Still others are caused by workers, homeowners, and friends of the owner. These include improperly installed tape on joints, insufficient compound over nails, and improperly prepared ceilings that cause paint to peel off.

Fire causes catastrophic problems on ceiling and walls. Even though drywall has a fire rating (if that type was used), it will burn. Beyond that, smoke rolls across the ceilings if the doors are left open during the fire. Firefighters cause damage to walls and ceilings to gain access to the flames and smoldering inside the walls and in the ceiling.

Other wall materials can also cause problems for the owner. Wood paneling fades when sun strikes the wall, and this means that some walls look good, others lackluster. Wainscot-covered walls look poor if numerous coats of paint or varnish have been applied. Adding more paint makes things worse. Ceramic tiles fall off the wall, grout becomes contaminated with fungus and mold and must be restored, and wallpaper either fades or falls free of the wall at joints and along borders and needs replacing. Finally, nail holes, window brackets, and valances create problems that require repair.

Any one or a combination of these conditions can require the expert assistance of a carpenter, painter, wallpaper hanger, tile setter, or drywall installer to restore the walls and ceilings.

Contractor's responsibility.   We, as contractors, can be faced with either of two situations pertaining to restoring walls and ceilings using the same materials or coverings in a residential home. The first problem occurs when the amount of work is insufficient to have a worker dedicated to the job. This happens when less than a day's work restores the damaged wall or its covering. The other is finding a perfect match for the wall materials or wallcovering. Manufacturers prepare materials in "lot quantities." This means that the chemical makeup used to manufacture tiles, wallpaper, paints, and other materials differs slightly from batch to batch or lot to lot. The differences are slight, but noticeable. Further considerations include the aging of the wall and its covering. Sun, smoke, cooking smoke and oils, and human oils change the character, feel, intensity, color and luster of wall coverings. Matching is almost impossible.

Restoring walls also presents other problems for the contractor. In many situations restoration would be cost prohibitive, causing the owner to rebel and feel taken advantage of. Some owners do not comprehend the cost of operating a company and the effects these costs have on the bid/contract price. A simple task of cleaning the dirt from ceiling deflectors can be done in minutes with the proper materials, for example. Yet we would not readily accept such a job since the minimum wages would be a full day's work at the contractor price. This price will vary from locale to locale and section to section of the country. In one area the price might be as low as $20 per worker hour. In another the price might be $65 per worker hour. Using an 8-hour day as a standard for this example, we readily see a total cost to the owner ranging from $160 in one area to $520 a day.

Yet we must find a way to satisfy our customer. One method is to satisfy more than one need when working with the owner. When the owner asks for help, the problems are usually well advanced. We usually find this to be the situation. Therefore, we can incorporate a wide variety of repair actions under the umbrella of a single contract. In this way we can reduce our costs and provide the owner with a reasonable price.

Finally, as contractors, we work with insurance adjusters and agents when they are called in by the owner. These people are generally expert in assessing the costs of various damages to ceilings and walls. They may also seek out contractors and other tradespeople to provide us with estimates.

Homeowner's expectations.   The homeowner expects two things from us: (1) the work must restore the wall or ceiling to its original state; and (2) the cost needs to be minimized. If the damage is the result of storms or fire where the homeowner's insurance covers all or most of the restoration, it is unlikely that the owner will be too concerned by costs, except for the standard deduction, which is usually a minimum of $250.

In many situations involving restoration of walls and ceilings, the homeowner is frustrated because contractors and jobbers will not respond to their needs. Once again we are back to the concerns cited above regarding the problems these workers would have in obtaining matching materials and the short duration of a very small project. The owner must rely on persuasion and constant follow up to have a contractor even take on a small job. Most of the time the work will be done between major construction contracts or on weekends as fill-in jobs.

It is very important for the owner to know that there are many tasks associated with each restoration. The following projects provide details that expose these tasks and provide an idea of the various decisions the contractor or jobber will use to make the wall or ceiling of first quality again.

Homeowners who elect to use this book as a source document to effect restoration will require considerable time and effort to accomplish even the simplest job. He or she will incur travel times, specialized tool requirements, special materials, and various principles of construction required to perform the tasks. In this area of consideration, the owner must compare the economics of do-it-yourself against using the contractor. Where the owner earns $240 a day for labor and a 2-day job costs $400, the owner will definitely elect to work rather than doing the job himself or herself.

Scope of projects.   There are so many materials used on walls that we cover a wide variety in the following projects. They generally fall into the categories of drywall, wood paneling, wallpaper, ceramic tile, and wainscot. We define problems with these materials and suggest corrective actions.

PROJECT 1. REVIEW THE ELEMENTS OF A CONSTRUCTION CONTRACT

Subcategories include: contract parties; location of work to be done; description of the work; price; any conditions or limitations; expectations of the owner and contractor; and sometimes, a warranty.

Preliminary Discussion with the Owner

Problems facing the owner.   In the first volume of this two-volume set, we described a great deal about the various parties entering into a contract. One important item worth repeating is the need to have a written contract rather than a handshake or oral contract. Often, the contractor will describe numerous solutions during the discovery phase of assessing the job. As an owner, you will naturally key in on the most desirable solution, which may be the most costly. Then when the subject shifts to price, you may well assume that the best solution was at the least cost, when in fact it was something else. This mix-up is very prevalent and happens most often when an owner is under stress or pressure to make repairs or restorations.

Owners must establish a clear set of parameters; these need to be stated clearly to the contractor. In fact, it would be good to have them written down. Your goal is to ensure that you have a fair and equitable contract.

Alternative solutions to the problem.   The contractor will often require the assistance of subcontractors to perform the work. He or she will act as general contractor in this case. A contract produced by the general contractor can be all-encompassing with little breakout. This may not be satisfactory to the owner, since the specifications of the subcontractors may not be stated. Thus the owner may want the contractor to provide alternatives where subcontractors' bids are defined. Or you may desire that the single contract have specific paragraphs pertaining to electrical work, plumbing and heating work, and painting work, for example.

Consider the fact that in some cases a contractor can provide a single-price contract that is of fixed-price type. In other situations he or she may offer a time-and-materials contract. There are also variations of each. In every case, the contractor is responsible to ensure a fair price for high-quality work.

Statement of work and the planning effort.   Every contract includes the essence of statements of work. These express, in words, what will be done by workers, the materials that will be used, and the quality and timeliness of the work. The body of the contract must include these factors in sufficient detail for your understanding. They also provide the contractor with parameters within which he or she must operate.

Contract.   The basic parts must be included in every contract. Next we examine the elements of a complete, legal contract.

1. *Parties and geographical location.*   The physical characteristics of any job—the names and locations of the principal parties and the location of the property where the work is to be done—must be included.

2. *Competent parties.*   As contractors, we are one-half of the "competent parties," and the building owner or homeowner or his or her legal agent is the other half of those who can enter into a contract.

3. *Lawful subject or object.*   The fact that we are contracting to restore a roof and cornice to its original condition is a lawful subject. We must describe the subject or object in sufficient detail to isolate it to avoid misunderstanding.

4. *Legal consideration.*   Both parties must receive a legal consideration. As the contractor, we receive a check for payment. The owner in this case gets a renovated roof and cornice.

5. *Mutuality of agreement.*   In this section of the contract, four parts must be considered and included as necessary:

a. The offer of acceptance must be unqualified—there must be no terms or conditions (no coercion).

b. With construction contracts the bidding documents usually constitute agreement and form mutual agreement when accepted.

c. Times, turnkey dates, payment schedules, and other schedules are elements of mutual agreements in construction contracts.

d. Quality standards may also become elements of mutual agreement. These standards could pertain to materials and workmanship.

6. *Mutuality of obligation or genuine intent.* Both parties must truly and willingly intend to enter into the contract. Both parties must be on the lookout for invalidation. Honest mistakes can and should be worked out reasonably. Since we, the contractors, are submitting the bid/contract proposal, we must make clear the conditions that fall under this element. We must not fraudulently state intent; and we must expect the owner to have the money to pay for the work before the job starts.

For example, a job contract could look like this:

Contractor   Building Contractors
                                              123 Main Street
                                              State, ZIP
                                           Ph 123/444-5555

Owner   Proposal for: Mr. and Mrs. Jones
Location   Address

Body   Description and Estimate: Replacement of roof shingles. This includes the removal of the old roof and installation of new shingles with a 20-year life span. The job includes complete removal of all waste and debris. The job also includes the replacement of fascia along the north wall of the building and repainting the entire cornice. This proposal is good for 30 days.

Price   Total cost, tax included: $2300.00.

Material Assessment

Normally, a contract does not list the direct, indirect, and support materials. Sometimes on larger restorations a specification sheet will be prepared to list the materials by type or manufacturer. In this chapter and the remaining ones, we expend considerable effort listing the materials needed to accomplish each project. This type of spec sheet provides owners with a frame of reference to judge whether or not all aspects of a specific job have been covered. We, as contractors, use the list to ensure that owners are assured of a clear understanding as to how we arrived at the materials cost of contracts.

As contractors, we would not list the purpose for each material or support item. But in text where the reader needs as much fact as possible and a complete model to work from, we include the purpose or use of the item listed. The major headings deal with *direct materials and their uses/purposes, indirect materials and their uses/purposes, support materials and their uses/purposes,* and *outside contractor support and their uses/purposes.*

Activities Planning Chart

Each job is a collection of activities. In this book we select the major activities that constitute a job. Each activity is a group of related tasks that must be done by the workers. As we shall see, some workers operate out of the contractor's office. They are his or her staff and assistants and include the scheduler, estimator, clerks, typists, accountant, and the like.

Each person who contributes to the job uses time that must be accounted for and paid for. Time may be calculated in many ways. Most often, office personnel time is calculated on an hourly basis. For example, the estimator may charge 4 hours to a job. But workers on the job are usually calculated on a full day's wages. Even if the job takes only 3 hours to complete, the contractor needs to charge a full day's wages, since there is a small likelihood that the worker can earn money for the contractor for the remainder of the day, yet he or she wants a full day's wages.

In our book we make an activities chart like the one below.

Activity	Time Line (Days)						
	1	2	3	4	5	6	7
1. Contract preparation	|_×_|	| ___ |	| ___ |	| ___ |	| ___ |	| ___ |	| ___ |
2. Materials and scheduling	|_×_|	| ___ |	| ___ |	| ___ |	| ___ |	| ___ |	| ___ |
3. Removing the old flooring	| ___ |	|_×_|	| ___ |	| ___ |	| ___ |	| ___ |	| ___ |
4. Installating the new flooring	| ___ |	|_×_|	|_×_|	| ___ |	| ___ |	| ___ |	| ___ |
5. Applying the floor finish	| ___ |	| ___ |	|_×_|	|_×_|	| ___ |	| ___ |	| ___ |

Reconstruction and Concluding Comments

In each project we provide significant detail about the work performed by the various tradespeople and office personnel. This detail helps explain the use of the materials and time associated with each phase of the job.

PROJECT 2. RESTORE DAMAGED DRYWALL

Subcategories include: drywall construction techniques; joint compound and its application; taping; repairing holes; repairing exposed joints; repairing inside and outside corners; and adding corner protection.

Preliminary Discussion with the Owner

Problems facing the owner.   Except for those houses that have plastered walls and ceilings, homes generally have walls covered with drywall. These are panels of paper-covered gypsum that are easily cut to fit and are easy to install.

Many years ago the standard $\frac{3}{8}$-in. drywall thickness was used for walls and ceiling in homes and light commercial buildings. Today the standard thickness is $\frac{1}{2}$-in., which provides better strength and has a higher fire containment rating. We also installed the pieces vertically years ago, whereas today, most contractors install the pieces horizontally. As in the early days, the manufactured long side/edge is recessed to accept the tape and joint compound. This all but eliminates visual traces of the joint.

Drywall installers apply several coats of joint compound to the seams and over the nail heads. Each coat fills progressively more of the materials to be covered.

This lead-in provides a simple understanding about the installation and basic finishing techniques. When an owner has problems with drywall, understanding the facts of installation can quickly lead to identifying the problems that can happen and their repair. For example, the problem of damaged walls or ceiling caused by door knobs, hard objects puncturing walls or ceiling, or other objects, such as furniture, tearing and gouging the walls all create one form of serious problem. Another set of problems is related to improperly applied tape and compound. When this happens the tape edges peel away from the drywall, corners built up with folded tape pull loose, and the wall's appearance becomes progressively worse.

The problem may be simple enough to use a self-help method. The supply house can provide new rolls of tape and ready-made cans of joint compound and the tools to make the repairs. We shall describe some of these procedures later. When it comes to larger damaged areas, though, the contractor may be best equipped to make the restoration. If, for example, there was water damage to the drywall, or large areas of wall or ceiling that sustained physical damage, we are describing extensive work. First the damaged materials must be removed, and this means that moldings and baseboards need to be removed as well. There will probably be electrical outlets, switches, TV outlets, and telephone outlets to cut out. There is much more fitting and cutting and thus much more taping and finishing. Whereas a small job can be attempted by the owner, the larger jobs should be done by people with special skills.

Alternative solutions to the problem.   The solutions to the list of problems identified above are standard. Holes can be patched and floated to all but eliminate any trace of damage. Loosened tape can be replaced with new tape and compound. Outside corners originally installed without protective metal corners can be made more durable by installing metal corners and then applying compound, eventually floating the wall about 12 in. from the corner. All water-damaged drywall must be removed and replaced with like kind. There is no alternative to this solution.

Statement of work and the planning effort.   For this project we will use a contractor not only to restore the drywall damaged by water but also to make long-needed repairs to other walls and to a place in the ceiling. This job will enable us to study how to make a wide variety of repairs. Our first statement of work is *remove and replace the damaged drywall in the utility room,* where the cause was a broken pipe in the wall. Removing and replacing it is not sufficiently clear. We must also include the statement to *finish the wallboard and apply a seal coat and two top coats of paint.* We must also stipulate the repairs to the dents and scars in the wall, such as *make repairs to dents caused by door handles in the bathrooms and middle bedroom, a 6-in. scar in the entrance wall, and after finishing the repairs, paint the walls with a matching color.* Our last statement must be directed at the damaged ceiling, where something heavy fell above and cracked the ceiling drywall, causing a line about 18 in. long and a sag of about 1 in. Our statement of work here is to *restore the ceiling to a flat surface and repaint it to match the rest of the house.*

There is enough work included in these statements to require the special skills of a drywall contractor and painter. We will assume that the plumber has already removed some of the drywall to make repairs to the broken pipe. When we arrive on the job site, we are guided to the utility room first, where we take measurements and then examine the other problems. We must plan to bring materials to the job, employ one drywall installer, take several days to make repairs, and then apply three coats of compound. Finally, we need to subcontract with a painter to repaint the walls and ceiling.

Our plans also call for a trip by the painter to determine the materials that he or she needs and the time estimate to perform the work. Finally, we will meet with the owner to agree on the contract price and sign the agreements.

Contract.   In this situation we can offer the owner a fixed-price contract. Both the drywall installer and the painter can readily determine the extent of work to be done. From this they can prepare their bids. We could be a general contractor who has persons with the needed skills and our office can prepare the contract offer, or we can act as general contractor and subcontract all the work. For this contract we would use our letterhead or company contract/bid offer form. Both would have our company name and location.

The owner's name and location would be the second party in the contract. If the location were different from the address of the owner, we would include both addresses.

In the body of the contract, we would describe the work to be accomplished from the statements of work. In this instance it could be similar to the following:

For the price indicated below, we agree to make repairs to the damaged walls and ceiling. These are as follows:

a. Repair the ceiling in the den where the drywall is partially broken through. The entire room's ceiling will be spray painted.
b. Replace the damaged drywall behind the washer and dryer. Work includes finishing the drywall and painting the entire wall.
c. Repair the three dents in the walls in the baths and bedroom and repaint the walls.
d. Repair the scar in the entrance and repaint the wall.

We will ensure quality work, safety to the possessions as much as possible, and leave no evidence of our materials. The owner agrees to remove the furniture from the room where the ceiling will be painted and any paintings or other personal belongings hanging on walls to be painted.

Due to the times required for the materials to set and dry, we will make several visits. At these times we will require a member of the family to be at home to permit entry and assist with any final decisions, should there be any.

We agree to perform the work for the total price of $xxx.xx.

Material Assessment

Direct Materials	Use/Purpose
$\frac{1}{2}$-in. drywall	To replace the damaged materials
Drywall nails	To nail drywall in place
Joint compound	To cover tape, joints, and nails
Drywall sealer	To seal the new surfaces
Wall primer	To prime the walls
Wall paint	Selected colors to match other walls
Ceiling paint	Textured-blown ceiling (spray paint)

Indirect Materials	Use/Purpose
Sheet vinyl (plastic)	To drape over furnishings
Masking tape	To tape vinyl in place
Roller	Paint roller head
Paintbrushes	Disposable brushes

Support Materials	Use/Purpose
Paint spray outfit	To spray ceiling
Ladders	For access to ceiling
Carpentry tools	For construction
Drywaller's tools	For construction
Painter's tools	For construction

Outside Contractor Support	Use/Purpose
Drywall	To make repairs
Painter	To restore the walls and ceilings

Activities Planning Chart

Activity	Time Line (Days)						
	1	2	3	4	5	6	7
1. Contract preparation	I _×_ I ___ I ___ I ___ I ___ I ___ I ___ I
2. Materials and scheduling	I _×_ I ___ I ___ I ___ I ___ I ___ I ___ I
3. Repairing the wall	I ___ I _×_ I _×_ I _×_ I ___ I ___ I ___ I
4. Repairing the ceiling	I ___ I _×_ I _×_ I _×_ I ___ I ___ I ___ I
5. Painting	I ___ I ___ I ___ I ___ I _×_ I _×_ I ___ I

Reconstruction

Contract preparation.   Our office personnel will expect two separate bids, one from the drywall contractor and the other from the painter. With these, we will add a small fee for administrative costs and permits and a small amount for profit and the hourly rate for times expended meeting with the owner.

Materials and scheduling.   The subcontractors will bring the materials they need to the job with them. All materials are readily available and there should be no delay in completing the job due to materials.

Since the drywall contractor will need 3 days and the painter 2 days, we need to have the owner assist us in scheduling the work. The activity list shows the contractors working in serial. When the drywall contractor is done, the painter begins. Actually when we agree on a schedule, there may be several days or more between the time the drywaller finishes and the painter begins. In total the job should take 5 working days.

Drywall repairs and preparation for painting.   We have several problems to solve. First is the utility room wall, second are the dents in the walls, and third is the scar in the hall.

In the utility room, we need first to establish how much more drywall must be cut away to have sound nailing for the new materials. Figure 1–1 shows some of these requirements. The new drywall must be soundly nailed to the studs. What we do is measure the opening and transfer the dimensions to the new piece, cut it, and nail it in place. Then we apply a piece of tape up from the floor and across the joint. (Figure 1–1 also shows this.) Since there is nailing in the stud not covered by the tape, we must drive the nail head slightly below the surface to allow us to apply

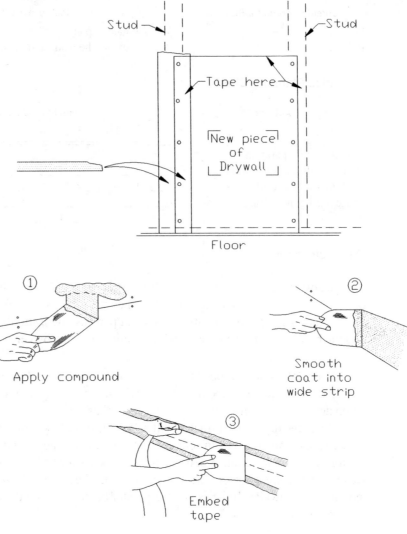

① Apply compound

② Smooth coat into wide strip

③ Embed tape

④ Skim coat of compound over taped joint

⑤ Float coat

Figure 1–1   Solving problems on drywall.

compound. Tomorrow a second coat of compound is added, and a third coat is applied the following day. Each of the second and third coats is applied wider than the undercoat.

Where the dents are not broken through, we can apply several coats of compound, allowing each to dry thoroughly to permit full shrinkage. However, when a dent turns out to be a puncture through the wall, a different technique is required. Figure 1–2 shows this as a series of actions. We may need to enlarge the hole to insert a patch. The patch is buttered and slipped into the opening, positioned appropriately, and pulled firmly toward the back of the drywall. When this dries, we cut another small piece of drywall to fit into the opening. Then we butter the back of this piece and carefully fit it into the opening. After the compound has dried, we will probably tape the edges, or we might apply several coats of compound, each successively wider. When all coats have been applied, we sand the surface smooth, removing all marks made with the trowel or putty knife.

Ceiling restoration.   In our project the ceiling was sprayed with a textured paint mixture. This might appear to make the repair more difficult, but it does not. We need to define where the ceiling joists are, and this can be done from the attic

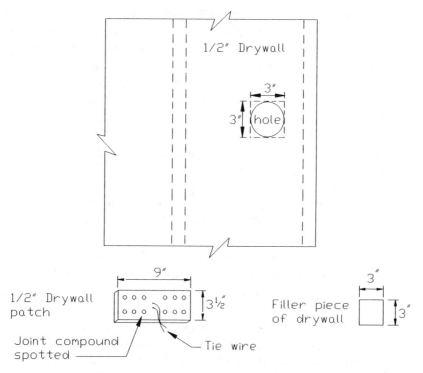

Figure 1–2   Repairing a hole in the drywall.

or by sounding the ceiling from below. We would draw lines indicating them. Then we can determine where to cut away the damaged ceiling. After the piece has been removed, we scrape away the ceiling paint around the hole about 6 to 10 in. back from the opening. This provides a flat surface on which to apply tape and float the joint.

After the new piece is installed, tape is used around the four sides. Then two additional coats of compound are applied on successive days. Finally, we sand the surface to remove all trowel marks. The ceiling is now ready for painting.

Scarred wall.   The long, deep scar in the entrance wall did not fully penetrate the wallboard. However, we must make the repair invisible by preventing a bulge, which could cause a shadow under some circumstances. For this job we employ a technique used in body and fender repair. We take a ball peen hammer and carefully dent the area around the scar to slightly wider than a strip of tape. We can do this without breaking the paper even though the plaster is crushed slightly. In the dented area we paste in a short strip of tape and apply some compound on top of the tape. From then on, we treat the problem as we would any other joint. Finally, we sand it smooth.

Painting the restored walls and ceiling.   The painter takes over the job now. New drywall needs to be sealed first so that the paint takes better. On the walls the painter applies several coats of latex paint which matches the opposite and adjacent walls. This could be a single color, or each room may have its own color. When custom-mixed colors are on the walls, the painter has more work matching. In this case, the job costs more. When the paint cannot be matched economically, the entire room is painted. This would have been stipulated in the contract.

In patching the ceiling, the painter has also stipulated in the price that the entire ceiling would be repainted rather than just painting the repair. The entire job proceeds in the following sequence:

1. The painter moves all remaining furnishings to the middle of the room.
2. The painter masks the walls with masking tape and large sheets of clear plastic/vinyl sheets.
3. The floor and furnishings are covered with drop cloths.
4. The spray gun and paint are prepared and the gun is loaded.
5. The painter starts at the patch area by applying a light coat over the area to begin the buildup.
6. The entire ceiling is sprayed (blown), including the repaired area.
7. The painter examines the entire ceiling for uniform density and coverage. If the repaired area is slightly less covered, he or she adds another thin application.
8. Cleanup follows.

Concluding comments.   The homeowner who has some skill could do personally many of the repairs described here. However, a painter should be employed for the ceiling. Considerable skill is required to operate the spray gun and to throw textured paint onto the ceiling.

One important element of the job that can make the finished product either perfect or a mess is the application of successive coats of compound and the sanding operations. No shortcuts can be taken, and the job cannot be rushed.

The job we have used in this example can easily cost more than $300. Even though the workers actually use less than 8 hours, the job is charged at the daily rate. However, a well-qualified jobber with the skills and tools may charge less.

As contractors, we would fit this job in between others when our schedules are jammed. When we do, we can sometimes perform the work as fill-in, or we might forgo profit for goodwill.

PROJECT 3. REINSTALL LOOSENED WALL PANELING

Subcategories include: types of wall paneling; techniques of applying paneling to studs, furring strips, and drywall; repairing loosened panels; and reapplying molding.

Preliminary Discussion with the Owner

Problems facing the owner.   Vertically installed wood paneling usually reaches from the floor to ceiling. The vertical joints are butted. Ceiling cove molding is used along the ceiling. Baseboard is used along the floor. In some installations the corners are fitted closely with no molding. In other installations corners are not closely fitted and cove molding is used to cover the poorly fitted corner. In most installations the door frames are removed and the paneling is fitted to the opening. Then the frame is reinstalled. This works well with modern adjustable-width door units. In earlier handcrafted jambs and casing installations, the casings are removed, a furring strip is used to widen the jamb the thickness of the paneling, and the casings are reinstalled. In installations with very old casings, the casings are subject to damage if removed. When this is true, the paneling is closely fitted around the casing and usually across the baseboard as well. When the workmanship is of good quality, moldings are not required since the fit is perfect. When the workmanship is less than perfect, small shoe or quarter-round moldings are stained and varnished and nailed to the wall to cover poor workmanship. Almost all of these conditions also apply to window treatment, except that windows are not supplied with casings as units.

In addition to the differences in installation, we are always faced with the type, style, color, and finish of the paneling. Most of the best panels are plywood, about $\frac{1}{4}$ in. thick, and have expensive hardwood veneers on the face side. Cheaper panels are made from particleboard covered with hardwood veneers or vinyl simulating wood grains. These panels are seldom $\frac{1}{4}$ in. thick; more often than not, they are $\frac{3}{16}$ or $\frac{1}{8}$ in. thick and thus have less strength than that of $\frac{1}{4}$-in. panels. The glues are almost always interior grade and thus are not capable of withstanding excessive moisture over a prolonged period of time or water over a short period. The particleboard varieties crumble when they become wet and are then dried.

Finally, some installations are applied over drywall with nails and glue, or just nails; other installations cover old and damaged plastered walls where nails or glue or both were used; and in some cases, not approved by building codes, the paneling is applied directly to studs.

From these descriptions, we can see that an owner who has paneling that has buckled, loosened, or through abuse does not fit well has to understand the conditions that existed when the paneling was installed before a sound judgment can be made about restoration. Numerous problems are possible:

1. The glue has dried and the joint has separated.
2. The toenailed edge nails missed the studs.
3. The paneling absorbed excessive moisture and buckled.
4. Something or someone fell into the wall and broke the glue seal or caused the nails to pull free.
5. During installation the workers did not make the joints over a wall stud (between studs) and the joint pulled apart over time.
6. The corner joints do not fit as well as before, due to settling in the house.
7. Storm damage freed the paneling.
8. Jarring by the door banging into the paneling broke loose the joint.
9. A panel was removed by workers to make repairs to electrical service or plumbing. Unfortunately, paneling is made by lots and by several different companies. After a relatively short period of time (2 years or so) manufacturers change colors, patterns, and finishes. Thus new panels that match the old are not available.

When so many variables exist in combinations, the owner is faced with selecting the one that corrects the problem at least cost and prevents further damage or extended damage to the finish on the paneling or its moldings.

Alternative solutions to the problem.   We, as contractors, need to examine the problem and ascertain the conditions under which the paneling was applied to the wall initially. Some of the answers can be obtained by questioning. The owner can tell if the paneling was installed over studs, drywall, or plaster. He or she can state if the under-wall surface was sound or damaged—the paneling may cover a mess. He or she may even have been home when the paneling was installed and can tell if glue and nails were used or just nails. Unless the owner is knowledgeable about construction, he or she may not know if the panel joints were placed over studs. However, we can tell readily by sounding the wall with a hammer.

Some of the alternative solutions are simple; others are more complex. The simple one is to free the joints from ceiling to floor and apply new ones. Fresh glue is used between the wall and the panel and then pressure is applied to the joint. Then we replace the ceiling molding and baseboard. Where the wall behind the paneling lacks soundness—for example, when plaster has deteriorated—we may be able to use color-coated nails to restore the paneling. But sometimes we need to remove the panel and put fillers in place, then reinstall the panel. In more difficult cases, we might need to remove and reglue a glued panel without breaking or cracking it. This is not simple.

The most expensive alternative may apply when the paneling has been split or cracked and a new piece must be found for replacement. This may not be possible. We need to convey this information to the owner and suggest that if we cannot match the panel, we replace the paneling along the entire wall with some that matches very closely. Due to light striking the walls and bouncing around, a slight difference may not be readily apparent. Finally, we can recommend refastening the loose panel and suggest that the wall be painted.

Statement of work and the planning effort.   For our problem we will assume that several conditions happened at once as the result of a damaging storm. The storm broke a window and allowed water to enter a room. It ran down the wall into a joint under the window and into the baseboard. The drywall under the paneling became soaked and now shows mildew. The paneling buckled, but the surface finish seems unaffected. Our first statement of work is a general description: *Restore the wall to its original condition.* This is not sufficiently detailed. We must stipulate several factors, such as *all damaged drywall will be removed and replaced, wall insulation behind the drywall will also be replaced, and window trim and baseboard will be removed, reinstalled, and refinished as needed to match the old finish.* We should state that *the original paneling will be reused.* But if the piece is broken when removed, we must make that a condition. Finally, we need to *restore damaged or water-stained window trim and baseboard to their original condition.*

Figure 1–3 illustrates the details that affect our work. As in this job the window trim, baseboard, and ceiling molding were installed over the paneling, we must remove them without breaking or splitting any pieces. We also need to anticipate that the paneling was glued and nailed to the drywall. For planning purposes we need to use our most experienced carpenter for this job. We may need to remove and reinstall more than the pieces that make up the joint. This means that several

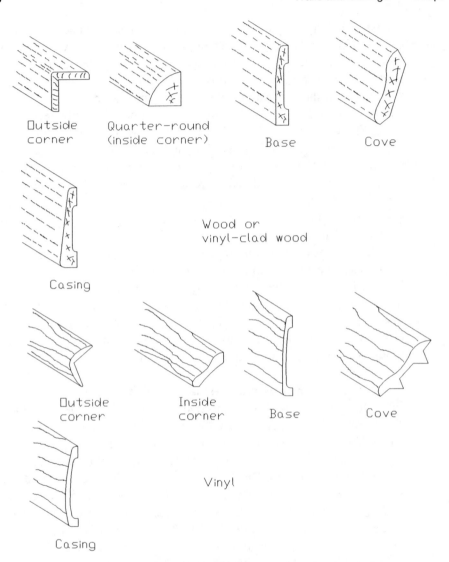

Outside corner   Quarter-round (inside corner)   Base   Cove

Casing

Wood or vinyl-clad wood

Outside corner   Inside corner   Base   Cove

Casing

Vinyl

Figure 1–3   Trim installed over paneling.

sheets of drywall may need to be removed and replaced. We won't know this until the paneling is removed. We would also have added problems meeting the statements of work if the paneling were particleboard and veneer, but by examining the joint, we found that we had high-quality $\frac{1}{4}$-in.-thick paneling with hardwood veneer.

We will need several kinds of materials but they can all fit into the back of a pickup truck and are readily available. The carpenter can pick up all the materials on the first day of work. The job should last only 2 days.

Contract.   A fixed-price contract is best for the work described in the statements of work. We have enough empirical data to price the work and materials accurately. The body of the contract should be simple to construct since only one wall of the room is involved in the restoration. We should, however, include a clause pertaining to possible unforeseen damage to the panels to be removed and reinstalled. The body could look like this:

We agree to restore the damaged wall to its original condition. We will preserve the original paneling to the greatest extent possible, but in the unforseeable chance that it is damaged, the cost of new paneling will be an added cost above the price stated below.

We also agree to remove and replace damaged drywall and insulation under the paneling. Where the window trim and baseboard is water stained, we will refinish it.

One member of the owner's family will be required to be home when the carpenter performs the work. A scheduled date will be agreed to.

Materials and labor: $xxx.xx.

Material Assessment

Direct Materials	Use/Purpose
Drywall and nails	To replace the water-damaged materials
Batting insulation	To replace the water-damaged materials
Paneling nails	To hold the panel to the wall
Panel glue	To stick panel to drywall
Stain	To touch up window trim and baseboard
Varnish	As top coat of window trim and baseboard
Colored wood putty	To fill nail holes in trim and panels
Furniture wax	To polish the trim and paneling

Indirect Materials	Use/Purpose
Sandpaper	To smooth wood putty and rough wood
Trash bags	To deposit used insulation
Plastic/vinyl sheet	To drape the floor while working on the wall
Mineral spirits	To clean paintbrush
Rags	To wipe excess stain
Steel wool	To polish the varnish to reduce the shine and to smooth
Blades for utility knife	To cut drywall

Support Materials	Use/Purpose
Carpenter tools	For construction
6-ft stepladder	To work at the ceiling
Paintbrush	To apply stain and varnish

<table>
<tr><td>Outside Contractor Support</td><td>Use/Purpose</td></tr>
</table>

None

Activities Planning Chart

Activity	Time Line (Days)						
	1	2	3	4	5	6	7
1. Contract preparation	_×_						
2. Materials and scheduling	_×_						
3. Replacing the damaged materials		_×_					
4. Replacing the paneling and trim		_×_	_×_				
5. Refinishing the paneling and trim			_×_				

Reconstruction

Contract preparation. This is a small restoration job, but the office personnel are still needed to prepare the contract. A bill of materials must be prepared to establish the price of direct and indirect materials and support materials. We must also apply our overhead costs, which would be prorated according to the size and duration of the job. Overall, we should expect the contract to be complete within 1 working day. The contractor would present the contract to the owner for examination and signature.

Materials and scheduling. The carpenter assigned to the job would drive to the lumberyard or builder's supply house and pick up the materials listed by the office personnel. As noted before, the materials will fit easily into a pickup truck. The sheets of drywall are the only materials of any size.

Replacing the damaged materials. The sequence used to replace the damaged materials is as follows:

1. Remove the baseboard along the wall.
2. Remove the ceiling 2-in. cove molding (or whatever kind is there).
3. Remove the window apron and casing.
4. Carefully free the paneling.
5. Remove the damaged drywall.
6. Remove the damaged wall insulation.
7. Install new insulation and drywall.
8. Reinstall the paneling.
9. Reinstall the window trim, baseboard, and ceiling molding.

Now let's discuss some of the special aspects of the tasks listed above.

When removing the baseboard, we must be extremely careful not to crack or split the piece or pieces or mar the paneling. For this job we use a combination of tools: a claw hammer, flat pry bar, thin nail set, and small square of thin wood. The best place to begin is away from the corner. Where the nail heads are easily identified by the putty in the nail hole, we use the nail set to drive the nail farther through the wood. This makes it easier to pry the baseboard free. Next, we carefully drive the flat bar between the top of the baseboard and the paneling, place the thin square of wood behind the bar, and push the bar toward the wall. The baseboard should pop loose. If not, we repeat the steps again and again until the baseboard is loose. Rather than drive the nails back through the front of the baseboard, we pull them through from the back side with a hammer or with lineman's pliers.

We use the same technique to remove the ceiling cove molding. Again we begin away from the corner. Then we work first toward one corner and then toward the other.

There are four pieces of window trim to remove. These are the apron, both side casing pieces, and the head casing piece. We can pry the top casing piece loose easily using the claw hammer. Again we use the thin block of wood to prevent damage to the paneling. Next, we use the claw of the hammer and free the side casing pieces by inserting the claw into the miter and prying the piece loose. Finally, we use the hammer's claw to pry off the apron.

The windowsill should not have to be removed. But if the paneling was glued along the window (usually not done because the casings hold the panel tight to the wall), we might have to remove the sill as well.

Next, we remove the receptacle covers on pieces of paneling we expect to remove. If the panel to be removed is a corner piece and there is a corner bead or cove molding, we would remove it using the pry bar as before. To remove the sheets of paneling, we can begin at the ceiling or at the floor. In the joint between two pieces where the ceiling cove or baseboard will cover any marks we make, we drive in a wood chisel and gently pry the paneling loose. If the edge was originally glued to the drywall some paper will come off the drywall with the paneling. This is okay. After the entire leading (vertical edge) is free, about 16 in. is freed from the 48-in. wide panel. We start again at the ceiling or floor, but this time we use a long-handle flat pry bar (not a crowbar) to reach the next point where glue and nails are located. We gently pry the panel loose. We repeat the steps at the 32-in. point, and finally, the other vertical edge is loosened in the same way. The result is that the piece has been removed with no damage to the face veneer and finish. Before we set the piece aside, we remove the panel nails. These nails have small heads, so pulling them through from the back side might rip the wood. Instead, we carefully drive them back out.

Removing the drywall is a simple task and so is removing the insulation.

Since the insulation has glass wool or fibers, gloves should be worn. To prevent insulation and drywall gypsum powder from being ground into the carpeting, we need to tape down vinyl sheet goods along the wall. The 6-mil-thick kind sold in lumberyards and builder's supply houses is best. Because we are installing the paneling over drywall, we do not need to tape the joints in the drywall or fill the nail holes. This saves considerable time and some material costs.

Replacing the paneling and trim.   The back of each panel should be examined, and loose drywall paper and dried-glue buildup need to be removed with a chisel. Then the panel should be reinstalled to the wall with new panel nails and adhesive. This adhesive comes in a tube that is inserted in a caulking gun. A bead is placed every 16 in. and along the edges. The panel is set in place, pressed against the wall, and then removed. After a few minutes it is realigned and pressed against the wall. Nails are then used sparingly to anchor the panel further.

We replace the casing, baseboard, and ceiling molding with casing or finish nails. Most of the time, 6d size nails work fine, but 8d nails are sometimes required.

Refinishing the paneling and trim.   If we have been successful, there is not much refinishing to do. We need to fill all nail-head holes with colored putty. We do this very carefully to avoid damage to the adjacent finish. Then we need to lightly sand the surface smooth. We then apply stain if needed to darken any areas where sanding removed the finish and stain. Once it dries, we smooth it with steel wool and apply a coat of varnish. Since varnish usually leaves a less than smooth surface, we come back and steel wool the surface and apply a coat of wax. Finally, we apply a light coat of wax over the entire wall and wipe it off to polish the surface.

Concluding comments.   As we have just read, the work of restoring a paneled wall requires considerable carpentry skill. One slip and the panel is ruined. When the paneling is several years old, obtaining a matching piece is next to impossible. Homeowners who lack these skills should not attempt the work. Also, in our problem we described working with $\frac{1}{4}$-in. plywood paneling. Any other kind would be much harder to work with and would be more liable to breakage.

PROJECT 4. STRIP AND REFINISH WAINSCOT

Subcategories include: stripping chemicals; stripping tools; finishing papers to smooth surfaces; priming and finish coating materials; and coating applications.

Preliminary Discussion with the Owner

Problems facing the owner.   A great many homes have wainscot on their walls. Some have it halfway up the wall, others have it from floor to ceiling, and some have it on the ceiling as well. Wainscot is made from solid wood and most is pine. In earlier times yellow pine was used, and it lasts and lasts. However, its longevity is part of the problem the owner faces when the wall begins to look shabby.

What makes the wall look shabby, marred, overpainted, or otherwise detracts from a good-quality appearance? Almost always it is multiple coats of paint or varnish. Figure 1–4 shows us what a new piece of wainscot looks like. Notice that there is a very pleasing bead in the center and along one edge. The wood is only $\frac{3}{8}$ in. thick and is tongue and grooved. When the wainscot is first installed, there are no hammer marks and the first finish enhances the curves and pattern in the wood. As the surface wears and is abused, additional coats of finish are added. Soon, the molded parts, whose lines were distinct, become blurred as the paint or varnish builds up. When this happens, owners are prone to rip the wainscot off or cover it with wallpaper. The owner who desires to restore the wainscot to its original quality is faced with a difficult and time-consuming job, as the wall's surface must be stripped.

Alternative solutions to the problem.   There are only two solutions that can solve an owner's problem with the wainscot. The first is to remove and replace it with new material. If the wood were dented, banged up severely, gouged, split, or rotted, this alternative would be the proper one. On the other hand, if the wood were in good condition but the buildup of multiple coats of finish is detracting from its appearance, we need to discuss stripping the finish away and applying new finish. In this project we describe restoring old wainscot.

Statement of work and the planning effort.   When we arrive at the home of the owner, we are shown the wainscoted walls. We make a careful examination to determine if the wall can be restored or if it must be replaced. Since we can restore it, our statement of work begins: *We will remove the old paint and varnish to the greatest extent possible in order to expose the natural wood.* After removing the old paint, *we will sand and prepare the wall for finishing and apply a base coat*

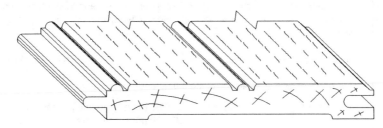

Figure 1–4   Wainscot design.

and two top coats of finish of the owner's choosing. Since the job is a messy one, we agree to *prevent damage to floors and surrounding areas.*

For planning purposes, we need to employ a painter. He or she needs to examine the surface and determine how to remove the old paint and varnish. This examination and decision process provides the painter with an estimate of time needed to complete the job. The process of heating and scraping the old paint from the surface and grooves is slow. This translates to several days' work to remove the finish and several more days to apply the new finishes. The time for performing the work is proportional to the number of square feet of wall covered with wainscot. The owner is to be required to have someone home while the painter is on the job unless the house is vacant.

There is also a safety consideration associated with this job. When chemical paint removers are used, proper ventilation is essential for the good health of the painter and the owner's family. When a heating iron is used to blister the paint, a fire extinguisher should be close by. Burns can also happen if proper care is not exercised. Finally, we expect to make special tools to scrape the paint from the grooves and beads. To do a clean job, these need to have sharp edges, but sharp edges can cut hands and fingers.

Contract.   Discussion with the owner regarding contract terms and pricing can be difficult. A painter with no experience in doing this work would, in good faith, probably want a time-and-materials contract. The owner would be reluctant, since he or she has no basis to judge when a fair day's work for a fair day's wages would be earned. Yet that may be the proper solution. On the other hand, a painter with past experience in doing the work would probably offer a fixed-price contract for the entire job or a fixed price per square foot of wall. Because of this possible situation, two contract samples are provided: the time-and-materials variety and the fixed-price type.

Time-and-Materials Contract

The job is to remove the old finish from wainscoted walls and adjacent wood moldings and baseboards and replace the finish with a latex paint of the owner's choice of color. We will use chemicals and heating tools to remove the old built-up paints, sand the surface, and restore the original designs in the wood to their original style. We will guarantee no damage to floors or adjacent walls or fixtures.

The owner agrees to have a member of the family at home when the workers are present.

This work will be accomplished using a time-and-materials method of computing costs:

Labor rates: $30.00 per hour for the painter
$22.00 per hour for the helper

Material costs will be calculated at average retail prices plus taxes.

Fixed-Price Contract

For the fixed price stipulated below, we agree to restore the wainscoted walls. We shall remove all old built-up paint and other finish to reveal the original design in the wood and agree to paint the wood with a latex paint system. The color will be chosen by the owner. Adjacent wood moldings and baseboards will also be restored using the same techniques.

The owner agrees to have a member of the family at home while the workers are present.

Total cost for labor and materials: $xxx.xx.

Material Assessment

Direct Materials	Use/Purpose
Sandpaper	To smooth the wall surface
Paint remover	To soften and remove paint
Latex primer and paint	To finish wainscoted walls
Wood filler	To fill cracks and nail holes

Indirect Materials	Use/Purpose
Trash bags	To gather old paint stripped from walls
Ground cloths	To protect floors
Masking tape	To hold protective materials in place
Vinyl sheet goods	To protect walls and woodwork

Support Materials	Use/Purpose
Paint-removing heat tool	To heat paint for simpler removal
Painter's tools	For painting
Special scrapers	Made to fit into the grooves of the wainscot

Outside Contractor Support	Use/Purpose
None	

Activities Planning Chart

Activity	Time Line (Days)
	1 2 3 4 5 6 7
1. Contract preparation	I _×_ I ___ I ___ I ___ I ___ I ___ I ___ I
2. Materials and scheduling	I _×_ I ___ I ___ I ___ I ___ I ___ I ___ I
3. Removing the paint	I ___ I _×_ I _×_ I _×_ I ___ I ___ I ___ I
4. Painting the walls and trim	I ___ I ___ I ___ I _×_ I _×_ I ___ I ___ I

Reconstruction

Contract preparation.   Since, in this project, we are the painting contractor and a general contractor was not called, we deal directly with the owner. In preparing the contract we discussed the job and its problems. We know that there are many, many grooves that must be cleaned of old paint and finish materials. This is time consuming, even when we use a combination of heat and chemicals. The final work must be done with steel brushes, scrapers, and sandpaper.

As we discuss the effort, we agree that we can clean a few square feet of wall per hour with a small team effort. If we send a painter and a helper, the overall cost to the owner is less than the cost of two painters.

We have most of the tools, but specially made scrapers to clean out the grooves need to be made. For this we will need a piece of wainscot for a model and a piece of steel to make several tools.

Our office personnel prepare the contract forms in the appropriate format, fixed price or time and materials. They make out the worksheets for the painter and helper, and they have the special tools prepared that the workers will need. The contractor then takes the contract to the owner for signature and to establish acceptable dates.

Materials and scheduling.   Due to the nature of this project, the materials can be picked up on the first day of the job from a paint supply store. The direct and indirect materials would both be bought at the same time, to avoid further trips for supplies.

From the activity chart we see that several days have been allocated for paint removal and repainting. The times shown are representative for experienced workers removing the old paint from the walls at about a rate of 4 square feet per hour and painting at a rate of 15 square feet per hour. In a real situation in a fixed-price contract, the owner does not care about these rates because the price is set. But in a time-and-materials contract this information can become a major area of concern for both parties. The contractor may extend the time by convincing the owner that the rate of 4 square feet per hour is unattainable as an average and specifying a different rate. As a result, the time line for all activities can vary considerably from the chart. Scheduling must also involve the availability of a member of the family, since the contract stated that the owner would have a member of the family at home at all times when workers were present.

Removing the old, built-up paint and other finishes.   We begin by making a list of the tasks to accomplish. They would be followed more or less in sequence.

1. Remove as much of the furniture from the room as possible.

2. Remove the drapes, curtains, wall decorations, and anythi. ɡ else hanging on the wall.

3. Fit vinyl sheets around the perimeter of the room on the floor and tape them to the baseboard or shoe molding.

4. Apply a strip of 2-in. tape just above the wainscot molding to protect the wall or wallpaper.

5. Create ventilation. This can be done with fans or naturally, with open windows.

6. Using a heat iron, scorch the paint over a small section while removing the scorched paint with a wide-blade putty knife.

7. Apply chemical paint remover to the surface in prescribed dimensions, and when the paint has softened, scrape it free from the grooves and other surfaces. Neutralize the chemical with wash as directed on the can. For safety reasons, some paint remover companies recommend wearing a mask to avoid breathing toxic fumes.

8. Sand the surface smooth with 100-grit open coat first and follow this with 150-grit sandpaper.

9. Examine the wainscot carefully and repeat as many of the foregoing tasks as required.

10. Apply a filler such as spackling to small blemishes and holes in the surface of the wainscot as required, and sand smooth.

11. Mix a batch of wood putty powder and water and apply this material to larger holes, splits, and other blemishes to restore the style of the wood. Let dry and sand smooth.

These 11 tasks constitute the total effort required for every square foot of wall and cap molding on the wainscoted wall. If we think of these tasks as a series of events taking place over a 4-square-foot area, we can make a judgment about the average time needed to do the work. Remember that there is a bead, and grooves on either side of the bead, approximately every $1\frac{3}{4}$ in.

Part of the job is to remove the paint to keep the job site clean. This is a messy job but needs to be done for several worthwhile reasons. First, the materials are mixed with chemicals that can cause a skin rash and create fumes that can affect breathing. Next, the waste materials can melt the vinyl covering the floor and stain the floors. Finally, we could track the materials into other rooms, causing damage to carpets and to vinyl-covered and wood floors.

Finishing the cleaned walls.   The contract calls for a basic three-coat latex wall painting system: a prime coat and two top coats. Since we are painting wood, we would recommend semigloss rather than a flat finish. But recall that the owner has the choice.

We will apply a prime coat with a thickness of approximately 1 mil. After a light sanding and inspection we would do the following:

1. Repair any blemishes that show up from the painting. Sometimes, painted surfaces show gouges, pockmarks, and areas of wood where the old paint was not fully removed, which create lines or ridges.
2. Apply each top coat at a thickness of 1.5 mils.

Concluding comments.   This project can be done by a homeowner who has the time and patience to do the work. As a rule, a painter can do the work much faster than the owner. This means that the household is disrupted for a shorter period. Also to be weighed is assuring proper and safe use of the heating iron and chemicals. Finally, there is the economic advantage to self-help over use of a contractor. Which is better?

PROJECT 5. REPAINT WALLS

Subcategories include: types and textures of paint suitable for walls; color coordination between walls and trim; painting tools: manual and electrically operated; and stripping, smoothing, and sealing walls.

Preliminary Discussion with the Owner

Problems facing the owner.   Generally, painting walls in a house is a simple, straightforward project. One simply goes to a paint store or discount outlet, picks up a couple of gallons of paint and a roller and brush, and does the job. Homeowners do this all the time, and often the job is done very creditably. But sometimes an owner is faced with problem walls and wants them painted. Exactly what needs to be done?

Let's make a list of the potential problems and what might be done:

Problem	Cure
Wall is papered	Remove the wallpaper or paint over paper
Wall is damaged	Spackle or repair drywall, then paint
Wall is covered with paneling	Remove the paneling and repair the wall
Wall has chair railing	Strip the railing or remove it, repair the drywall, and paint
Wall has water damage	Replace or paint with oil-based paint
Wall has rotted drywall	Remove and replace drywall, seal, and paint
Wall paint must match	Repaint entire room
Wall must withstand moisture	Select an appropriate paint type
Wall is subject to mildew	Select an appropriate paint type
Wall and trim must blend	Select companion colors and types
Plaster wall is cracked	Repair cracks and repaint

Alternative solutions to the problem. From the painting contractor's viewpoint, for every problem identified above there is at least one alternative that will produce a satisfactory job. In those situations where the drywall is damaged, we would make the necessary repairs to the wall and prime and paint the wall to the owner's satisfaction.

Where the wall was previously wallpapered, we would prefer to strip it free of wallpaper and then prepare the wall for painting. We understand that one prime and two top coats of paint total only 4 mils in thickness. Paint is never used to cover blemishes or irregularities in wall surfaces. It is used to add beauty to a room or hall. The seams in the wallpaper will always show through.

Where moisture or a buildup of mildew is the problem, we would attempt to locate the cause and offer a cure before restoring the wall. Somehow air circulation is being blocked, and if we can eliminate the blockage and let air flow across or up the wall, we can be assured that the problem is fixed. When we cannot eliminate the moisture, we must use a painting system that can maintain its covering quality and withstand moisture. We might have to use oil-based rather than latex paint.

Where a painted plastered wall has cracked, we have a severe problem. A plasterer would need to make repairs and probably have to apply a new top coat of plaster to the entire wall to ensure that a uniform surface is available for painting.

In addition to the problems examined above, we frequently must work with an owner who desires the best of paints and custom colors. Not all paints are the same. Some have very excellent covering qualities because they include substantial quantities of pigments and body. Others have greater quantities of thinner and less body, and therefore will produce a poorer-quality job. Some manufacturers alert the customer by including coverage estimates on the label. For example, one label might state that a gallon of paint will cover 300 to 350 square feet, whereas a second lists the coverage as 350 to 400 square feet. The one with greater coverage has more body. In any event, considerable skill and understanding of walls and paints is required for truly high-quality restoration.

Statement of work and the planning effort. For our project, we shall assume that a bedroom with papered walls is being converted into a den with painted walls. The first statement of work is: *Remove all wallpaper and paint the walls.* We can improve on this by stating that *work will be done to prepare the wall surfaces to be free of blemishes prior to applying paint.* We also need to state that *the painting system will consist of a seal/prime coat and two top coats of latex paint.* We should also state that *the paint will be top quality, and the applications will not show any brush marks, runs, or wall surface imperfections.* Finally, we need to state that *the woodwork is to be refinished using semigloss latex.* These statements of work describe the essential elements of a high-quality job using quality paints and quality workmanship. The owner wants the best and is willing to pay for quality.

Planning is important for this job. The painter needs to determine the extent of work and the other conditions implied or stated in the statement of work. Workers can be expected to work for several days to get the room ready and for a couple of days to apply the new paint. A trip to the job site is required to obtain measurements and conditions from the owner. Some time is required to prepare contract/bids and agree to a price. Then the work needs to be scheduled. All in all, the job will not take very long.

For this project we are contracting to paint two rooms. One room is 12 by 15 ft and the other is 18 by 24 ft. There are six door frames to repaint, baseboard, and four double-hung windows with casings and sills.

Contract.   Since the painter can observe the walls that must be restored, he or she can measure the wall surface, determine the condition of the walls, determine what has to be done, and find out from the owner what type and color of finish is to be applied to the walls and woodwork. Because of this firsthand knowledge, the painter can offer a fixed-price contract.

The body of the contract can be very simple, almost a series of notes. For example:

For the fixed price of $XXX.XX, we will restore the walls with paint. We will remove or repair any blemishes to the walls and apply a three-coat latex system. We agree to repaint the woodwork with a semigloss latex paint. The owner has selected the colors and type of paint during preliminary talks, and these will be the ones applied.

The owner agrees to move all furnishings away from the walls or out of the rooms to be painted. We guarantee a high-quality job and no damage to the ceilings or floors as a result of our work or the materials used.

Material Assessment

Direct Materials	Use/Purpose
Latex primer	To prime walls
Latex wall paint	For top or finish coats
Latex semigloss	To paint the woodwork

Indirect Materials	Use/Purpose
Sandpaper	To sand walls as required
Spackling	To fill holes
Masking tape	Various uses as required
Vinyl sheet goods	To protect floors
Drop cloths	To protect floors and furniture

Support Materials	Use/Purpose
Paint roller and tray	Standard for painting walls
Power sprayer	Optional method of spraying
Assorted paintbrushes	To paint along corners and trim
Stepladders	To reach to ceiling
Painter's toolbox	For painting and preparation
Wallpaper stripper	As required to remove old wallpaper

Outside Contractor Support	Use/Purpose
None	

Activities Planning Chart

Activity	Time Line (Days)
	1 2 3 4 5 6 7
1. Contract preparation	| _×_ | ___ | ___ | ___ | ___ | ___ | ___ |
2. Materials and scheduling	| _×_ | ___ | ___ | ___ | ___ | ___ | ___ |
3. Preparing the walls and trim	| ___ | _×_ | _×_ | ___ | ___ | ___ | ___ |
4. Painting the walls and trim	| ___ | _×_ | _×_ | _×_ | ___ | ___ | ___ |

Reconstruction

Contract preparation.   This contract was easy to prepare. We had all of the details about the job when we left the owner. At the office we prepared a worksheet for materials and labor, with an allowance for overhead and profit, and prepared the actual contract/bid. The entire job did not take more than 4 hours. After completing the contract, we returned to the owner and presented the document for concurrence and signing.

Materials and scheduling.   Tools and materials for this job can easily be carried in the painter's truck. We used the estimate of materials to obtain the required gallons of paint, rollers, tape, and other materials for the job on the first day of the scheduled work. All materials were purchased from a single supply house:

Latex primer: 3 gallons to cover 1440 square feet at 350 square feet/gallon

Latex wall paint: 7 gallons for two coats

Latex semigloss: 8 gallons to cover approximately 1450 square feet of door, window casings, and baseboard with two coats

The activity chart shows 3 days for performing the practical work. The 2 days dedicated to wall preparation is reasonable for the size of these rooms. If the rooms were smaller, less time would be programmed. The 3 days for applying new paint is also reasonable for the size of the rooms. Some primer can be applied on the second day of work, after one room has been prepared. As a rule, the trim paint is applied after the walls are covered.

Preparing the walls and trim.   The following tasks are involved:

1. Cover the floor to ensure that there will be no damage to floor coverings.
2. Strip walls of all applied materials except old paint.
3. Fill all nail holes, blemishes, dents, gouges, and so on, with spackling or drywall compound.
4. On plastered walls, fill all cracks with a final coat of plaster.
5. Sand all walls to a smooth finish. Old paint should be sanded as well to remove loose particles.
6. Vacuum the walls and floor to remove all dust.
7. Inspect and prepare all baseboards, door and window casings, and sills with fillers as needed. Sand all surfaces smooth with sandpaper. Vacuum.
8. Perform a final inspection on each wall:
    a. All holes, dents, and the like are filled, smooth, and flat with the wall surface.
    b. All surfaces of the wall are even, with no ridges, leftover paper, uneven cracks, and so on.
    c. All trim is smooth and even to the touch: no dents, mars, nail holes, and so on.
    d. No dust is present on walls and trim.

Painting the walls and trim.   We begin with the primer and apply it with roller, power roller, or spray gun. The edges and corners are painted with a brush since many rollers create marks on adjacent walls when corner painting is attempted. Most latex primers dry within 1 to 3 hours, so we can evaluate the adequacy of the job in a very short time. Usually, a single coat is sufficient to create a base for the top coats to adhere to properly.

The final or top coat is applied twice at a 1.5-mil thickness. We attempt never to apply heavy coats or skimpy coats, as they both cause problems and give the wall an uneven finish.

When the walls are painted, we paint the woodwork with the semigloss paint. Since there were already several coats of semigloss latex paint on the wood, we have a much better foundation. By sanding the surface, we expose some of the base paint, and new paint usually adheres to it very well. Sometimes, though, we need a primer, especially when the color change is from very dark to very light.

Near the end of every day we need to clean the tools very thoroughly. The paintbrushes and equipment are costly and must be reused again and again. Only rollers are thrown away. To complete our work we remove all vinyl and drop cloths and ensure that no paint has splattered onto adjacent walls or floor. Our contract guarantees this.

Concluding comments.   Many homeowners repaint a room or an entire house themselves. For some this is an easy task; however, the quality of the job varies considerably. All too often, the wall is a new color but the blemishes in the wall are still noticeable because they were not repaired as the painter would do. Painters apply their skill and knowledge to create the best-looking walls and wood-work they can create. Sometimes owners can do the work very well, but often a job needs to be done by a professional painter.

PROJECT 6. REPLACE WALLPAPER

Subcategories include: stripping techniques and tools; types of wallpaper and their suitability; planning the installation; determining the amount of wallpaper required; pasting techniques; sizing walls; cutting and applying wallpaper; and applying bor-der papers.

Preliminary Discussion with the Owner

Problems facing the owner.   An owner may be faced with one of several problems related to wallpaper: (1) it is desired to paper a room or several rooms that are now painted; (2) a change of paper is wanted; (3)choice among the wide variety of papers available is difficult; and (4) the owners must decide if they can hang the paper themselves or need to contract out the work.

When we desire to paper a room or several rooms that currently have paint, what problems will we face? We can begin with the idea that applying wallpaper over a painted wall is not uncommon; so there is plenty of information to read and experienced people to talk to. This helps us determine the ease or difficulty of the job and all the side issues, much as selecting the paper. When we look into the costs, we find discount papers for very few dollars per roll, up to extremely expen-sive paper. Experts in this area are readily available at the numerous wallpaper outlets, and many of their employees have experience in selecting the right kind. Only by using a systematic planned approach can homeowners make a sound, reli-able, and economical decision.

When we want to paper a wall that is already papered, we must decide if we will attempt to paper over the old paper, or strip the old paper off first. Sometimes we can paper over paper, but the decision must be made based on several important considerations. If the old pattern and colors are strong and dark, we must determine if they will show through the new paper. This we do with a small scrap of new paper. When the old paper is glued very securely to the wall, we might be able to repaper, but when pieces are loose or there is damaged and missing paper, we face real problems trying to make a high-quality job. Irregularities always show through and cast shadows.

There are untold rolls of paper available but not many different basic kinds. Almost all papers are now preglued at the factory. This generally ensures a uniform application of glue on the back of the roll. Further, prepasted paper is very convenient to install. Many of the old tasks, such as mixing paste and applying the paste to the back side of the paper, are eliminated. If the paper is not prepasted, we would have to add paste with a brush. Today, modified wallpaper pastes are smooth and rarely have lumps. The older wheat paste had to be worked until it was 100 percent lump-free. Papers are also pretrimmed at the factory. In years past, the paperhanger had to trim the excess before hanging the paper. Much time is saved with pre-trimmed paper.

Another characteristic today is that most papers are $20\frac{1}{2}$ in. wide and are sold in double rolls of 32 ft 8 in. or slightly more. This means that we can get four 8-ft pieces from a double roll. Knowing how many strips we can get from a roll helps determine how many rolls we need for a room. (We discuss this further later in the section on reconstruction.)

Owners also need to decide whether to do the work or contract it out. Wallpaper hangers do not work cheaply, but they generally work fast and complete a room in several hours to less than a day. Even a bathroom, which is the worst room in the house to paper, can be done in a day or less. If the old paper has to be removed and the wall sanded and repaired, added time and costs will be incurred.

Alternative solutions to the problem. As a wallpaper contractor, we would first solve the problems described in previous paragraphs. All of the conditions that the owner needed to be concerned about and solve are standard conditions that we face in any paperhanging job.

We offer the owner knowledge of how to prepare the walls, how to remove the old paper, how to repair to the walls as needed, and how to ensure a high-quality job. We can accurately determine the quantity of paper needed, which would be a help to the owner. With this information he or she can order the proper amounts for each room. We can also determine the amount of border paper if the owner desires to add that to the job.

The one thing we cannot do is select the paper. However, we can recommend reliable stores and people (perhaps interior designers) in the stores who have excellent reputations for assisting owners with paper selection. Paper styles, colors, and patterns vary greatly, and these people can often lead a customer to the right selection group. Wallpaper is designed in groups by many manufacturers. Each group usually has a floral, solid, and stripe pattern as well as a border. Some groups have several color schemes, to satisfy a wide variety of customer tastes.

We also cannot select the weight or quality of the paper for an owner; however, we can make recommendations. Each manufacturer produces papers of varying quality and prices the papers accordingly. There is usually a chart in the front or at the rear of each sample book that shows the grades from A to E or F. Each grade has an associated price per roll. From the manufacturer's viewpoint, the higher the price, the better the paper. The price reflects the costs to produce the paper. These costs are derived by the investment in designs for the paper, dyes used to print the paper, the paper content and number of layers, any protective vinyl coating, the texture of the paper, and other manufacturing expenses.

There are alternatives, and we believe that two separate considerations should be used in every job. First, is it economical for an owner who has experience hanging paper to do so? For example, if we can do the job of preparing the walls and hanging the paper for $1 per hour and the owner makes $2 per hour at his or her job, we should do it—the owner would be money ahead. Second, several people need to be involved in each job: the owner, the interior designer, and the paperhanger. This team, working together, can make a job successful.

Statement of work and the planning effort.   For our project, we will remove old paper, prepare the wall, and hang new paper in a room whose dimensions are 10 by 14 ft, with a hall 4 ft wide by 18 ft long. The ceilings are 8 ft 1 in. from the floor. There is a $3\frac{1}{2}$-in.-wide baseboard and no ceiling trim. The room and hall have the usual doors and windows. The old paper was not the strippable kind. Generally, our first statement of work is: *We will remove the old paper and prepare the walls for new paper.* Specifically, *we will ensure a sound, blemish-free wall before new paper is installed.* Next, we stipulate that *we will use quality workmanship, guarantee matching seams, and guarantee 100 percent adhesion for one year unless the wall is damaged by mechanical failure or natural causes.* Finally, we need to state that *there will be no damage to ceilings or floors and we will remove all old materials from the job site.*

We could have been called by the owner or by an interior decorator we frequently work with to assist the owner with the job. If we were called by the interior decorator, some of the details regarding the job would be provided by the decorator. If we were called by the owner, we would need to determine all of the details. The first expedites our interview with the owner; the second requires a little more time. Either situation is perfectly acceptable. From the meetings we determine the extent of work and make several planning judgments. Because of the type of old paper, we require several days to strip the walls. Then we need to make repairs with spackling, and sand the walls. We need to size the walls to make sure of a sound base. Finally, we should schedule 2 days to hang the paper.

We can send one paperhanger to the job, or a paperhanger and a helper, or two paperhangers. The number of days to complete the work depends on the number of workers on the job. We cannot perform any work until the owner or decorator has informed us that the new paper is at the house or store. With this information, we can program the time block needed to do the work.

Contract. In this situation we can provide a fixed-price contract. We can provide all the services and materials but usually the owner selects the paper. The body of the contract could look like this:

For the price stated below, we will furnish all labor and costs except the wallpaper purchased by the owner. We will strip the old paper from the walls and prepare them for the new paper.

We guarantee first quality workmanship and servicability for one year.

Total Price: $xxx.xx

Material Assessment

Direct Materials	Use/Purpose
Wallpaper	New treatment of a wall
Sizing	To apply to wall as required
Border paper	If used, at ceiling or other places

Indirect Materials	Use/Purpose
Knife blades	To trim paper
Water tray	To soak prepasted paper
Vinyl sheet or drop cloths	To protect floors
Paper-stripping fluid	If used, softens old paper and glue
Spackling paste	To fill holes
Sandpaper	To smooth walls before wallpapering

Support Materials	Use/Purpose
Electric paper stripper	To simplify paper removal
Paperhanger tools	For construction
Paper cutting table	To cut paper

Outside Contractor Support	Use/Purpose
None	

Activities Planning Chart

Activity	Time Line (Days)						
	1	2	3	4	5	6	7
1. Contract preparation	| _×_ |	___ |	___ |	___ |	___ |	___ |	___ |
2. Materials and scheduling	| _×_ |	___ |	___ |	___ |	___ |	___ |	___ |
3. Removing old paper and preparing the walls	| ___ |	_×_ |	_×_ |	___ |	___ |	___ |	___ |
4. Applying new paper	| ___ |	___ |	_×_ |	_×_ |	___ |	___ |	___ |

Reconstruction

Contract preparation.   This is a relatively small job, but the contract preparations are consistent with this type of work. In the office we would work with the owner or with the owner and a decorator from the paint store to determine the details and timetables, as explained earlier. With this information we can apply our rates for paper removal and installation of new paper. Since the owner is providing the paper, our material costs are limited to those needed in preparing the walls. We would add the cost of the expenses involved to obtain the contract and an allowance for profit.

Preparing the contract should not take longer than 2 to 3 hours. This time includes making out the worksheet for estimating the materials, programming the paperhanger's work schedule, and preparing the contract/bid document.

Materials and scheduling.   The materials are obtained from two sources. The owner provides the rolls of paper and we provide the remaining materials. We would probably have most on hand in the shop as normal stock. In some cases we would have to purchase chemical stripper or sandpaper and vinyl sheets.

A schedule of work needs to include access to the house. As soon as it is confirmed that the paper is available, we would suggest a series of days. The owner would agree and have someone at home while we were there unless the house were empty.

From the activity list we see that our schedule would require 3 days. This is based on using a paperhanger and a helper. The helper can assist to both strip and prepare walls and cut and hang the new paper. The owner benefits because of the overall lower labor costs.

Removing old paper and preparing the walls.   Let's begin by listing the tasks as they would be done:

1. Remove all pictures and hangers, drapes and curtains, and their holders.
2. Move the furniture to the center of the room.

3. Lay out drop cloths or vinyl sheets to cover the floor along the walls. This means from the wall out a minimum of 4 ft.

4. Soak or heat the old paper and pull from the wall. Sometimes several tries will be required to get it off.

5. Pick up the old paper and bag it as it is torn from the wall to minimize tracking it to other rooms.

6. Inspect the wall for damage and flaws to be corrected.
   a. Spackle all nail holes.
   b. Identify dents and fill with spackling.
   c. Use joint compound to fill the larger dents and gouges.
   d. Sand irregularities and the wall surface.

7. Size the wall with a wall sizing mixture

The work of preparing the walls is clearly labor intensive. Each of the seven tasks requires the labor of the paperhanger and helper.

Applying new paper.   Before we list the tasks associated with hanging the paper, we need to define several conditions pertaining to wallpaper and how to use it economically.

Normally, wallpaper is purchased in double-roll quantities (it is precut in double rolls) for economical use. Since a double roll is generally 32 ft and a few inches long, we can generally cut four full-length pieces from it.

The pattern on most papers falls into one of the following five categories:

1. Solid with no pattern
2. Stripes with no repeat pattern
3. Stripes and designs alternating (can include flowers) with a repeat pattern in the flowers or designs
4. Design (floral or other) with a straight-across match
5. Design (floral or other) with a drop match

Patterns 1 and 2 are the simplest types to apply. As long as seams do not overlap, there is no matching to do. Pattern 3 requires us to match the design either straight across (usual) or as a drop match. The stripes have no bearing as long as we repeat their sequence with full-width pieces.

Patterns 4 and 5 are those requiring most of our concern and skill. In Figure 1–5 we see an example of a straight-across match. The straightedge is level and the points on the left and right have the same design. So every sheet starting from the ceiling will have the same pattern. In other words, we would make sure that the tip of a leaf or design was X inches from the cut. Then we would measure down 94 to 96 in. and make the bottom cut. In Figure 1–6 we see an example of a drop-match

Figure 1–5   Wallpaper: straight across match.

wallpaper. Corresponding points on the left and right edges are offset by an amount specified by the manufacturer. However, we can determine this ourselves. These may be as small as 5 or 6 in., up or up to 18 in. In Figure 1–6 we see that the offset or drop match is 16 in. What problems does this pose? First, we can cut four full-length pieces from the first roll but only three from the second roll, since we must move the sheet up 16 in. to obtain a match. The remaining piece from the roll may

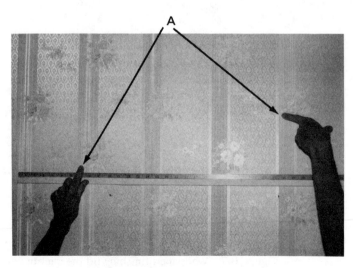

Figure 1–6   Wallpaper: drop match.

be used over the door (probably not unless it is a double door) or below and above the window. When decorators and paperhangers see that the owner wants to select a drop match with a large drop, he or she usually recommends buying at least one more double roll than the number used in a straight-across match. The rule to follow is this: "Always buy more than is calculated and have some left over to ensure a complete job." If the job takes part of one more roll than was ordered, (1) the job is stalled, and (2) obtaining another roll from the same dye or roll lot may be difficult, impossible, or incur days of delay.

Another rule to follow is this: "Use only full-width pieces everywhere except in corners." Nonskilled paperhangers may try to splice a piece alongside a door trim from floor to ceiling rather than cut it to fit above and alongside the door. The results are bad. The sequence of the pattern is broken, and a professional must never do this. Sometimes we make the turn in a corner with a one-fourth of the width of sheet. We can begin the adjacent wall with the remainder of the sheet and avoid losing good paper. Figure 1–7 shows how to plan for and finish an interior corner. Notice that the first sheet is cut sufficiently wide to return about $\frac{1}{2}$ to $\frac{3}{4}$ in. Then the next sheet is trimmed to fit into the corner while still establishing the

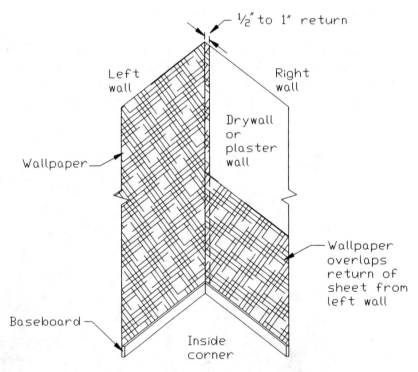

Figure 1–7   Wallpaper: finishing off the interior corner.

plumb reference for the remaining sheets on the adjacent wall. Why do we cut the paper rather than creasing it into the corner? All to often walls that may have been plumb during construction are out of plumb. We cannot see this with the eye, and when paper is applied as we just recommended, one does not notice any irregularity. However, when a piece is forced into the corner that is not plumb, the plumb reference is lost for the remaining sheets and we will always notice a tilt, especially at the ceiling or along the baseboard. It looks like pattern creep.

When we think about the rule just explained, we can easily estimate the number of rolls of paper needed for the room or hall. Let's use our project room and hall as an example. Recall that they were 10 by 14 ft and 4 by 18 ft, respectively. Therefore, we have

$$(10 + 14) \text{ times } 2 = 48 \text{ linear feet for the bedroom}$$

$$(4 + 18) \text{ times } 2 = 44 \text{ linear feet for the hall}$$

1. If the paper is straight across or pattern 1, 2, or 3, we need

$$48 \text{ linear feet divided by } 20\tfrac{1}{2} \text{ in. (paper width) or 28 strips at 4 strips}$$
$$\text{per double roll} = 7 \text{ rolls}$$

$$44 \text{ linear feet divided by } 20\tfrac{1}{2} \text{ in. (paper width) or 26 strips at 4 strips}$$
$$\text{per double roll} = 7 \text{ rolls}$$

$$\text{Total} = 14 \text{ double rolls}$$

2. If the paper is drop match, one double roll produces 4 strips, and one produces 3 strips, for a total of 7 strips.

$$48 \text{ linear feet divided by } (7 \times 20\tfrac{1}{2} \text{ in.}) \text{ (total paper width for}$$
$$\text{two double rolls)} = 8 \text{ double rolls}$$

$$44 \text{ linear feet divided by } (7 \times 20\tfrac{1}{2} \text{ in.}) \text{ (total paper width for}$$
$$\text{two double rolls)} = 7.2 \text{ rolls, rounded up to 8}$$

$$\text{Total} = 16 \text{ double rolls}$$

We see that drop-match paper can increase the cost of the job. Now let's list the tasks involved to paper the room.

1. Measure the length of each wall and divide by the width of the paper; or step off the wall with a stick whose length is the same as the paper's width. This tells us how many pieces we must cut and also tells us if we end up with a piece 4 in. or less. We want to avoid narrow pieces in corners.
2. Measure the height of the wall to be papered and add $\tfrac{1}{2}$ in. at the top and 1 in. at the bottom, but do not be wasteful since we must use our paper economically. (Always try to minimize waste.)

3. Set up the worktable and examine several rolls to see if they all start at the same design point. Then unroll one and cut the four pieces. In straight match or pattern 1, 2, or 3, simply lay one sheet on top of the other and make them all the same.

4. In drop match, open a second roll and align it next to the first piece cut and mark the top and bottom for cuts. Then using the piece just cut, make several more just like it. Mark these as B or 2 on the back side near the top for identification.

5. Measure out from the corner the paper width less $\frac{1}{2}$ in. and draw a plumb line using a level and pencil. Make sure that no point from the line to the corner is more than the paper width.

6. Soak the first piece in a trough of water until it is fully wet. The prepasted glue must absorb water thoroughly. Some of the water in the glue will soak into the wall or be absorbed by the sizing. Failure to wet the back of the paper adequately will result in loose spots and edges.

7. Hang the first piece along the pencil line. Use a brush or squeegee to remove air between the paper and the wall, and trim the excess at the ceiling and along the baseboard.

8. Hang piece 2, 3, and so on until the wall is done.

9. When prefitting pieces around doors and windows, some paper can be cut away on the bench. Sometimes this makes handling and hanging simpler. Many paperhangers never bother. Close fitting is required and there is no substitution for good-quality fits.

10. When adding pieces above and below the window, we always ensure a 100 percent match. When pieces are added into the window area on the head and along the sides, we:
   a. Make a self-corner on the vertical corners.
   b. Add small strips along the head and extend these up onto the wall $\frac{1}{2}$ in. The wall piece overlaps the $\frac{1}{2}$ in. When dry, the overlap is almost invisible and curtains will hide everything.

One cardinal rule we never violate is this: "All vertical joints are *butted together,* never overlapped or left to gap."

Concluding comments.   Many owners paper their homes and do excellent work. Many try and make serious mistakes that ruin paper and the quality of the work. The reader of this book could follow the ideas and guidelines and with some practice do a creditable job, maybe a perfect job. But given the expense of many good-quality papers and the economics of earning a salary versus hanging paper, a contractor might be the best solution. Many paperhangers are excellent at their trade and should be able to provide anyone with references to that effect.

Paper is beautiful, it changes a room or hall dramatically, and it costs more than paint. Therefore, we must strive for high-quality work.

PROJECT 7. REPAIR DAMAGED LATH AND PLASTER WALLS
OR CEILINGS

Subcategories include: identifying the three coats of plaster; understanding how to apply each coat; preparation of scratch, brown, and final top coat; preparing the wall or ceiling for repair; tools used in plastering; and testing the soundness of the plaster.

Preliminary Discussion with the Owner

Problems facing the owner.   Owners who have problems with plastered walls or ceilings face substantial costs to restore them. The problems range from simple stress cracks, to cracks made by settling forces, to failure of the scratch coat to bond to the lath. Each problem is caused by different conditions and each requires a different solution.

Let's examine a lath wall or ceiling in terms of construction. In residential homes dating back to the nineteenth century, walls and ceilings were plastered. Today some are plastered, but most walls and ceilings are covered with drywall.

In homes 60 years old or older, wood lath was nailed to studs and plaster was applied to the lath. Figure 1–8 shows a cross-sectional view of this type of wall. Notice several important things.

1. Wood lath was separated about $\frac{1}{4}$ to $\frac{3}{8}$ in. and was rough cut.
2. Three coats of plaster were applied: a scratch coat first, then a brown coat, then a top or finish coat.
3. The scratch coat had to be pushed through the lath to sag and form clinkers. These held the plaster to the wall or ceiling.
4. The scratch coat was applied about $\frac{3}{8}$ in. thick. After a large section of wall was applied, the mason or plasterer would make scratches in the surface to give the brown coat more anchor.
5. The brown coat was applied over the scratch coat after the first coat dried. It was left smooth, but because of the materials used, it was porous.
6. The final top coat was applied in several ways: some with texture but most with a fine, nonporous smooth surface about $\frac{1}{8}$ in. thick.

Plastered walls and ceilings built less than 60 years ago to the present consist of various base materials. Drywall companies made 2 × 4 ft sheets with rounded edges and holes evenly distributed throughout the sheet. Plaster was forced into the joints and through the holes, forming clinkers. Wire mesh stamped in cold-running or stamping mills was made in 2 × 8 ft pieces. These were cut and nailed to the studs. As plaster was applied, hundreds of small clinkers were formed.

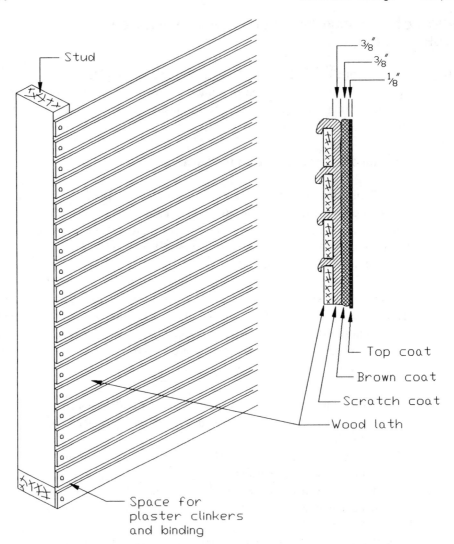

Figure 1-8   Wood lath plaster wall.

Now, that gives us an idea of the construction, and with it we can better understand an owner's problems. Let's briefly identify several causes for each of the three major problems identified in the opening comments.

First, a surface crack that occurs immediately (within 6 months) after the wall or ceiling is installed is caused by an improper mixture or improper application techniques. The top coat materials were placed under conditions of stress, and with the advent of certain temperature and humidity conditions, the most stressed areas cracked. These types of cracks are the easiest to repair. The owner can sometimes use a plaster of paris mixture to fill such cracks. Or the owner can call in a plasterer and have him or her restore the wall with a new top coat.

Second, a crack in a plastered wall or ceiling that occurs well after the original installation is caused by movement of the house. Almost all causes are natural. The pressure or direct effects of a tornado move the walls or ceiling and crack the plaster. The pressure or force of a hurricane does the same. Settling of the ground under the foundation causes the walls and ceilings to stress; this causes cracks from the corners. Finally, houses built with improperly cured lumber can have studs and other members shrink, twist or sag. This pressure causes cracks through all layers of the plaster.

In addition to natural causes, there are problems caused by workers who fail to prepare the plaster mixes properly, apply them improperly, or try to apply them over a larger surface area than standards permit. Some of these cracks are surface types, but many go through the three layers.

The owner is faced with two problems with cracks from these causes, and neither is easy to identify. Is the crack a surface type, or does it go to the core? In either event, what can he or she do? The owner can call in a contractor for an examination and consultation, or the owner can attempt to make repairs himself or herself.

Third, the workers failed to apply sufficient scratch or base coat to form sound clinkers. When this happens, the owner can press the wall or ceiling and feel the wall give. Small or large sections may be affected. This is the worst situation. The owner must face the reality that the section must be removed and replaced. The outcome may be that the entire wall or ceiling will have to be taken off and an entirely new wall or ceiling built. Repairs to sections are possible.

Alternative solutions to the problem.   Each of the three conditions detailed in the preceding section has one or more solutions. If the wall or ceiling must be restored with plaster, we must repair the crack or replace the wall or ceiling where the damage is located. Where the owner has decided that the wall or ceiling must look like new but objects to the costs associated with extensive repair, the wall or ceiling can be covered over with drywall. A third alternative is to apply plywood paneling over the damaged wall. We have already discussed drywall installation and finishing and repair of a plywood paneled wall.

Let's, therefore, restrict the discussion to restoring a wall that has cracked and loose plaster. In this situation the work can be performed by the owner with the help of family, neighbor, or friend, or the owner can hire an experienced mason or plasterer. If the option is do the work personally, some parts of the job are completed easily and others are difficult. The easy part is tearing out the old materials and applying the base and second coats. The difficult part is applying the top coat and matching or blending it into the old top coat. A mason has the skill to perform all parts of the job.

By using modern plastering materials and standard techniques, the work is much simpler than in days past. The materials can be purchased premixed dry and wet. We discuss this later in the section on reconstruction, but the mason has several choices. For example, he or she can choose a neat, wood-fibered, ready-mixed, or bond base coat. He or she can select from a variety of finish plasters, including gauging plaster, gypsum, Keene's cement, prepared gypsum finish plaster, and veneer coat (thin) plaster.

Statement of work and the planning effort.   The effort is to restore the wall, so our first statement of work should be: *We agree to restore the damaged wall to its original plastered condition, free of defects.* We then add several conditional statements beginning with *all old plaster will be removed to expose the lath, and where the lath is rotted or decayed, it too will be removed.* We then specify that *new lath will be applied to studs and a three-coat plaster system will be applied.* The next conditional statement must describe the finish and quality, such as *the finish coat will be troweled smooth to match the surface of the rest of the walls.* If the wall were textured, we would state that in our work description. Next, we specify the quality of the work: *We guarantee our work and agree to ensure that there will be no physical damage to floors and surrounding walls or furnishings.* Finally, we need to agree to paint the room or wall if the owner desires this done with a latex painting system.

For planning purposes, we need to employ both a mason/plasterer and a painter. We must also expect the two contractors to perform their work at separate times. The wall must have time to cure before the paint is applied. The mason could do the job without help, but this is a situation where the labor cost of a helper or apprentice reduces the total labor costs of the job. We know that much of the work is ripping out old materials. For this kind of work, we can use less expensive labor. The apprentice can even help apply the mew materials under the watchful eye of the master mason.

Due to the materials used, there can be a lot of dust while tearing out the old materials and plastering. We need to plan to restrict the dirt and dust to the room being restored. For this we plan to cover all openings leading to other rooms, to cover rugs, furniture, and fixtures, and to prevent tracking on floors in other rooms by covering the floors with vinyl.

Since the work is indoors and we expect to use premixed materials, we are not restricted by weather or temperature. This helps in scheduling the masons and painter. The painter will be the subcontractor to the mason contractor for this job. Therefore, the painter must submit the bid to the mason so that a single total price can be determined.

Contract.   After discussion with the owner and determining the amount of wall to replace, we can offer the owner a fixed-price contract. This makes it easy for the owner to decide to have us perform the work or seek elsewhere for a solution. We should incorporate the painter's bid in with ours to arrive at the total cost. The body of the contract could look like this:

For the fixed price stated below, we agree to restore the damaged plastered east wall in the living room. We agree to remove the damaged materials and replace them with a good-quality three-coat system of plaster. The finish or top coat will match the original and adjacent walls for smooth texture. The room will be repainted with a latex painting system by the painter after a minimum of 24 hours for setting and hardening. We further guarantee the work for one year and accept responsibility for damage to furnishings and flooring made by our workers.

Total price is $ XXX.XX.

Material Assessment

Direct Materials	Use/Purpose
Base coat plaster	For scratch and brown coats
Finish top coat	For the final coats on the wall
Water	For mixing
Lath	Wood, metal, or gypsum boards
Lath nails	To secure lath to the studs
Casing or finish nails	To renail trim in place

Indirect Materials	Use/Purpose
Vinyl sheet goods	To protect floors, block off doors, and cover furniture
Masking tape	To secure vinyl in place
Drop cloths	To cover furniture
Mortar board	As required to apply base coats

Support Materials	Use/Purpose
Mortar box	To mix plaster
Stepladder	To access upper parts of the wall
Mason tools	For masonry

Outside Contractor Support	Use/Purpose
Carpenter	To replace baseboards and door or window trim
Painter	To paint the entire room

Activities Planning Chart

Activity	Time Line (Days)						
	1	2	3	4	5	6	7
1. Contract preparation	❘ _×_ ❘	___ ❘	___ ❘	___ ❘	___ ❘	___ ❘	___ ❘
2. Materials and scheduling	❘ _×_ ❘	___ ❘	___ ❘	___ ❘	___ ❘	___ ❘	___ ❘
3. Removing the old wall	❘ ___ ❘	_×_ ❘	___ ❘	___ ❘	___ ❘	___ ❘	___ ❘
4. Applying the new plaster	❘ ___ ❘	___ ❘	_×_ ❘	_×_ ❘	___ ❘	___ ❘	___ ❘
5. Reinstalling the trim	❘ ___ ❘	___ ❘	___ ❘	___ ❘	_×_ ❘	___ ❘	___ ❘
6. Painting the room	❘ ___ ❘	___ ❘	___ ❘	___ ❘	_×_ ❘	_×_ ❘	___ ❘

Reconstruction

Contract preparation. We know that the office personnel must coordinate with the painter to arrive at a single contract price. This will take several phone calls, and the painter and carpenter may drop off their estimates rather than mailing them in. The office personnel must convert the specifications obtained from the job site into specific quantities of direct and indirect materials and price them out. They must also price out the labor costs for masons, helper, and company estimator and overhead. Then the written bid/contract is prepared for owner approval or negotiation.

The estimator must prepare the bill of materials and obtain costs to arrive at the total materials costs. He or she will make several calls to local suppliers or refer to a current price listing if the company has a database of this kind. He or she will also price out the worker costs and overhead. Most of these will be direct-labor, on-site costs, but some will be fixed costs.

Materials and scheduling. After receiving the contract acceptance, we would procure the materials and establish a time frame for doing the work. Since this is not a very large job, we would want to make use of workers when they were available. We see from the activity chart that we need two workers (a helper and a mason) for 3 days. Once they are done, the carpenter will need a day to reinstall the woodwork. Then the painter must spend 2 days priming and painting the walls and woodwork.

For this effort we enter the data into a production timetable. Then we coordinate with the subcontractors to see if they can work on the specific days. If not, we notify the owner when the subs will do their part of the job.

Removing the old wall. On the first day of the job, the helper and mason spend considerable time protecting the rest of the house and any furnishings left in the room. The removal process creates a great deal of dust and debris. They will cover all door openings with plastic/vinyl sheet goods. They will cover all furniture with cloths and carpeting with tape-down heavy-gauge vinyl. They will also tape down strips of heavy-gauge vinyl in the halls and other rooms between the room to be restored and the exterior door they plan to use to bring in and remove materials.

Next, they need to remove all woodwork from the wall to be restored. This means removing the baseboard, door casings, and window casings if the wall has a window. There may also be a fancy built-up crown molding at the ceiling. If so, it must be removed without damage as well. Throughout this effort the workers must avoid damaging the woodwork. Since the wall's plaster will be removed, the workers can ensure that their tools, such as crowbars and flat irons, dig deeply into the plaster before applying pressure against the wood. If there is any indecision in the mind of the mason contractor that his or her workers would damage the woodwork, he or she must call the carpenter in to do the work.

Since in our project, the ceiling and walls are plastered, we must take precautions to prevent cracking the ceiling and adjacent walls. The masons would score the joints with hand or power tools. This groove is important to the task. When the groove is complete, the old plaster is removed with hammers and crowbars.

Several problems can occur when removing the plaster and are worth identifying.

1. If the plaster was applied over wood strips, there will be a chance to crack pieces, and we should avoid this if possible. However, we do need to clear the clinkers between the strips to ensure a proper bond when we apply the new scratch coat.
2. If the plaster was bonded to gypsum boards, we will probably need to pull the boards off with most of the old plaster. This means that we need to remove it all and replace it.
3. If the plaster was applied over riblath (stretched wire), we can expect to replace some or all of it to save labor hours.

As the materials are removed from the wall, they are placed in a wheelbarrow and taken out to a truck for disposal. A vacuum such as a large shop vac should be used to trap the dust and clean up the floor area. When this part of the job is complete, we have an exposed wall with or without lath.

Applying the new plaster.   Since our project wall is an interior wood-framed wall, we will use the three-coat system. We plan to use packaged or job-prepared plaster mixes for the job. The base coats are made from bags of ready-mixed which contain the fibers needed for those coats. The finish coat is made from bags of prepared gypsum finish plaster. The sequence is as follows and is shown in Figure 1–9:

1. Bags of ready-mixed are opened into a small mortar box and mixed with the appropriate amount of water. Then the mason applies the mixture to the wall with a wide trowel. After it sets for an hour or so, the mason makes cross-rakes into the plaster to

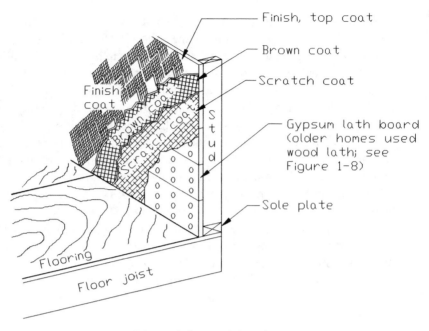

Figure 1–9   Applying plaster.

rough it up. Then the plaster is allowed to set and harden (not more than 8 hours total).

2. The same materials are used to apply the second base coat, or brown coat. It is not raked like the scratch coat, since the finish coat that is applied next is very thin.

3. The finish coat materials are mixed with water and applied with a trowel. Since this is an interior wall that will be painted and the other walls are smooth, the masons must use finishing trowels to create a smooth flat surface.

When the finish plaster has hardened, the masons need to clean up the job site and remove their equipment. They can take up the sheet goods, since the carpenter and painter will not require them.

Subcontractor work.   The carpenter must take the woodwork materials and reinstall them. If any were cracked or broken, he or she must replace them and set all nails. The painter must seal the wall and then apply the painting system, which is a flat latex paint on the walls and semigloss on the woodwork.

Concluding comments.   Plastering is not a job suited to a novice or do-it-yourselfer. It requires considerable knowledge to prepare the materials, and skill to apply them. Mistakes are not permitted. Timing is important, the proper consistency of mixture is important, and the method of application is important. All must be done expertly.

CHAPTER SUMMARY

In this chapter we studied and examined a wide variety of situations and problems that homeowners experience with walls and a few with ceilings. We looked at the problems from the owner's point of view, with the idea of defining the problems and trying to figure out solutions. Then we looked at the problems from the contractor's point of view and discussed many alternatives. Then we selected a solution and began to take corrective actions.

We outlined the statements of work, prepared a sample contract, and selected a type suitable for the job. We prepared a materials assessment to better understand the variety of materials needed, and prepared an activity list to plot out the major tasks and times. We then described the reconstruction activities by providing task sequences and technical details. In the concluding comments we commented on owners doing the work in relation to having it done by experienced contractor personnel.

2

CEILINGS

To repaint a textured or blown ceiling
To replace a severely damaged plaster ceiling with drywall
To restore a tile ceiling
To restore a drop ceiling

OPENING COMMENTS

Conditions or circumstances that necessitate corrective action. Many of the causes of wall damage also apply to ceilings. Smokers cause nicotine to accumulate on walls and ceilings. If the ceiling is made of drywall and is spray painted, the nicotine permeates the paint and vermiculite in the paint. Once there, it remains unless the materials are removed. Physical damage happens to ceilings just as it does to walls. Storms and fires cause the same damage to ceilings as to walls. However, other problems are uniquely ceiling problems. In this chapter we focus on them. They range from repainting a textured ceiling that has been damaged to restoring a suspended ceiling. Problems with these involve removal and replacement of materials fastened to the joist members or suspended from the joists, to problems with loose or fallen ceiling tiles that must be replaced.

Contractor's responsibility.   As we stated in Chapter 1, we, as contractors, can be faced with either of two situations pertaining to restoring ceilings or their coverings in a residential home. The first is where the amount of work is insufficient to have a worker dedicated to the job. This happens when less than a day's work would restore the damaged ceiling or its covering (however, this happens less frequently than when we restore walls). The other is finding a perfect match for the ceiling materials or the texture or paint on the ceilings.

Contractors face the same cost problems with ceiling restoration as they do with walls. Small jobs may be cost-prohibitive for the owner. For this reason many contractors refuse to take on such jobs. In some situations, the restoration work would involve just minor repair that requires expert help. The contractor may be willing to perform the work as a fill-in job and eliminate the allowance for profit. In such situations the job is done to create goodwill. Even so, the price may be substantial.

Homeowner's expectations.   The homeowner expects us to restore the ceiling to its original condition. He or she also expects us to locate the appropriate materials to match the damaged ones or to match the paint or texture of the ceiling. In some cases this is time consumming for our estimators and the people at the builder's supply house where we do business. Nevertheless, those are the expectations. Yet the owner also expects a fair price for the work performed and materials used. Finally, the owner expects a good-quality job with no damage to the rest of the home or its furnishings.

Scope of projects.   The objectives list the four types of problems with ceilings that we cover in this chapter. We have separated them from Chapter 1 because they are uniquely ceiling problems and have no association with walls.

PROJECT 1. REPAINT A TEXTURED OR BLOWN CEILING

Subcategories include: spot painting; general painting with power tools; roller painting; types of paint or special mixtures; preparation and protection of walls and floors; safety factors; and cleanup requirements.

Preliminary Discussion with the Owner

Problems facing the owner. The owner looks at the ceiling every day without seeing it. It slowly gets dirty from smoke, infiltration of outside dust particles, and dust or organisms brought in on the clothing of the occupants. Slowly but surely it darkens, and eventually the owner recognizes that it is not bright as before. It needs painting. The owner can also recognize that the ceiling needs painting when repairs are made to it and the new paint is much brighter than the old.

The owner also recognizes that the ceiling is not a smooth surface but is textured. This presents several problems. First, if it is rolled improperly with new paint, the texture will fall off and the surface will look bumpy rather than textured. Second, he or she does not have the equipment, knowledge, or skill to respray it. Finally, how does one spray the ceiling without getting the mixture all over the walls and floor?

Alternative solutions to the problem. There are several alternatives to this problem. To retain the texture of the ceiling, the owner can rent the equipment and practice using it with the proper mixture of textured paint until he or she has mastered the technique, then apply paint to the ceiling; the owner can employ the expertise of a painter to do the job who has the equipment and can do the work; or the owner can obtain the proper type of roller and paint the ceiling while retaining a majority of texture on the ceiling. In addition to applying the paint, protection of walls and floors is a serious concern. Protective vinyl sheet goods needs to be taped to walls and cover the floor.

We need to remember that the cost of hiring a painter must be weighed against the salary earned for the same period. If the cost equals the salary earned, it's a toss up. But if the salary earned is greater than the cost, the painter should do the work. This assumes that the skill needed to apply the paint is equal between owner and painter. For our project, we assume that the painter will perform the work.

Statement of work and the planning effort. The primary statement of work is to *restore the ceiling to its primary quality by repainting it.* To accomplish this, we need to *remove all light fixtures and deflectors/directors.* We must *tape vinyl sheets to the wall to prevent overspray or direct spray from damaging the walls.* We must *prevent damage to floors by covering them with drop cloths or heavy-gauge (6 mil) vinyl.* We need to *apply a good-quality paint mixture whose color is white and whose texture is medium.* The dry-mix ceiling paint is available in light, medium, and heavy texture. This means that the size of the vermiculite is different in each type. Finally, we need to *provide a high-quality job and complete cleanup.*

For this job, the painter must discuss the work with the owner, which requires an examination of the ceilings. Then the ceilings must be measured so that pricing can be determined. If the work involves one room only, the job could be done in a day, but normally the entire house is done at one time. An entire house of 2000 square feet, for example, could take up to 3 days for a painter and helper. The actual spraying time is only a fraction of the total time. Most of the time is used for preparation and cleanup.

In addition to the production time, we need to schedule the job after contract negotiations are complete.

Contract.   The contract for this project could be of the fixed-price type. There are no hidden aspects that could drive up the price. We would expect the body of the contract to encompass the statements of work:

For the price listed below, we will paint the ceilings in the house with a spray that restores the original textured surface to the ceilings. The paint will be applied once.

We guarantee that no overspray will touch walls or floor or any furniture remaining in the rooms. All materials used to protect the interior will be cleaned up upon completion of the job.

The owner is expected to present a check or cash at the completion of the job unless special arrangements are made ahead of time.

Time and materials costs: $XXX.XX.

Material Assessment

Direct Materials	Use/Purpose
Textured or acoustical dry-mix ceiling paint	Mixed with water and sprayed; some brushing around perimeter
Water	To mix with the dry paint

Indirect Materials	Use/Purpose
Vinyl sheet goods	To protect walls, floors, and furniture
Masking tape	To hold vinyl in place
Mixing pails	To mix paint

Support Materials	Use/Purpose
Stepladders	To paint around the perimeter and apply vinyl covering to the walls
Spray outfit and hoses	To spray paint onto ceiling
Brushes	For hand painting

Outside Contractor Support   **Use/Purpose**

None

Activities Planning Chart

Activity	Time Line (Days)						
	1	2	3	4	5	6	7
1. Contract preparation	I _×_ I ___ I ___ I ___ I ___ I ___ I ___ I
2. Materials and scheduling	I _×_ I ___ I ___ I ___ I ___ I ___ I ___ I
3. Preparing the room and ceiling	I ___ I _×_ I _×_ I ___ I ___ I ___ I ___ I
4. Spray-painting the ceiling	I ___ I _×_ I _×_ I _×_ I ___ I ___ I ___ I
5. Cleaning up the job site	I ___ I ___ I ___ I _×_ I ___ I ___ I ___ I

Reconstruction

Contract preparation.   The painter or his or her office staff would prepare the contracts after developing estimates for materials and labor. Since the job involves simple repainting of existing ceilings and there are no repairs, the estimate should be straightforward. The worksheet should list the direct and indirect materials, and these need to be quantified and priced.

The allowance for overhead and profit should be determined for the method used by the contractor. This can be a percentage of the annual expected fixed cost of operations and the application of variable costs associated with this contract.

Finally, the labor rates for the helper and painter are computed and the worksheet is ready for tallying. With the total of fixed and variable expenses and the appropriate tax rate applied, the total price is derived. The contract/bid document can now be typed.

Materials and scheduling.   The materials are simple to obtain from a paint supply house. One stop of less than an hour on the morning of the first day should suffice. The order could be placed the day before to preclude workers wasting time in line for supply pickup. There will only be several bags of dry paint mixture, masking tape, and vinyl sheet goods.

Scheduling this job is not difficult since only painters are involved and no outside subcontractors are involved. What we would do is program the work after the next job completion or between larger jobs.

Preparing the room and ceiling.   We are guaranteeing a first-quality job of spraying the ceilings with textured paint. Therefore, we must take every precaution to avoid overspray. The paint from the gun will go forward (in this case upward) and outward. Any paint not adhering to the ceiling will fall to the floor or adhere to the sides of the walls. Our task is to place a vinyl sheet barrier against the walls and on the floor to trap the overspray.

We tape the vinyl sheet goods to the wall along the ceiling–wall line. This is an exacting task, especially when the walls are painted a color other than white. But even when the walls are white, we need to prevent overspray since the spray contains vermiculite (the texture material), which will create bumps. We need to overlap each piece of vinyl about 12 in. and apply small strips of tape to the seams.

After completing the walls, we apply a layer of vinyl over the floors to protect the carpets, vinyl, or other flooring. This completes the cocoon in which we will spray the ceiling. We repeat the process with the other rooms.

Spray-painting the ceiling.   The painter begins by mixing the paint. Normally, the dry mix is mixed with proportioned amounts of tap water. Most skilled painters use a pressurized container spray outfit. This type of unit features hoses attached to a gun and cannister. Many painters use stilts such as those used by drywall installers, to eliminate the need for a low scaffold or stepladders.

The quality of the spray job is determined by the even flow from the gun to the ceiling. When it is not sprayed evenly, there will be built-up areas that may create shadows or thin spots where the the texture is very thin or nonexistent. In our situation of repainting the ceilings, a light coat of paint will probably permit the old, darkened ceiling to bleed through. Should this happen, we would need to apply another coat. From the contractor's viewpoint, this adds cost to the job and reduces profit. From the owner's viewpoint, this problem can only be fixed by repainting.

Cleaning up the job site.   We would inspect the ceiling after the paint has set and dried sufficiently. This is important to do before cleaning up the room. We would normally peel masking tape off the walls and let it build up on the floor. While doing so, we would ensure that the painted side lay face down and toward the center of the room. Then we roll up the vinyl and cart it outside. We load the empty bags and vinyl and any other waste materials into the truck for disposal. Finally, we clean the equipment to ensure proper operation on the next job.

Concluding comments.   Homeowners can rent the equipment and can buy the paints needed to spray the ceiling. With careful room preparation as we described here, the owner can perform the work of the painter. However, the equipment must be used properly and the conditions that create a poor job must be avoided. Painters can do the job efficiently and quickly. They usually apply an even or uniform coat to the ceiling so that one coat covers it all and has the correct texture.

PROJECT 2. REPLACE A SEVERELY DAMAGED PLASTER CEILING WITH DRYWALL

Subcategories include: furring techniques and materials; leveling the ceiling; lowering the light fixtures; installing the drywall; taping and floating the joints; and adding cove or crown molding.

Preliminary Discussion with the Owner

Problems facing the owner.   The owner with the severely damaged plastered ceiling has the option of having the ceiling replaced with plaster or having it covered over with drywall to eliminate forever the problem of cracking. In this project we are going to examine the alternative of replacing the ceiling with drywall. Next the owner must decide whether he or she will do the work or have it done. Some of the following conditions or considerations may aid in answering the question.

The weight of plaster is considerable. The fact that it hangs on the ceiling by the clinkers between the wood lath or metal holes makes it relatively heavy dead weight. Throughout the years of service, the weight has had an effect on the ceiling joists. They almost always have some sag. Where good-quality wood such as virgin yellow pine or Douglas fir was used for the joists and the sizes were ample to support the weight, there will be little sag. However, the wood quality often proves insufficient to support the ceiling and there will be sagging. The sag would ordinarily be enough to cause cracking. The more the sag, the greater the amount and severity of cracking. The important point here is that there is no reversal.

The ceiling must be replaced, but it may also need leveling. This is not a difficult part of the total job, but it does take some construction knowledge and skill. The ceiling is stripped with 1 × 3s or 1 × 4s on 16-in. centers. Blocks are used between the plaster and the back side of the 1 × 3 or 1 × 4s as furring pieces. These permit leveling the ceiling. Then drywall panels are nailed to the strips. Taping and painting operations follow. Finally, the border trim is added.

Alternative solutions to the problem.   From the contractor's viewpoint, what are the alternatives that the owner can select? The contractor needs to show the owner that applying a drywall ceiling is the solution. He or she needs to explain that the ceiling will be lowered by 2 in. or more depending on the severity of the sagging. In some cases the contractor would recommend removing some of the plaster and lath to avoid lowering the ceiling too much. This point must be agreed to by the owner and contractor.

Using molding to cover the joint between the wall and ceiling is optional. If the option is to use molding such as crown or cove, repainting the side walls can be eliminated as a requirement. This may save some costs. If the owner desires no molding, the contractor must tape the ceiling drywall and wall and apply three coats of joint compound. This operation will necessitate repainting the walls. This single set of conditions is a trade-off. Both incur costs and affect the character of the ceiling and must be chosen by the owner.

For our project, we will apply molding so that the reader can learn how ceiling perimeter molding is prepared and applied to the ceiling–wall joint.

Statement of work and the planning effort.   The preliminary statement of work is *to replace the damaged ceiling with a new one built from drywall.* To perform this work we need to state that *the new ceiling will be level and that sagging now present will be eliminated.* The specifications also include *furring out the ceiling to eliminate the sag and to provide a sound base for nailing the drywall.* Next, we need to state the final appearance of the ceiling: *The ceiling will be taped and floated and painted with a flat latex ceiling paint. Around the perimeter we will install $3\frac{1}{2}$-in. crown molding. It will be painted with semigloss latex.* Finally, we add the quality statement: *We guarantee no damage to walls, floors, or furnishings, and the job site will be policed thoroughly.*

The planning effort for this job involves soliciting estimates from subcontractors: drywall installers, painters, and carpenters. A coordinated effort will produce the desired outcome. There are no special materials needed that could delay completing the work. The contract preparation should not be excessively long. Since this is a small job, we can plan to fit it into the schedule fairly easily.

Contract.   Although there are three contractors needed to perform the various parts of the project, each should be able to prepare a fixed-price type contract. Each can be given a description of the job and with it they can calculate the materials and labor required for their part. These bids will be forwarded to us, the general contractor, for consolidation into a single fixed-price bid/contract. The body of this contract could look something like this:

We will replace the damaged plastered ceiling with drywall. The completed ceiling will be level, properly floated, and painted with a three-coat system of ceiling paint. Around the perimeter of the room, we will install and finish a crown molding. For its finish, we will apply a semigloss matching painting system.

We guarantee a good-quality job and complete cleanup. We will be responsible for any damage to walls, floors, or furnishings that cannot be removed from the room.

The schedule of work will be coordinated between us and the owner. The owner agrees to have a member of the family home while workers are present.

The bid/contract price is $XXX.XX.

Material Assessment

Direct Materials	Use/Purpose
1×3 or 1×4	Furring strips
8d common nails	To nail furring strips to ceiling joists
$\frac{1}{2}$-in. drywall	Sheets of drywall to cover old ceiling
Drywall nails or screws	To secure drywall to furring strips
Drywall tape and compound	To cover joints and float joints
$3\frac{1}{2}$-in. crown molding	Applied around ceiling and wall
6d or 8d finish nails	To nail molding to wall/ceiling
Flat ceiling latex painting system	To paint the ceiling
Semigloss latex painting system	To paint the molding

Indirect Materials	Use/Purpose
Filler blocks	Shims to level the ceiling
Roller	To apply paint to the ceiling
Masking tape and vinyl	To apply to floor and, if needed, to walls
Drop cloths	To protect furnishings

Support Materials	Use/Purpose
Carpenter tools	For construction and trim installation
Painter tools	To apply the painting systems
Drywall installers	To install and finish the drywall

Outside Contractor Support	Use/Purpose
Painter	To paint the ceiling and woodwork
Drywall contractor	To perform the drywall installation

Activities Planning Chart

Activity	Time Line (Days) 1	2	3	4	5	6	7
1. Contract preparation	×						
2. Materials and scheduling	×						
3. Stripping the ceiling		×					
4. Installing and finishing the drywall			×	×			
5. Installing the crown molding					×		
6. Painting the ceiling and trim					×	×	
7. Cleaning up the job site						×	

Reconstruction

Contract preparation.   This contract is an assembly of the estimates of the three contractors involved. Therefore, our office workers must provide specifications to the drywall installers and painter. With them the subcontractors can provide fixed-price bid/contracts. Our office personnel must compile an estimate of materials from the materials list and price the materials. Then they need to price the labor and overhead, and finally, the worksheet price-out is used to arrive at the contract price. We have already shown how the statements of work are formulated into the body of the description. The final typing produces a bid/contract proposal. The prime contractor uses this to arrive at a consent agreement with the owner.

Materials and scheduling.   The materials are all standard types that are readily available at any local builder's supply or lumberyard. Due to the limited quantities involved, each contractor will pick them up the day before work begins or on the first scheduled day.

The schedule is shown in the activity list above. The work is performed sequentially; this extends the total time for completion somewhat but is unavoidable.

Stripping the ceiling.   The carpenters must install strips on the ceiling on 16-in. centers, as shown in Figure 2–1. The first piece is nailed alongside the wall and the direction is usually perpendicular to the direction of the ceiling joists.

The sequence of tasks is as follows:

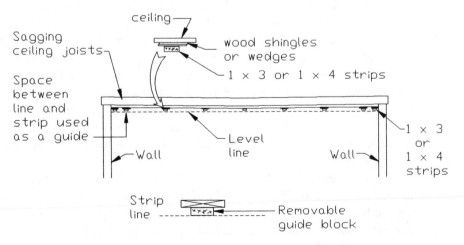

Figure 2–1   Applying wood strips to an old ceiling.

1. Ascertain the amount and point of ceiling sag.
2. Determine how best to eliminate the sag and strike chalk lines around the perimeter accordingly.
3. Mark opposite walls at 16-in. centers.
4. Cut a fairly large stack of wedges as shown in Figure 2–1. These will be used in pairs as needed.
4. Cut 1 × 3s or 1 × 4s to fit the room's length and nail centered on the marks. Insert a pair of wedges close to the nail and drive the nail in.
5. Use the mason line as a guide to determine how far to drive the wedges to create a flat ceiling.
6. Finalize the installation with a piece against the wall.
7. Perform a cross-check with the mason line opposite the direction of the run of the 1 × 3s. Make adjustments as required.

Installing and finishing the drywall.   We will not repeat this process since the subject was covered earlier. However, installing full-length sheets of drywall onto the ceiling is a strenuous task and usually requires two workers. After the drywall is nailed in place, the three-step process of taping and floating is done.

Installing the crown molding.   The carpenter needs to return to the job for a couple of hours to cut and install the $3\frac{1}{2}$-in.-wide crown molding. This task requires a great deal of skill and a certain amount of knowledge. Figure 2–2 provides several clues that show how the carpenter thinks and works. Notice that the molding has to fit flat against the wall and ceiling. The molding is manufactured so that the convex part is near the ceiling and the concave part is near the wall. If you look closely, you will also be able to distinguish a difference in the width of the wood's surface that fits against the wall and ceiling. The orientation must be carefully maintained when each piece is installed. If not, the union of joints will not be exact.

The carpenter does not use miter joints in the corners, but does use them when two pieces must be used along one wall. The miter is accomplished simply with the use of a miter box. However, the joint at the corner is made differently: The "coping" technique is used, which produces a closer fit. Figure 2–2 also shows how this joint is made. Notice that the carpenter places the crown molding into the miter box upside down. Then a 45-degree miter is cut, which reveals the coping line. He or she then uses a coping saw and severely undercuts along the line between the face grain and the end grain.

The pieces are nailed to the wall with 6d or 8d finish or casing nails which are toed slightly upward. This upward direction is crucial to pull the molding firmly against both the wall and the ceiling. Where the final piece is a single length, the carpenter must cope both ends, and this requires great skill.

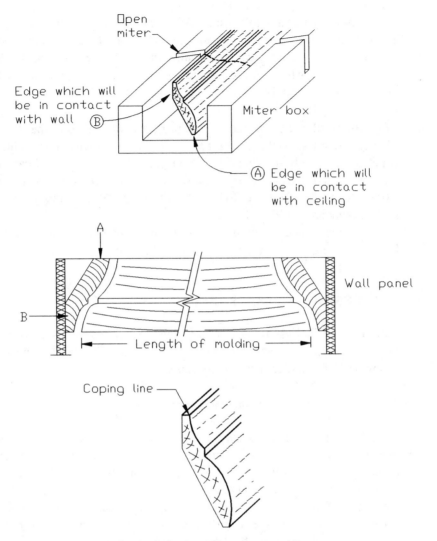

Figure 2–2   Installing crown molding.

Painting the ceiling and trim.   The painter will apply a base coat or under-coat to both the wood and the drywall. Since all materials will be painted with latex paint, the same base-coat paint can be used. After the paint dries, the painter must fill the nail holes with spackling and sand the surface.

The final two ceiling coats of flat paint are applied with a roller and paint-brush. The molding is given two coats of latex semigloss as per the specifica-tions.

Cleaning up the job site.   After the work has been completed and in-spected, the contractor removes all vinyl sheet goods, drop cloths and tools from the job site. We guaranteed a high-quality job, so the cleanup must be thorough and complete. All waste and excess materials must be removed from the job site and disposed of accordingly.

Concluding comments.   This project is not suited to the do-it-yourselfer. There are many steps that are best solved by the experienced. In addition, all work is performed overhead. This is strenuous, and the inexperienced can suffer severe muscle strain or worse. Some of the work is performed on low scaffolds, some on ladders, and some from the floor with stilts. This means climbing and working on surfaces that are not like a floor.

The job can be costly, but the solution can be the best one over the long run. Certainly, there will be no more cracking of plaster.

PROJECT 3. RESTORE A TILE CEILING

Subcategories include: understanding how tile ceilings are installed; removal tech-niques; installation of new tiles with cements, nails, or other fasteners; cutting and fitting new tiles; and reinstalling moldings.

Preliminary Discussion with the Owner

Problems facing the owner.   The owner of a home with one or more ceil-ings covered with ceiling tiles that have been damaged must replace them or have them replaced. The owner who has a tile ceiling that has darkened with age or is smoke damaged from cigarette, pipe, or cigar smoke or cooking smoke can repaint the ceiling. We will not discuss repainting, since painting ceilings was discussed earlier in the chapter. We need to focus on a ceiling that has sustained physical damage. This damage can be the result of fire, storm, or water, or a failure of ce-ment. Of all of these, water damage is the most prevalent.

Owners who know installation techniques can sometimes replace damaged tiles with new ones. If we know that the tiles were stapled to 1 × 4 strips, we can remove and replace them. If we know that they were cemented to a plaster or drywall base, we can replace them. If we know that they were of interlocking type, as shown in Figure 2–3, we can replace them by trimming off certain interlocks. If we know that they were of noninterlocking type, as shown in Figure 2–4, they can easily be removed and replaced.

The next problem we face is matching the tile on the ceiling with new tiles. For this we would remove a tile and take it to a builder's supply house for a match.

Figure 2–3   Ceiling tiles with interlocking design.

Employees there can usually identify the tile by manufacturer and style number and name. With luck, we will find that the style has not been discontinued and that replacements are available. One company manufactures these with a count of 40 per box. A builder's supply house rarely sells less than a full-box quantity.

This work is classified as finish work, which means that a certain amount of knowledge about ceiling tile construction is necessary. A considerable amount of skill is required to remove and replace damaged tiles without creating additional problems or expanding the damaged area.

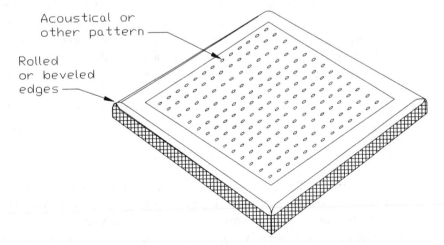

Figure 2–4   Noninterlocking ceiling tiles.

Alternative solutions to the problem.   The first alternative to the problem is to make a personal evaluation regarding knowledge and skill. When the owner lacks either, he or she should seek help from a carpenter or contractor. The experienced carpenter knows how to remove and replace damaged tiles without enlarging the damaged area and causing further expense. He or she also knows how to remove and reinstall ceiling moldings without cracking or breaking them. Every ceiling covered with tile squares has a border cove or crown molding.

When the tiles can be matched with new ones, the cost of the job is less than when all new tiles must be purchased. In the event that the tiles cannot be matched, the owner must replace the entire ceiling, even if only a few tiles are damaged. The owner could also call the manufacturer, who may know of a distributor or outlet that has some discontinued stock on hand.

Even when the replacement tiles are a match, the old ones may be discolored and the colors are off. In that case, this is a two-phase job: to replace the damaged tiles and then to repaint the entire ceiling.

For our project, we will assume that replacement tiles are available and that the ceiling is clean and bright. The ceiling uses an interlocking tongue-and-groove tile that is stapled to 1 × 4 strips. The border trim is 2-in. cove.

Statement of work and the planning effort.   The ceiling tiles in a corner of the room were damaged due to a plumbing leak and have turned black with stain. Our job is to *replace the damaged tiles with new ones of the same style and color.* We must also *remove and replace the cove molding and fill all nail holes as appropriate.* Finally, we must *repaint the cove to match the current color.*

The planning effort for this job is not extensive but requires locating replacement tiles, preparing the estimate and contract, scheduling the carpenter for the work, and making the final inspection. The carpenter or contractor may recognize the tile by sight or may have to remove a piece for a sample. Locating the match may be simple, or as we stated above, may take several phone calls and a week or more for shipping. The owner may have to agree to have the entire ceiling replaced, and this will increase the worker's time on the job. The carpenter may be able to repaint the cove that was removed. If not, the painter will perform the work, or the homeowner may elect to do the painting. This decision must be known in the planning stages.

Contract.   This job can be bid with a fixed-price contract. Even though there may be some time lapse locating the matching tiles, we, as contractors, would not consider this an unusual circumstance. Once the tiles were located or we found out for certain that none were available, we would proceed with contract preparation. We will assume that the tiles are still available and construct the body of the contract accordingly.

For the price stipulated below, we agree to replace all damaged ceiling tiles with matching tiles. We will perform all carpentry work and ensure a high-quality job. The owner will provide the paint for the carpenter to repaint the cove molding at the ceiling.

In the event that the matching tiles are significantly brighter in color than the rest of the ceiling, a separate contract or an amendment to this contract will be prepared for painting the entire ceiling.

Time and materials: $XXX.XX.

Material Assessment

Direct Materials	Use/Purpose
Ceiling tiles	To replace damaged tiles
Staples or cement	To fasten tiles to ceiling or $1 \times 4s$
Paste wood filler	To seal nail holes in molding
Paint	To repaint the molding

Indirect Materials	Use/Purpose
Drop clothes	To cover floor and furniture

Support Materials	Use/Purpose
Carpenter tools	For construction
Stepladder	To reach ceiling
Paintbrush	To apply paint to trim
Workbench or table	To measure and cut tiles
Staple gun	To insert staples

Outside Contractor Support	Use/Purpose
None	

Activities Planning Chart

Activity	Time Line (Days)
	1 2 3 4 5 6 7
1. Contract preparation	|_×_|___|___|___|___|___|___|
2. Materials and scheduling	|_×_|___|___|___|___|___|___|
3. Removing and replacing the damaged tiles	|___|_×_|___|___|___|___|___|

Reconstruction

Contract preparation.   Due to the simplicity of the job, there would not be many requirements of office personnel in preparing the contract. A standard work-sheet would be used for this 1-day effort. However, if there were a problem obtaining matching tiles, the cost would increase slightly due to office hours and long-distance phone call charges against the job. The contractor could have the contract ready in less than a day, after which he or she and the owner could agree on the stipulated work and price.

Materials and scheduling.   The minimum number of tiles charged to the job would be determined by the total full boxes of tiles required. Even if a half-box were all that were required, the owner would be charged for a full box. (The contractor would probably leave extra tiles with the owner since another call for that style may never arise.)

Scheduling this one-day job would probably be a simple matter. In all likelihood the contractor would schedule a carpenter on a fill-in day between other jobs.

Removing and replacing the damaged tiles.   The tasks for this job are as follows:

1. Remove the ceiling cove molding along the wall or walls where the tiles need to be replaced.
2. Remove the damaged tiles, being careful not to extend the damaged area.
3. Install the replacement tiles.
4. Reinstall the cove molding and fill the nail-head holes.
5. Paint the molding.
6. Clean up the job site.

One major concern in doing this job is to maintain perfect tile alignment. The tiles are made of fiber that is very fragile; it is easily crushed and damaged. This means that when a tile is installed with its tongue sides (two sides have tongues) into the adjacent tile's grooves, the carpenter must ensure proper alignment. If he or she applies too little or to much force, the ceiling goes out of alignment and becomes crooked. Alignment is essential.

There are two tongue sides with wide flat surfaces (consult Figure 2–3 if necessary); the staples are driven into these surfaces. Normally, three staples are used on the side parallel to the 1×4 and one more is used on the side in the adjacent 1×4.

End pieces and pieces that fit around openings in the ceiling must be individually cut to fit. Sometimes the old pieces can be used as a model. These pieces are easily cut with a handsaw or very sharp utility knife. The carpenter measures and fits each one, then staples it in place.

Where the damaged tiles cannot be slid into place because of the tongues, the tongues are carefully trimmed away. The tile is placed into the opening and a 1-in. white or buff colored nail with a very small head (wood paneling nails could be used) is driven into a crevasse in the tile and into the wood. Then it is set slightly below the surface to hide it. In most cases, no spackling is needed, but some may be used if the nail head is visible.

Concluding comments.   This project is one that a homeowner can do if he or she has some skill with tools and a clear understanding of the job. None of the work is heavy, but all of it requires careful planning and execution.

A contractor would have no problems performing the work with minimum interruption to the family and house. His or her work skills would ensure no change from the straight lines currently in the ceiling.

PROJECT 4. RESTORE A DROP CEILING

Subcategories include: materials used in drop ceilings; techniques used to hold up the rails and ties; reinstalling border strips; removing damaged tiles; and fitting and installing new tiles.

Preliminary Discussion with the Owner

Problems facing the owner.   Many homes have drop ceilings—also called suspended ceilings—in kitchens, basements, dens, and even bathrooms. In these installations ceiling lights are usually flush with the acoustical tiles. The owner who has a ceiling of this type can simply change the tiles when they are damaged, stained, or have sagged from getting wet. Each tile, whether 2 × 2 ft or 2 × 4 ft, lays in a metal frame that is suspended from the joists. Manufacturers of suspended ceiling components prepare the runners and cross tees, wall angle pieces, and common wire used to tie up the frame. (See Figure 2–5 for typical members of a suspended ceiling.) In every case the frame is painted. Most often the color is white since most tiles are white. However, there are decorator schemes that use anodized frames and decorator tiles.

When the owner needs to change the tiles, he or she would buy a box of tiles

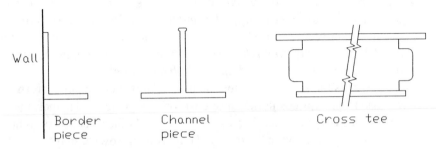

Figure 2–5   Members of a suspended ceiling.

and replace them as needed. Many will need cutting to fit. These are the ones adjacent to the walls, next to lights, and around heater/air-conditioner deflectors and distributors.

When the ceiling has sustained more severe physical damage that involves the frame, the replacement job becomes more difficult and certain skills and knowledge are required to make the repairs. At this point the owner may call in a contractor to appraise the damage and recommend a solution.

Alternative solutions to the problem.   There are conditions that create alternatives to solving the problem for the owner. The contractor needs to identify them; they can include:

1. Locating the matching tiles or decorator panels
2. Reestablishing the original flat and level frame
3. Replacing the lighting that was suspended with an exact replacement
4. Helping the owner determine the minimum effective solution to the set of actual conditions

One alternative would be to replace the damaged piece of frame and insert new tiles or panels into the frame. Another might be to remove the damaged frame and install a completely new one. Another would be to install a slightly different frame and tiles/panels where the frame is not seen. This slight modification could enhance the ceiling's appearance but could add to the cost of the restoration. For our project we shall consider the ceiling to be storm damaged and in need of full replacement.

Statement of work and the planning effort.   The project is straightforward; we must *remove and replace the damaged drop ceiling.* We need to include several specifications pertaining to the job, such as: *All new light fixtures will be included in the estimate, and ceiling tiles and panels will match the old ones for pattern and color to the maximum extent possible.* The owner needs to have an input in this matter, so we state that *the owner must provide acceptance for the pattern and color of the ceiling tiles and fixtures.* Where the old fixtures were 2×2 incandescent types with white flat surface plastic panels, *the owner may opt for 2×2 surface lights, spotlights, track lighting, or a combination of these.* The contractor also *guarantees a high-quality job and full cleanup.*

We, as the contractor, must plan to have one carpenter perform this job. But we also need to price out the labor cost for a carpenter and helper; there might be a cost savings to the owner. We will need to clarify the selection of lighting and style and color of ceiling with the owner. To this end the owner may need our help locating suitable places to look. Beyond this, we need to prepare the estimate and worksheets, schedule pickup of the materials, and time for completing the job. We must also plan for a final inspection and presentation of bill.

Contract.   This contract should be a modified fixed-price type. We should allow the owner a price range for ceiling light fixtures. We also need to allow a certain latitude in pricing for ceiling panel style and color. The ranges we provide should be set with the owner and should fall within his or her budget. We should also help the owner avoid selecting lights or styles that do not blend well architecturally.

The body of the contract should contain these specifications and statements of work:

We will restore the damaged ceiling within the price range specified below. The owner may select the electrical lights in any combination from flush 2 × 2 recessed types, recessed spotlights, and track lighting with a total value not to exceed $XXX.XX. The owner can also choose the style and color of ceiling tiles or panels from suggested vendors provided by the contractor.

The contractor will provide all other materials and will pick up selected fixtures and tiles and panels after contract signing.

The contractor will also replace the damaged ceiling and provide a guarantee of high-quality work. Site cleanup is included in the estimate.

The total price will not exceed $XXX.XX as long as the owner remains within allowances specified in this contract. The final price will be adjusted according to the actual price of owner-selected materials.

Material Assessment

Direct Materials	Use/Purpose
Suspended ceiling frame	Various pieces that make up the frame
General-purpose wire	To tie up framing members
6d common nails	To nail L-shaped pieces to wall
Tiles and panels	To set into the frame
Light fixtures	To replace old lights
Wire nuts and electrical tape	To make electrical connections

Indirect Materials	Use/Purpose
Drop cloths	To protect the floor

Support Materials	Use/Purpose
Stepladder	To reach the ceiling
Carpenter tools	For construction
Workbench	To mark and cut tiles and panels

Outside Contractor Support	Use/Purpose
Electrician (possibly optional)	To install new lights

Activities Planning Chart

Activity	Time Line (Days)						
	1	2	3	4	5	6	7
1. Contract preparation	I _×_ I	___ I	___ I	___ I	___ I	___ I	___ I
2. Materials and scheduling	I _×_ I	___ I	___ I	___ I	___ I	___ I	___ I
3. Removing and replacing the old frame	I ___ I	_×_ I	_×_ I	___ I	___ I	___ I	___ I
4. Installing the lights	I ___ I	___ I	_×_ I	___ I	___ I	___ I	___ I
5. Installing the panels	I ___ I	___ I	___ I	_×_ I	___ I	___ I	___ I

Reconstruction

Contract preparation.   The office staff will develop the estimate of materials and set the labor costs based on the statements of work and activity list. They will be in contact with the owner to determine what style and color the ceiling should be and what fixtures to include in the contract. Recall from the suggested body of the contract that the owner had certain rights.

The actual typing and coordination of the contract will take only an hour or slightly more to prepare from the estimating worksheet. Then the contractor can take it to the owner for acceptance.

Regarding the lights, in some situations a carpenter who has the electrical knowledge to reinstall fixtures would do the job. However, if new wiring must be run where light fixtures were placed differently than before, the contract price would include the cost of an electrician.

Materials and scheduling.   Materials will be picked up by the carpenter assigned to the job, since they can easily fit into a pickup truck. These will be the same as those listed in the materials assessment. The estimator would have provided a complete quantity list along with specific style and color data. The carpenter would also pick up the lights.

From the activity list we see that the carpenter will be at the job for 3 days and the electrician (if required) would be there for several hours to not more than a day. Some coordination is required if two workers are used. To avoid delays and minimize wage costs, the carpenter must not be delayed from completing his or her work. If, however, the electrician is not available when needed, the carpenter would require two specifically assigned days.

Removing and replacing the old frame.   The frame pieces of the suspended ceilings are manufactured in long strips and cross strips. The long strips are hung from the joists with wire and spaced 2 ft apart. The cross pieces fit into slots in the long pieces. This arrangement forms either 2×2 squares or 2×4 squares, as shown in Figure 2–6. Around the room's perimeter, an L-shaped piece is fastened to the studs.

The only difficult part of the job is the layout. When performing this task we must determine how much each border panel's width is to ensure that both sides of the room have equal-width border panels. The simplest way is to measure the room's width and divide by 2 to obtain an answer for the number of whole pieces. Then we divide the remainder to define the width of each border panel. We use this same approach to define the length of each border on the end walls.

Installing the lights.   Where light fixtures are installed flush with the suspended ceiling, they are set in place before the panels are installed. They may be either a 2×2 assembly or round spot or area light fixture. The 2×2 type occupies one entire 2×2 panel opening or one-half of a 2×4 opening, as Figure 2–7 shows. The spotlight assembly is also flush with the suspended ceiling frame with the light bulb recessed in the housing. These lamps are customarily placed in the exact center of a panel opening. This unit is less than 12 in. across, which means that a hole must be cut into the panel to fit the lamp. All wiring to the fixtures must be completed and tested before the panels are set in place.

Figure 2–6   Replacing suspended ceiling frames.

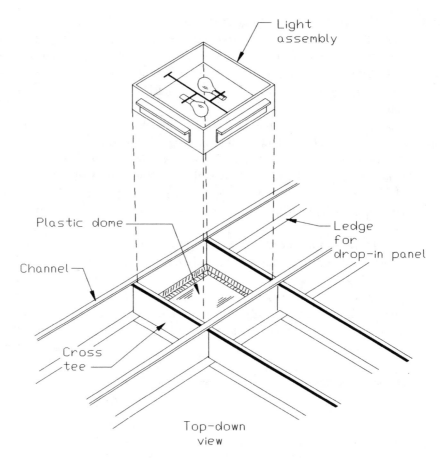

Figure 2–7 Installing a light in the frame.

Installing the panels.   Installing the panels is a simple task. They are usually installed at the worker's preference. Sometimes the border pieces are cut to fit and placed first. Sometimes the border panels are installed last. Sometimes, because furniture must be moved, a section of the room's ceiling is completed and then another, and another, until the job is done.

Concluding comments.   Homeowners with some skills in carpentry can perform this job and produce a high-quality ceiling. The manufacturer of the components produces standard parts and instruction sheets for their installation. No special tools are needed. Previous lines along the walls can be used as references to simplify the job further.

The layout is important and must be planned carefully. Lights must be installed correctly within the frames, and this may pose problems for the owner. Yet these often come with installation instructions as well.

The experienced carpenter can perform the job efficiently and accurately. This may be a better solution. Where new wiring is needed, local building codes may require a licensed electrician install the new fixtures. Then the local inspector would approve the work. This is something to be discussed between the owner and the contractor.

CHAPTER SUMMARY

We have examined and studied four types of ceiling problems. Each has a unique set of conditions that either the owner or contractor must deal with and solve. As a rule, restoration of ceilings is moderately expensive and frequently requires skillful workers. Some owners can perform some of the restoration work: where, for example, panels or tiles need to be replaced in a suspended ceiling.

We have also found that matching ceiling materials and colors may become a problem that drives up the cost of the job. We also learned that a skilled worker often brings a helper or apprentice to the job. This can frequently reduce the overall cost for labor. The skilled carpenter, painter or other professional can provide owners with a high-quality job at a reasonable cost.

3

FLOORS

To restore strip-wood floors and their finish

To restore parquet floors and their finish

To remove and replace vinyl flooring over a wood base

To improve the soundness of a floor system

To retile over a concrete floor

To replace carpeting

To clean and restore terrazzo, marble, ceramic/clay, and brick floors

OPENING COMMENTS

Conditions or circumstances that necessitate corrective action. Regardless of how they are covered, floors wear with aging and ultimately must be replaced. Some last much longer than others because of the fibers or materials from which they are made. Let us compile a short list of conditions or circumstances about floors that require corrective action.

1. Abrasion is a primary cause for wear and failure of flooring. Particles of grit or sand act like sandpaper. The movement of the sand or grit across the surface of the floor creates fissures based on the shape of the particle. Other particles are trod upon and are forced into the flooring, causing pockets or indentations. Abrasion or wearing away of first, the surface materials and later, the base materials, happens. The severity of the action, in large part, dictates or limits the options in restoration.

2. Adhesion failure is also a primary cause. Cements are developed to secure flooring to a subsurface. When conditions exist that deteriorate the cements the flooring will fail. The degree of failure is dependent on the degree of damage to the cementing properties of the mixture and the seal created originally by the cement. Some restoration work requires only reapplication of cement, while other work requires a change of cement due to the changing conditions surrounding the floor.

3. Matting is another form of floor failure. This is generally found in carpeting and is caused by prolonged use of heavy traffic areas. Generally, the restoration involves replacement since the fibers are no longer resilient and able to retain their original shape and twist.

4. Subsurface problems are also causes of floor failure. Some are primary and others are secondary. To the homeowner this does not make a difference. The results are generally the same. Some of these are sagging floor joists, improper underlayment or improperly installed underlayment, moisture penetration from subsoil conditions, and inadequate or cheap undercarpet padding which fails from surface force or chemicals in the air.

5. Finally, a floor can fail due to improper installation. The quality of work has a direct bearing on the life expectancy of the floor. Wood floors squeak because of improper installation of joists and subflooring. Traffic areas subject to water can have floor failure due to the improper selection of flooring and adhesive needed to secure it.

All of these are problems of the homeowner. He or she may have inherited the problems when the house was purchased, or the problems could have developed over many years through normal wear and tear. The magnitude and severity of the problem will dictate to the owner an action that provides the most economical cure.

Contractor's responsibility. Because of the wide variety of materials applied as flooring, owners tend to call on a specialist contractor rather than a general contractor. These include carpeting contractors, vinyl flooring contractors, tile setters, carpenters for wood floors and parquet, and masons who specialize in tiles and terrazzo. Regardless of the type of contractor called to the home, our responsibility is to examine the condition of the floor and provide the owner with one or more solutions that would restore the floor to its original condition. We would advise the owner when repairs can be made, such as resanding wood floors and refinishing them. We would advise the owner when an old floor needs to be removed and a new one of the same kind laid down. We would advise the owner when a change of flooring materials would result in a longer life cycle, yet blend with the architecture. We would also advise the owner how prices for materials and labor will be affected by the various solutions.

Homeowner's expectations.   The homeowner expects to have the floor restored at a reasonable cost and with minimum disruption to the people living in the house. Most of the time the owner hopes the problem can be fixed with a very limited solution and is often very unhappy when we contractors advise him or her that the costs are quite high.

Scope of projects.   There are seven types of projects identified in the objectives at the opening of the chapter. We study each of these to identify how best to achieve the best-quality floor at the most reasonable cost. They include refinishing the wood floor, terrazzo, ceramic, and masonry floors; replacing vinyl floors; taking the squeaks out of a floor; and carpeting.

PROJECT 1. RESTORE STRIP-WOOD FLOORING AND REFINISH THE SURFACE

Subcategories include: testing a floor for soundness; removing and replacing defective flooring pieces; factory-manufactured oak flooring; adding nails to remove squeaks; sanding floors; sandpapers and machines used; sealing and finishing materials and their applications; and removal and replacement of shoe moldings.

Preliminary Discussion with the Owner

Problems facing the owner.   Most homes that have wood floors have hardwood floors made from oak. Some have floors made of walnut, ash, and other hardwoods. Some also have yellow pine floors (a soft wood). All of these woods have a high degree of density that makes them especially useful for flooring, and they all wear very well.

The visual inspection of the floor performed by the contractor will locate several possible causes for restoration. The first of these is rot. Where water has laid on the floor for extended periods, some will eventually seep through the finish, or if the finish is worn away, seep into the joints between rows as well as into the surface fibers (cells). Other minerals and substances in the water also seep into the wood, and these add to the rotting problem. These conditions are usually found in bathrooms, laundry rooms, and near exterior doors. The symptoms are usually a dark stain to black, disintegration of the wood cells, and sometimes a sinking or depression. In solving this problem we must recommend removing and replacing the defective pieces. The pieces used in flooring are premanufactured, as shown in Figure 3–1. Notice that there are groves on an end and side and a tongue on the opposite end and side. The carpenter making the repairs must deal with this characteristic when removing and replacing the damaged pieces.

The next problem that can face the owner is loose flooring. As the owner or his or her family and guests walk on the floor, it squeaks or seems to give. This condition results when the flooring is stressed and nails work loose. Usually, the floor joist beneath the floor and subfloor has sagged or was installed crown down instead of crown up. Figure 3–2 shows this possibility. The solution for this problem is often to add shims between the subfloor and joist. But if the problem is not sagging joists, the problem was an insufficient number of nails to hold the flooring to the subfloor.

The carpenter must sometimes renail the flooring. Surface nails, even those countersunk and filled with putty, can detract from the overall appearance. When this method is used the carpenter can sometimes use a wood chisel and lift the wood along the grain sufficiently to permit driving the nail. Then he or she uses glue to bond the wood. Thus the nail is covered.

Many floors simply need to be resanded and refinished. For this operation the carpenter rents two sanders. One is a disk sander, used to sand the corners and borders. The other is a drum sander, which uses sandpaper that is rolled onto the drum. The drum rotates and sands the old finish and some of the wood away. This reveals the new wood. In this operation successively finer papers are used, first to

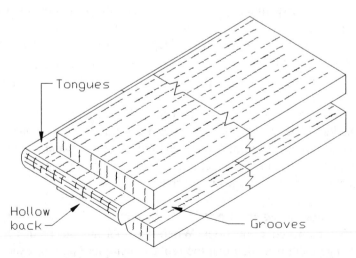

Figure 3–1   Oak tongue-and-groove flooring: end and side.

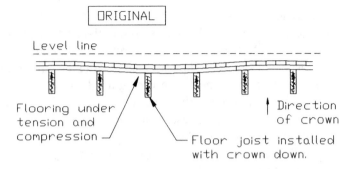

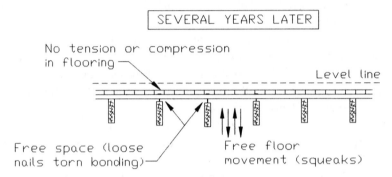

Figure 3–2   Joist: crown installed down versus up; floor squeaks.

remove great quantities of materials, and finally, to smooth the surfaces. Carpenters usually gain experience over time performing these sanding operations. Inexperienced persons create grooves, deep gouges, troughs, and scars with the drum sander. These results cannot always be overcome cheaply. In other words, if you are the owner and are inexperienced, you are well advised to pay to have the work done.

Refinishing a floor is not difficult. Most people leave the floor a natural color and let it darken with age. However, floor finishes can be purchased with stains in various colors. The finish material is in liquid form and is applied with a brush or as directed by the manufacturer. Several coats are applied to build up sufficient thickness to provide a lasting surface.

Alternative solutions to the problem.   There are a few alternatives to repair a damaged wood floor. When the floor has pieces that have rotted, we can change them provided that the replacement pieces are of exactly the same width. Sometimes we encounter a situation where the standards have changed from 20 or more years ago. In such situations we would recommend removing the entire floor from the damaged area to the closest wall and throughout the length of the room.

Where the floor squeaks, we would attempt to force the boards down, but if pressure is felt, we might need to relieve the pressure by trimming the ends of the row or taking up the flooring and reinstalling it with less pressure. Where the floor is only surface damaged, we can offer the simple solution of light sanding and refinishing rather than fully restoring the floor.

Statement of work and the planning effort.   In our project we will restore a bathroom floor that has some rot around the sink and water stains in other places. Our first statement of work is to *restore the bathroom floor to its original finish.* To define the work further, we need to add some detail, such as: *We will remove all damaged pieces and replace them with like kind. Then we will sand the entire surface and finish it with a high-quality clear finish capable of sustaining casual water for short periods.* The work will be guaranteed with a statement similar to: *We will guarantee the work and the manufacturer warranties the finish.*

The planning effort for this project requires many of the usual activities. As the contractor, we would discuss with the owner the things identified above, to determine the extent of work needed to restore the floor. We would need to price the job for materials and labor and overhead. We would make our contract bid/offer and present it for acceptance. At that time we would advise the owner how long the job will take and how many workers would do the work.

Contract.   Although our project is small, selection of a fixed-price contract for this type of job is applicable to larger jobs as well. We have all the requirements and can easily determine the types and quantities of materials needed. Calculating the labor costs is easily done.

The body of the contract should contain the following elements and can be expressed this way:

For the fixed price shown below, we agree to replace damaged flooring in the bathroom. We will remove and replace fixtures as required. We will sand the floor and apply two coats of high-quality finish.

The owner agrees to have someone at home while the workers are in the house unless the house is unoccupied. The schedule of repairs will be coordinated between contractor and owner.

Payment is expected at completion of the job.

Labor and materials: $XXX.XX.

Material Assessment

Direct Materials	Use/Purpose
Hardwood flooring	To replace the damaged pieces
Nails or staples	Nails if hand nailed; staples if machine nailed, and 4d finish
Floor finish	High-quality polyvinyl or varnish finish

Indirect Materials	Use/Purpose
Sandpaper	Disks, drum paper, sheet paper
Mineral spirits or water	For cleaning brushes as required
Brushes	To apply finish

Support Materials	Use/Purpose
Carpenter tools	For construction
Vacuum	To clean up dust
Sawhorses and plank	Work surface to cut flooring
Sanders	Disk and drum sander for stripping and sanding the floor

Outside Contractor Support	Use/Purpose
None	
Sander rental	Usually rented if seldom used

Activities Planning Chart

Activity	Time Line (Days)
	1 2 3 4 5 6 7
1. Contract preparation	I _×_ I ___ I ___ I ___ I ___ I ___ I ___ I
2. Materials and scheduling	I _×_ I ___ I ___ I ___ I ___ I ___ I ___ I
3. Removing and replacing the flooring	I ___ I _×_ I _×_ I ___ I ___ I ___ I ___ I
4. Sanding and finishing the floor	I ___ I ___ I _×_ I _×_ I ___ I ___ I ___ I

Reconstruction

Contract preparation.   The preparation of the contract for this small job requires some office personnel actions. The bill of materials must be made and priced. Then the labor costs must be applied to the schedule for labor. In this job we estimate 3 days for the carpenter. Next we apply the fixed costs for overhead using the basic percentage established as our standard. Since there are no subcontractors, we can finish typing the contract quickly and present it to the owner for comment and acceptance.

Materials and scheduling.   The several materials we need for this job can be obtained from a builder's supply company. The flooring is usually easily obtained. Nails are also readily available. The floor finish is usually sold in 1-gallon cans. One can of finish should be enough for this job.

The carpenter needs to be scheduled for 3 days. Practically, the work should be completed in three successive days. However, if the drying of the finish is hampered by the weather, applying the final coat could be delayed a day.

Removing and replacing the flooring.   The following series of tasks are performed by the carpenter:

1. Remove the quarter-round molding from the baseboards and save.
2. Remove the commode if it sets on the flooring to be removed.
3. Remove the vanity cabinet after disconnecting the water and drain lines if the flooring passes under the cabinet.
4. Remove the damaged flooring.
5. Install the new, replacement flooring.
6. Reinstall the quarter-round.

The flooring should be removed from the wall outward, if possible. We usually do this by driving a flat bar or wide chisel between the last strip of flooring and the next one. After the last piece is out, the rest are easily lifted out with the use of a hammer or crowbar.

Replacing the flooring is simple and straightforward when the tongue is showing. If the groove is showing, we can cut a filler tongue and insert into the exposed groove. Then we can nail the piece to the floor and proceed with the remainder of the installation.

Sanding and finishing the floor.   After all the floor pieces are in place, we sand the floor. First we select a 40-grit drum paper, for its coarseness and cutting capability. Then we change to 80 grit and, finally, to 100 grit. We do the same around the perimeter and near the door openings with the disk sander. Finally, we scrape the corners clean with a sharp wood chisel.

After closely examining the sanded floor, we vacuum the room and prepare for applying the finish varnish or floor-covering material. We follow the manufacturer's recommendations for first and top coats. After the second coat has dried, we reinstall any appliances or cabinets removed.

Concluding comments.   This project was relatively easy to accomplish since subflooring and the joist frame were not involved. Most of the work can be done by persons with limited skills, except for sanding. Improper use of the drum sander can create unrecoverable problems that could result in replacing more flooring.

If the project included several rooms and there were extensive removal and replacement requirements, a contractor could probably perform the work more cost-effectively. Also, due to the large number of square feet per room, a very qualified worker should sand the floors. This is important since the wood floor is usually exposed except for small throw rugs.

PROJECT 2. RESTORE PARQUET FLOORING AND REFINISH THE SURFACE

Subcategories include: understanding how parquet floors are built; removal and replacement techniques; and sanding methods and finishing methods. Sanding machines and finishing materials are the same as for strip-wood floors.

Preliminary Discussion with the Owner

Problems facing the owner.   The owner who has problems with a parquet floor may be in for expensive restoration work. Parquet floors are made of strip tongue-and-groove flooring strips glued together and trimmed into squares, some 9-in. and some are 12-in. These units are laid onto a solid, flat base in an alternate or checkerboard pattern. Often, the units are unfinished, and after being secured with nails or cemented in place, they are sanded and varnished. There is also the possibility that units are prefinished, so that after being installed, no added finish is required.

The owner can have several problems. These include loosened units, split units, rotted units, and damaged finishes. The causes might range from storm and rain damage to normal wear and tear over a lifetime of use. Where the units are loose, split, or rotted, the carpenter must replace them. Where the units are surface worn, the sanding and refinishing technique explained in the first project is used.

Alternative solutions to the problem.   When the contractor or carpenter is called to the job and examines the floor, he or she will determine the extent of damage and offer several solutions. Some of these will depend on the type of flooring that he or she finds. There are three basic types: the unit block, made from strips of flooring; the laminated block, made in three or more plies; and the slat block, which are shown in Figure 3–3. All of these may be made with simple wood or be very decorative. But the most decorative are the slat type. The carpenter will also determine the dimensions of the parquet flooring. These may range extensively by type from $\frac{5}{16}$ to $\frac{33}{32}$ in. thick; and from a small 6×6 inch square to blocks 30 in. long or wide. Not all parquet is made in squares; some is rectangular. The carpenter must determine the exact type used in the damaged floor. Further, he or she needs to

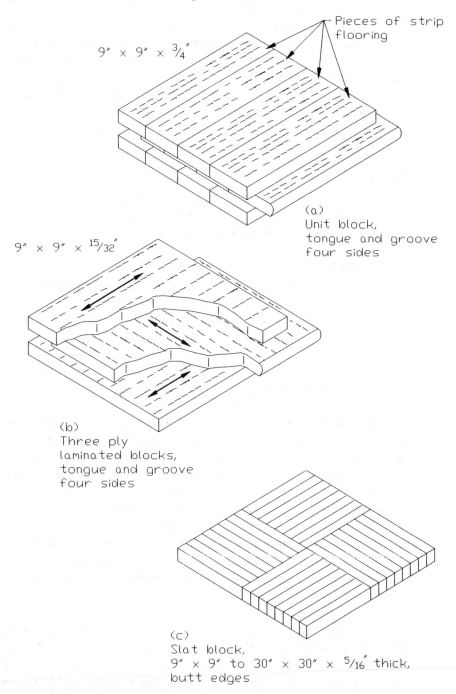

9″ × 9″ × ¾″

Pieces of strip
flooring

(a)
Unit block,
tongue and groove
four sides

9″ × 9″ × ¹⁵/₃₂″

(b)
Three ply
laminated blocks,
tongue and groove
four sides

(c)
Slat block,
9″ × 9″ to 30″ × 30″ × ⁵/₁₆″ thick,
butt edges

Figure 3–3   Three types of parquet flooring: (a) unit block; (b) laminated block; (c) slat block.

determine how the flooring's edges are shaped. Some are square and simply butt against each other, while others are tongue and grooved with tongues on adjacent sides and grooves on the other two sides. A third type employs four sides with grooves and the manufacturer supplies filler splines. The contractor carpenter needs to define the method of application. Most often the units are cemented in place. They may be cemented over a wood subfloor or on a properly prepared concrete floor. In some cases the units are nailed to the subfloor.

With all these variables the carpenter identifies the type, size pattern, wood species used, and thickness. Then an effort is made to locate replacement units that match those on the floor.

The carpenter or contractor decides how much of the floor must be replaced and combines the knowledge of the units with their installation method and tells the owner which solution will produce the best results. These are

1. Replace the defective units and refinish the floor.
2. Replace an area larger than just the defective units to compensate for the variations between the new and old units, and refinish the floor.
3. Replace the entire floor with a new pattern unit since the old ones cannot be located; then finish the floor.

These three alternatives are arranged in order of least to most costly. For our project we will use option 2.

Statement of work and the planning effort.   The statement of work begins as follows: *We agree to replace the damaged unit of parquet flooring by removing and replacing the entire section containing damage.* Further, we can try to obtain prefinished units, but due to the natural aging of the floor, the color would probably not match. So we need to *refinish the floor completely after making repairs.* We also will *use high-quality cement to lay the new units in place.*

For the planning effort, we must attempt to locate matching units of parquet flooring. This may require us to contact the manufacturer or his or her local distributor. Then we need to send a finish carpenter to the job since this is high-quality finish work. We also need to plan, with the owner, when, after contract signing, the work can be done and the duration of the job.

Contract.   In some cases, locating the replacement parquet blocks will be very simple and this will directly influence the contract price. Where our office personnel need to trace down the manufacturer to locate replacement blocks, we will need to add overhead costs. In the event that no matching blocks can be found, even though we desire to make partial repairs, we need to advise the owner of the situation. This solution will, as we already pointed out, result in a higher pricing.

We, as contractors, would delay preparing a bid/contract until suitable materials were located. Once this part of the project is defined, we should offer a fixed-price contract. All the details are available that concern the removal and replacement activities and the finishing requirements. The body of the contract should state the conditions and price:

For the fixed price stipulated below, we agree to remove and replace the damaged section of parquet floor and replace the blocks with matching ones. After installing the new blocks, we will sand the entire floor, stripping the old finish, and apply two coats of floor varnish (polyurethane). We guarantee the restoration for one year for failure of the workmanship.

The owner agrees to clear the room of all furnishings and personal property hanging on walls. The owner also agrees to have a member or agent at home when the workers are present, unless the house is uninhabited.

Total cost is $XXX.XX. Payment is due upon completion of the job and acceptance by the owner.

Material Assessment

Direct Materials	Use/Purpose
Parquet blocks	Replacement blocks
Cement	To cement the blocks to the subfloor or underlayment
Varnish (polyurethane)	Floor finish
Finish nails	To renail shoe molding
Shoe molding	Only if some is broken during removal
Mineral spirits	Cleaning solvent

Indirect Materials	Use/Purpose
Sandpaper	Sanding disks and drum paper
Vinyl sheet goods	To block off doors during sanding operation
Masking tape	To tape-up vinyl
Underlayment	To replace damaged materials, as required

Support Materials	Use/Purpose
Carpenter tools	For construction
Electric sanders	Drum and disk
Paint brushes	To apply finish

Outside Contractor Support	Use/Purpose
None	

Activities Planning Chart

Activity	Time Line (Days)						
	1	2	3	4	5	6	7
1. Contract preparation	| _×_ |	___ |	___ |	___ |	___ |	___ |	___ |
2. Materials and scheduling	| _×_ |	___ |	___ |	___ |	___ |	___ |	___ |
3. Removing the parquet block	| ___ |	_×_ | _×_ |	___ |	___ |	___ |	___ |	___ |
4. Installing the parquet	| ___ |	___ |	_×_ | _×_ |	___ |	___ |	___ |
5. Finishing the floor	| ___ |	___ |	___ |	_×_ | _×_ |	___ |	___ |

Reconstruction

Contract preparation.   The estimator will be required to find the replacement parquet blocks. This time may be spent scanning catalogs and phoning the local builder's supply and other distributors or retailers until a match is located. When this is done, he or she will prepare a cost estimate sheet for materials, labor, and overhead. The worksheet will include direct and indirect materials, rental of sanders, and labor taken from the activities list of a standard for labor estimates. Overhead will be applied in two forms: the standard fixed and variable costs of operation and the added time used by the estimator to locate the matching parquet blocks, if the time exceeds allowable standards.

The typing of the contract/bid will only take an hour or more, which includes verification by the estimator and validation by the contractor. Then the contractor and owner must meet and concur with the specifications and conditions in the document.

Materials and scheduling.   Materials would be picked up earlier than the first day to ensure that they are on hand on contract startup day. Cements and finishing varnish could be picked up the day work begins. The sanders would be rented for a day when needed.

The carpenter would be scheduled for 4 days. If a helper were also sent to the job, the time could be cut to 2 days. Working by himself or herself, every task would be done in series, that is, as listed below.

The carpenter would be notified of the start day and the need to pick up the blocks from the office and other supplies from the supply houses.

Removal activities.   On arriving at the job site the carpenter would discuss the conditions and area of floor to restore. The tasks would follow this sequence:

1. Ensure that the room is completely empty of furnishings.
2. Remove the shoe molding along the walls where blocks of parquet will be ex-

changed. Normally, the molding covers the small gap between baseboard and block. In some cases the blocks extend under the baseboard as well. When this happens, some of the baseboard will have to be removed as well.

3. Starting along the wall, pry up the blocks one at a time.

4. Smooth the subfloor or underlayment. Replace severely damaged underlayment with new materials as needed.

The actual removal of blocks involved requires that the carpenter use a wood chisel and hammer or flat bar and hammer. He or she drives the chisel under the block, placing force on the cemented joint. If the cement is old or was applied minimally, the block will pop loose with little damage to the underlayment or subfloor. On the other hand, if the cement was liberally applied and the bond is still excellent, the carpenter may have to chisel the entire block free. This action will probably cause damage to the underlayment.

If the blocks were toenailed in place, they will lift quite easily. The chisel will produce enough pressure either to pull the nails through the block or come away with the block.

Where the blocks butt against each other, prying them loose usually does not cause damage to adjacent blocks. But when they are tongue-and-grooved, the top piece in the groove usually splits off and the carpenter needs to remove that block as well. Skill must be employed in this activity. The removal activity is complete when all blocks are up.

Restoring the parquet floor.   After all the blocks are up and out of the way, the carpenter must prepare the subfloor for the new blocks. This is done in one of several ways. The subfloor can be sanded slightly with electric sanders to remove bits and pieces of old blocks and cement. Or the subfloor, if badly damaged, can be removed and replaced with a good-quality underlayment. Or the carpenter can prepare a paste filler to fill in all dents, splits, and other imperfections that make the floor uneven. After the filler dries, the floor is sanded smooth.

Then, reinstallation of the blocks can begin. The carpenter makes several chalk lines on the floor to ensure that the blocks remain in alignment as they are installed. The carpenter follows the directions on the can of cement. Usually, a relatively small section of floor is covered with cement, which is applied with a serrated trowel. This tool makes beads of cement. Each block is laid in place and pressed into the cement. Where the blocks have a tongue and groove, the carpenter taps them into each other without damaging the groove.

The skill in this effort is to maintain perfect alignment until all blocks are installed. The border row will probably need trimming to fit. This is done with a finetooth saw.

After all the blocks are in place, the shoe molding is replaced. Normally, the molding is nailed in place with 4d finish nails and the heads are set. If there was baseboard over the old blocks, it would be replaced before the shoe molding.

Finishing tasks are sanding and applying two coats of varnish. This information was detailed in Project 1 of this chapter.

Concluding comments.   The job of restoring a parquet floor is much more complicated and demanding than that of installing vinyl tile blocks, for example. Considerable carpentry skills and knowledge are required for a perfect job. This is a decorator floor and mistakes are not permitted. The owner who attempts to perform the work must have considerable skill with tools and sanding machines. He or she must also expect to spend some time locating the exact match of parquet blocks.

PROJECT 3. REMOVE AND REPLACE RESILIENT (VINYL AND OTHERS) FLOORING OVER A WOOD BASE

Subcategories include: types and sizes of roll vinyl; tile squares, cork and rubber tile; stripping sheet vinyl flooring from a wood-based subfloor; sanding and filling the underlayment; laying out the new flooring; cutting and fitting the flooring; cementing the vinyl to the underlayment; and reinstalling the shoe molding or adding vinyl baseboard.

Preliminary Discussion with the Owner

Problems facing the owner.   The owner of a home with resilient floors may have vinyl-asbestos, sheet vinyl, tile vinyl, rubber tile, or cork tile. All of these are cemented in place. Many are squares of 9×9 in. or 12×12 in. Others, particularly vinyl, are made in sheets of rug sizes and rolls, both 6 ft and 12 ft wide.

Cement failure is always a problem with resilient flooring. The bond may hold well in the beginning but lose its capacity over time due to various causes. Once the bond is broken, the tile or sheet goods are easily lifted from the floor. Tiles often skip out of place. Sheet goods often buckle because of foot pressure applied constantly in the same direction.

Failure of the surface is another condition, but its cause is usually abrasion. Bits of sand tracked over the floor act as sandpaper and erode the finish. Where tiles are not color-through, the change is most pronounced. Where the tile is color-through, the wear may be the same in terms of depth, but the colors remain true. Where the surface is no-wax, a dull appearance begins and spreads as more of the surface is eroded.

When tiles become brittle with age, they often crack. The chemicals evaporate very quickly at first and much more slowly over time. The cracks may start at the corners on tile squares. Later, they may stretch across the entire tile.

Some vinyl tiles and sheet goods are very soft, even after being exposed to the air. Sharp objects dropped onto the surface can damage a floor, as can high-heel spiked shoes. This is especially true when the vinyl has recently been laid.

Rubber tiles have additives for stiffness and durability. These tiles wear as do others but do not often crack.

Cork tiles are coated with vinyl to improve durability. When the surface vinyl is worn through, the core usually wears away at an accelerated rate.

Alternative solutions to the problem.   The contractor who is called to the home of a homeowner needs to provide a solution to the flooring problem. Based on the paragraphs above, we see that he or she needs a fairly wide background on the types of resilient flooring. Most contractors can easily recognize the type of flooring materials and with this knowledge can offer solutions. Some of these are:

1. Replace the damaged or worn tile squares where matching tiles are still available.
2. Replace the entire floor with a similar tile when the exact match is no longer manufactured.
3. Remove and replace the damaged vinyl sheet tile over the entire floor.
4. Using scraps of the original vinyl tile, remove and replace small sections by cutting carefully along pattern lines.
5. Remove the damaged tiles and eliminate the cause for cement failure. Then recement the tiles if still serviceable.
6. Apply a new floor over the old floor if the base adheres soundly to the subfloor. This may require some sanding of the old floor to create a better bond.

The owner can either perform the restoration work or the contractor can do it. If the owner has carpentry skills or a fundamental knowledge of working with hand tools and cementing tools such as trowels, he or she can pry up the old tiles and apply the new ones. Vinyl tiles are easily cut with a utility knife, so fitting the border tiles should not be a problem. Machines are available for rent that make lifting the old tiles easier. Otherwise, they would be chiseled off one at a time.

Statement of work and the planning effort.   For the restoration of a resilient floor having any of the problems identified above, we would state that the *restoration of the floor requires removal and replacement of the entire floor.* If the baseboard were wood, shoe molding would cover the gap between the wall and the flooring. When that is the case, the statement of work needs to include: *remove and replace shoe molding and if necessary refinish the molding.* If the baseboard is vinyl, we would also recommend that *we replace vinyl baseboard.*

Sometimes the subfloor needs to be repaired or covered with underlayment. When this is the case, we would *prepare the subfloor prior to installing the new flooring*. Finally, we *guarantee all work for three years (or longer) and the flooring manufacturer adds a warranty as well.*

Our planning effort begins after the initial inspection and meeting with the owner. We determine the extent of restoration and make arrangements with the owner to select the flooring. He or she can chose at random or can ask us for assistance. Once the flooring is selected, we can either purchase it and all the associated materials, or we can have the owner purchase it and the cement, too. Then we prepare and sign contracts. Next we arrange to install the new flooring and schedule the workers.

Contract. A fixed-price contract would be appropriate for this job. However, the body of the contract would include a separate condition pertaining to who selects and purchases the flooring. The body could look something like this:

The job is to remove and replace the kitchen floor at the owner's residence. We also agree to replace the baseboard with vinyl baseboard. Because of the condition of the subfloor, we will make corrections and apply an underlayment before installing the new flooring.

The contract price stated below does not include the price of the vinyl flooring or baseboards. The owner elects to select and purchase these materials based on the dimensions provided by us. We will provide all other materials and all the labor.

The total price is $XXX.XX. Payment is due upon completion of the job.

Material Assessment

Direct Materials	Use/Purpose
Underlayment	To cover old wood floor and provide a smooth flat surface for the new flooring
6d and 4d common nails	Ring shanked are best for nailing the old floor and underlayment
Cement	To bond the vinyl flooring and baseboards to the subsurfaces
Vinyl flooring	(supplied by owner)
Vinyl baseboard	(supplied by owner)
Metal edging	To cover the tile edge at door openings

Indirect Materials	Use/Purpose
Spackling paste	To fill nail heads and dents, joints, and so on
Sandpaper	To smooth floor after spackling dries

Support Materials	Use/Purpose
Tile remover	Rent one to remove old glued tile
Carpentry tools	For construction
Tile cement spreader	Serrated trowel and wide-blade putty knife

Outside Contractor Support	Use/Purpose
None	

Activities Planning Chart

Activity	Time Line (Days)
	1 2 3 4 5 6 7
1. Contract preparation	I _×_ I ___ I ___ I ___ I ___ I ___ I ___ I
2. Materials and scheduling	I _×_ I ___ I ___ I ___ I ___ I ___ I ___ I
3. Removing the old flooring and preparing the subfloor	I ___ I _×_ I _×_ I ___ I ___ I ___ I ___ I
4. Installing the new flooring	I ___ I ___ I _×_ I _×_ I ___ I ___ I ___ I

Reconstruction

Contract preparation.   The preparation of the contract for this project has been made simpler since the owner has elected to pick out the flooring. We would have had to bring various samples to the house for selection purposes. This would have increased the overhead costs for the job.

Since all we have to do is pick up the flooring, we can assign costs to the remaining materials and estimate the labor. Although one flooring specialist can perform the job without help, we can also elect to supply a helper at a reduced overall rate.

The estimator would prepare the worksheet for the job with cost figures for both a single worker and for a worker and helper. The contractor would make the final decision about which to select, based primarily on worker availability. The contract would then be typed on the company contract/bid form and presented to the owner for signature.

Materials and scheduling.   As we already stated, the owner would go to the flooring outlet and select the style and pattern of his or her choosing. We would pick up the flooring and cement on the first day of the job. We would also pick up the other materials at the lumberyard and the flooring remover at the rental equipment location.

Scheduling should be a simple matter. At the time of contract acceptance the owner and contractor would agree on an installation date. The contractor would already know when the workers would be available to perform the work. The owner would have knowledge of who will be home to let the workers in and be there while they work. (*Note:* Even when the contractor is bonded, it is still a good idea to have a representative of the owner or owner at the job site while workers are present.)

Removing the old floor and preparing the subfloor.   The first part of the job is to take up the old flooring. Some of the conditions the workers may find are:

1. Wood baseboards and shoe molding
2. Vinyl baseboard
3. Tile flooring laid loose (linoleum is sometimes laid this way)
4. Tile squares or sheet goods

The first task is to remove the shoe molding or vinyl baseboard. To accomplish this, the first task is to remove any appliances and cabinets resting on the floor. While removing the shoe with hammer and wood chisel, the workers will attempt to prevent breaking any pieces. However, some may break and need to be replaced. The old vinyl baseboards, which are cemented to the wall, will be pulled away from the wall and discarded.

The flooring should be fully exposed and ready to be removed. There is no prescribed starting place; any place will do. Usually, the workers will look for flooring that has become loose over time and use this as a starting point since the machine for lifting resilient flooring must have its shoe between the flooring and the subfloor. However, the machine can cut through the flooring if no place to start is obvious. An experienced floor installer will operate the machine without making gouges in the subfloor. An amateur or novice might make gouges that would later have to be filled and sanded.

In our project the workers will lay underlayment on top of the old floor to eliminate the joints in the subflooring, which was strip pine flooring. Underlayment should be at least $\frac{3}{8}$ in. thick, but $\frac{7}{16}$ in. would be better. It must be nailed every 4 in. around the perimeter of the sheet or piece and at 6 in. on centers across the sheet. Ring shank nails are preferred because of their holding power.

A filler is applied over the seams and nail heads to eliminate dents and depressions. After it dries, the entire floor is lightly sanded and vacuumed.

Installing the new flooring.   The tile or vinyl sheet flooring is laid in place and fitted. A discussion of each type follows:

Tile Squares.   Most tile squares used today are 12 in. square. In the past many were 9 in. square. We would proceed with the layout as follows:

1. We measure the width of the room and length of the room to determine the width of the border tiles as shown in Figure 3–4. Our objective is to have more than a half tile

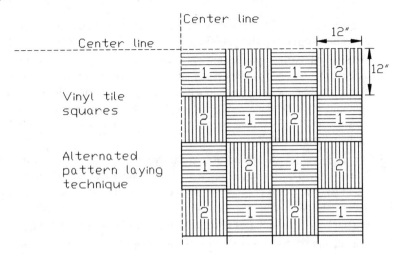

(a) Layout of tile squares and
setting pattern: 1, 2, 1, 2,

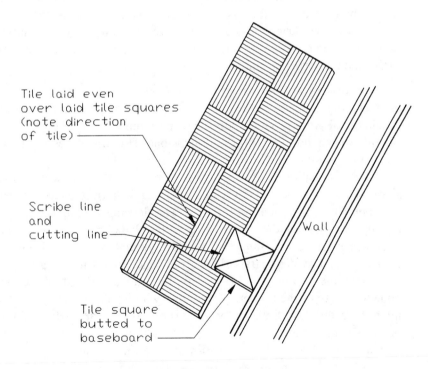

(b) Border tiles

Figure 3–4   Resilient tile floor, border tiles.

as a border tile, since this makes the best appearance. Starting in the corner with a full tile is unacceptable unless the floor is exactly of an even foot dimension.

2. We snap chalk lines on the underlayment to provide guidance as to where to install the tiles. These lines can be in the middle of the room and cross each other perpendicularly. Or two lines can be snapped adjacent to each other along the border line. For example, if the border tile on wall a is 7 in. wide, the line would be snapped 7 in. out from the wall. If the border tile on the adjacent wall b is $8\frac{3}{4}$ in., we would snap the line $8\frac{3}{4}$ in. in from the wall.

3. We apply cement to the underlayment over a space about 3 ft wide along one line. Then we lay the tiles beginning with the one that touches both snapped lines. This is the most critical tile to set. It sets the conditions for the remainder of tiles. However, tiles can be twisted or slid some within a short time after they are laid.

4. We apply cement and tiles until the entire floor is laid with full tiles.

5. We cut and fit the border tiles one at a time and cement them in place. A small gap can exist between wall and tile since the shoe or vinyl baseboard will cover the gap.

6. We reinstall the shoe or vinyl baseboard to finish the job.

Where there is a door opening, the flooring must be finished off. There are two methods used to do this: using a metal strip that is screwed to the floor, or using a vinyl or rubber strip that is cemented over the end of the flooring and adjacent flooring. When the flooring butts against the carpet, it is usually passed under the carpet and the carpet has the metal strip.

Resilient Sheet Flooring.   Sheet flooring is sold in 6-ft and 12-ft widths. Most products sold today do not require any or just a small amount of *relaxation* before installation. Earlier products almost always required it. The relaxation allowed the flooring to expand to its full flat dimensions. This was necessary to prevent bubbling after installation.

The installation of sheet goods is more difficult than tile squares installation since all cuts must be laid out with a ruler and then trimmed to fit when placed on the floor. There is no margin for error. The flooring specialist or carpenter would lay out the pattern on the new flooring with a chalk line and framing square. Some reference must be used and this would normally be the wall with no required cutouts. This provides a straight line from which to begin measuring.

Next, the installer would measure the width and length of the room to determine the width of the border. All flooring with a pattern has a repeat sequence. It might be every 4, 6, 8, 9, 10, or 12 in. or more. We are obligated to ensure that opposite ends of the room have the same width border in the pattern. The flooring is measured and cut with a small allowance for final trimming.

All cutouts are measured and cut individually. Again the installer might prefer to allow a little for final trimming when the vinyl is in place.

Then the flooring is brought into the room and positioned where final trimming is made. Once the installer is satisfied with the fit, which should be within $\frac{1}{8}$ in. from the wall or baseboards, the cementing operation can begin.

Using a serrated trowel the installer spreads cement on one half of the floor after rolling back the flooring to expose the underlayment. Then the flooring is slowly rolled into the cement. The process is repeated on the other half of the floor. Finally, a heavy roller is used to anchor the flooring to the cement and drive out all air pockets or bulges. If the floor is wider than a full 12-ft sheet, a splice is made by matching the two pieces exactly during installation.

The shoe or vinyl baseboard is installed next, and this would complete the installation. The rest of the job is to clean up the job site and take all old and waste materials to the dump for proper disposal.

Side Issue.   One significant point to be concerned about is the travel of doors. Most interior doors have about $\frac{3}{4}$ to 1 in. of bottom clearance, which aids in return airflow. Reducing this dimension some usually does not have any adverse effect. However, exterior doors might be affected if they have a low threshold. When this might be the case, the use of underlayment to cover a problem floor might not be the best solution. Everyone should use caution in the planning stages.

Concluding comments.   Some owners can plan and install a new resilient tile floor even if they need some help. The data in this project would be sufficient. However, installing sheet flooring is another matter. This type requires a great deal of knowledge and skill. The flooring is expensive and one mistake can be costly. All the tools, tile, and cement can be purchased at stores that sell flooring. The underlayment would be purchased in a supply house or lumberyard, as would the nails and replacement shoe molding.

Any floor will cost more than $100. Good-quality work and materials will definitely drive up the price. Yet, both of these are important to a long-lasting floor.

PROJECT 4. RETILE OVER A CONCRETE FLOOR

Subcategories include: removal of asphalt tiles; cleaning concrete; laying out new floor; cutting and fitting new tiles; cementing new tiles; and reinstalling vinyl baseboards or shoe molding.

Preliminary Discussion with the Owner

Problems facing the owner.   Whereas replacing the resilient flooring over a wood floor base presented problems of an uneven floor, a sagging floor, or a floor with movement, replacing the tile on a concrete floor presents us with a new set of conditions. Properly preconditioned concrete floors can be covered by a variety of floorings. Improperly prepared concrete floors present continuous problems for homeowners.

A concrete floor is usually used below grade level, as in a basement, and at grade level, as in the first floor of a home. In both situations the slab lays on the ground and is subject to moisture penetration from underneath. In addition, surface moisture from temperature and humidity variations cause problems. A prior selection of floor covering with a ragged back installed in a basement can develop mold. The effects are loosened tiles and a bad odor. Loosened tiles can also occur when the wrong type of cement was used in laying the tiles. For example, water-based adhesives will not set up in the presence of moisture or wetness. Finally, a below-the-surface floor installed too soon after the concrete has been poured will probably fail due to the moisture content of the concrete. Although most (90 percent) of the curing takes place in 30 days, it takes almost 6 months to reach 99 percent. During this time, thermal action continues as moisture continues the process. Eventually, the moisture is abated from the heat generated. Loosened tiles or sheet goods must be removed and replaced.

Alternative solutions to the problem.   Building codes today prescribe the installation of vinyl sheet goods at least 6 mils thick under concrete slabs. Where laps have to be used, they must be at least 12 in. This material is impervious to the capillary action of water. Thus the concrete maintains a dry state. However, in basements, as we know, moisture can accumulate from temperature and humidity when the dew point is reached. Walls will sweat and moisture will accumulate on the cold surface of the floor. Therefore, the selection of flooring must be resistant to the leaching effect of alkalis from the concrete and moisture. Products with organic backing such as ragged back must never be selected because of the potential for mold growth.

In the case of a ground-level slab, any of the modern types of flooring can be used to replace worn or damaged flooring, although those with a ragged back must be avoided. For a below-grade slab, cork and vinyl cork tiles do not do well and are not recommended.

In an older home we would find mostly asphalt or vinyl-asbestos tile squares. These were installed with an asphalt cement. The installers would have a torch and would heat each tile until it was flexible. Then they would place it on the floor and press it into the cement. Today, heat is applied after the tiles are set in place, thus saving some time. Today, more flexible tiles are usually used, as are vinyl sheet goods.

In order of selection, the best-to-least desirable are (1) for below the surface, solid vinyl tiles, asbestos-backed vinyl tiles, and filled or clear surface vinyl sheet; (2) for other surfaces, any of (1) and vinyl asbestos and ragged-back solid vinyl and both sheet vinyl types with a ragged back.

The type of cement we would use depends on the conditions at the job site, but the various manufacturers would offer a variety of adhesive compounds from which to choose.

When the floor is in the basement, we can be called upon to eliminate the cause of water seepage from outside underwater accumulations by trenching, or to eliminate sweating on the walls and floor due to the dew-point conditions of cool temperatures and high humidity.

Statement of work and the planning effort.   Arriving at the job site, we would make a very detailed inspection and determine the cause of floor failure. With that information we can declare: *The floor will need to be replaced and conditioning of the slab or other cause of flooring failure eliminated.* We would require that *the selection of flooring and cement must be appropriate for the below-surface conditions or surface conditions.* The other properties we can include might be that *the tile will have excellent alkali resistance, durability and resistance to stains, grease, and indentation.* We would also state that *the installation will be performed by skilled workers, thus guaranteeing a high-quality job.*

We might need to include the statement: *If the work involves trenching around the foundation to eliminate the subsurface water, we will eliminate the cause.* This might be necessary to eliminate leaching of groundwater through the blocks and concrete floor. We might also need to include a statement pertaining to altering the interior conditions, such as *we will take action to eliminate the buildup of sweat on walls and floor.*

For the planning effort, we would need to make up our mind about which solution for dealing with the dampness would be most productive. We might need to select one solution or a combination of more than one to eliminate the moisture problem permanently. Once the approach has been agreed to by the owner and by us, we can plan for the types of workers needed to complete the job. We would need to allow the owner time to select the flooring. Then we would plan on submitting bid/contract prices and determine an appropriate time for the owner to select the time frame for installation. After that we would schedule the electrician, laborers and carpenters, and the flooring specialist.

Contract.   The type of contract best suited for this job is the fixed-price type. Parts of it could be just like the one for replacing resilient flooring on a wood-base floor. The owner could select the style and pattern. But we would guide him or her in selecting the proper type and backing. We would include all materials and labor. A separate paragraph would be added to satisfy the need to eliminate groundwater as the cause of seepage, or for improving the interior conditions that cause sweating on walls and floors.

Material Assessment

Direct Materials	Use/Purpose
Flooring	Vinyl asbestos, vinyl solid, asbestos backed, or sheet vinyl
Cement	To glue tile to the cement floor
Muriatic acid	(Optional) To etch floor for cleaning old surface and alkalinity, grease, and organic particles

Indirect Materials	Use/Purpose
Gravel	(Optional solution 1) To create a natural drain
PVC pipe	(Optional solution 1) To shunt water away from the house
Ventilators	(Optional solution 2) To permit airflow to reduce humidity
Power dehydrator	(Optional solution 3) To remove the excess humidity for the basement
Electrical circuit	(Optional solution 3) New circuit for dehydrator

Support Materials	Use/Purpose
Carpentry tools	For construction
Floor-laying tools	To install flooring
Digging tools	For trenching
Electrical tools	To install new circuit

Outside Contractor Support	Use/Purpose
Electrician	To install new circuit if required

Activities Planning Chart

Activity	Time Line (Days)						
	1	2	3	4	5	6	7
1. Contract preparation	I _×_ I	___ I	___ I	___ I	___ I	___ I	___ I
2. Materials and scheduling	I _×_ I	___ I	___ I	___ I	___ I	___ I	___ I
3. Removing the old floor	I ___ I	_×_ I	___ I	___ I	___ I	___ I	___ I
4. Eliminating the moisture problem	I ___ I	___ I	_×_ I	_×_ I	___ I	___ I	___ I
5. Preparing the floor and installing the new flooring	I ___ I	___ I	___ I	_×_ I	___ I	___ I	___ I

Reconstruction

Contract preparation.   For this job the office estimator would build a worksheet for each type of work to be done. On every sheet, he or she would include the materials and labor associated with that phase of the job. If the electrician were a subcontractor, the estimator would prepare specifications for the electrician to make a fixed price bid. This estimate/bid would be added as a worksheet. The office person data processor or secretary would then build a contract/bid offer for presentation to the owner.

Materials and scheduling.   The contractor would suggest several outlets where the owner could make the selection of flooring. The owner would have a list of suitable types which would aid the salesperson in directing him or her in their efforts. The contractor would also provide the dimensions so that the proper amount of flooring and cement can be ordered. The other materials would be brought to the site by the workers.

As the activity list shows different workers can be on site at the same time. So, the particular activities we must accomplish depend on which solution we decide to use. Here is how it could go:

1. Carpenters improve the ventilation system with ducts and vents
2. Laborers dig the trench and place the gravel and piping along side the foundation.
3. Labors apply tar or asphalt to exposed basement block walls.
4. Flooring specialist removes the old floor, cleans the concrete slab and applies the new flooring.
5. The electrician installs the power dehydrator unit and new circuit.

Removing the old flooring and preparing the concrete.   The installer would use a machine to remove the flooring. In all probability there would be vinyl baseboard as well. This would also be torn away. All materials would be bagged and carted off. The installer would then clean the floor with a mild solution of muriatic acid and water. For this job, he or she would wear protective clothing such as long-sleeved shirt and long pants, good-quality worker shoes, and would wear a face mask to filter the fumes. He or she would create very good ventilation with fans, if necessary.

The acid solution is usually broomed onto the floor, permitted to soak in for a short time, and washed up with a clean water solution. The acid is mixed in a plastic container because a metal one would be damaged by the acid. A corn broom or floor broom with stiff bristles works the acid–water solution into the surface of the floor and on the walls where the baseboard will be cemented. A mop, pail, and clean water are used to remove the acid, alkali, old cement, and dirt from the floor. Then the floor is allowed to dry overnight.

Trenching and piping.   Since we know where the wetness comes into the basement and onto the floor, we have to assume that the underground water accumulates at that point. The laborers dig a trench about 2 ft wide and deep enough to reach the footings. First they apply a fresh coat of asphalt to the exposed basement wall. Then they place PVC pipe with holes in each piece along the wall and cover it with gravel. After this they replace the dirt and any shrubs removed.

Installing electrical service.   The electrician first determines the voltage and current requirements of the dehyrator from the label on the unit or from the instruction sheet. He or she then installs in the panel a new circuit breaker of appropriate size, such as 20, 25, or 30 amperes. He or she then runs a new cable to the point in the basement where the unit will be placed. This might range from setting on the floor to hanging from the floor joists or hanging between joists. The electrician then connects the unit to the power and tests it for proper operation.

Installing ventilators.   The carpenters would add the new ventilation. These might be powered ventilators installed in the wall above ground level, or convection passive types that permit airflow and air circulation. In some cases the new ventilators would actually be piped into the heating and air-conditioning ducts so that a drying effect would be created. The objective is to remove or reduce the amount of moisture, thereby eliminating the accumulation of moisture and water.

Concluding comments.   The actual job of installing the new tile onto a concrete floor is the same as installing resilient tile onto a wood-based floor. The major differences are the concern with moisture and eliminating it, preparing the concrete for the new tile, and using the proper type of tile and cement. Owners with carpentry skills can perform all the different tasks, including installing ventilators. They can even trench alongside the house and create water sheds. An electrician might need to install a new circuit for the dehydrator unit.

A contractor would know how to solve all the problems. This might be an advantage to the owner. Also, the owner might earn more in wages than the contract costs. If this is true, the work should be done by the contractor.

PROJECT 5. REPLACE CARPETING

Subcategories include: types and properties of carpeting; types and properties of undercarpet or pads; residential carpets and commercial carpets; kitchen carpets; removal techniques; installing tack strips; and fitting, joining, cutting, and installing methods for residential applications.

Preliminary Discussion with the Owner

Problems facing the owner.   In years past, replacing carpet was a simple task of lifting it off the floor and either cleaning it or buying a new area carpet and laying it flat on the floor. Today, area carpets are used frequently over special floors, such as wood, parquet, inlaid marble, and tile.

In this project we are concerned with the problems facing the owner when wall-to-wall carpet is installed. There are two basic installation techniques to installing carpet. One is cementing the carpet to the subfloor. This is done in kitchens, bathrooms, and sometime dens or utility rooms. It is even used on patios and exposed areas outside the home. The other technique employs tack strips around the perimeter of the room or hall and a pad under the carpet. The workers nail the tack strips along the border of the wall or baseboard, and when they stretch the carpet over these strips the nails in the tack strips grab the underside of the carpet and hold it in place. As an owner with a worn-out carpet, we would need to determine if the carpet is cemented in place or installed with tack strips. We can lift a corner and find the answer easily. The ramification of this is that when replacing the worn carpet, the cost is less per square yard if the old carpet is not cemented to the floor.

Another problem we face is the selection of replacement carpet. In almost every case, we will need to substitute another make and style, due to the changes made in manufacturing carpets. Along with this problem comes the questions of quality, durability, color-fastness, resistance to stain, expected life of the carpet—and the list goes on. We almost need to make a complete study of the manufacture of carpets. Sometimes we can rely on local suppliers, who, if trained, can help us select a carpet suitable to our needs and desires.

All too often we are faced with damaged carpet due to the ravages of a storm. Sometimes the water causes stains. Sometimes mud, vegetation, and other organic materials are deposited on the carpet. Sometimes building materials such as glass, roofing materials, wood, brick, stone, cement blocks, and the like are embedded in the carpet. In all of these situations we might be able to have the carpet cleaned professionally, or we might need to throw it away and start over.

Let's also discuss the problem with the backing on carpeting. This often leads to problems for us. Jute is used as the backing for some carpeting. Being a natural fiber, it cannot withstand moisture and usually rots when wet. Many times the combination of the fiber, moisture, and heat form the conditions for fungus growth. The jute turns black and smells bad. Even if we can remove the odor, the backing is damaged and the carpet needs to be replaced. Today, manufacturers employ several substitutes for jute. Part of the reason was a lack of jute some years ago. Also, the chemical industry assisted by supplying alternative backing materials made from oil. One such backing is called action back. It is a polymer material and so is impervious to moisture. This means that the carpet can be soaked, then allowed to dry, and the backing will not sustain damage. Carpets damaged as we suggested earlier can be salvaged if the backing is a polymer.

Some carpets have a bonded rubber backing. However, most are not pure rubber but a combination of synthetics or cellular rubber (foam or sponge). These had a high rate of disintegration in carpets made several years ago, but the better grades today hold up better. Nevertheless, once the rubber backing begins to disintegrate, nothing can be done to stop the action. Replacement is the only solution.

Burns in carpets are another problem we face. Most burns result from dropped cigarette ashes or burning cigarette stubs. Most carpet will not ignite because federal standards require that the burn area remain small. But burns affect carpet pile differently for different fibers. A common solution to small, less severe burns is to snip the pile fibers to remove the damaged ends and follow with a good brushing. This solution also causes the carpet to wear faster in these areas. Larger burned areas will probably require patching or complete replacement.

Crushed pile is another problem we face. Hallways and areas inside doorways usually have the greatest crush rate. If this has been a problem, we must consider selecting a quality of carpet with a high pile density, which is the closeness of the tufts and tightness of the yarn. Commercial carpets tend to have these characteristics.

Finally, we can have the problem of paint spilled on the carpet. When the paint has a latex base, we can recover the carpet quite easily by keeping the area thoroughly wet until professional assistance arrives. But when the paint is oil based and requires mineral spirits for cleaning, we may damage the colors or backing with added mineral spirits.

Alternative solutions to the problem.   As we can see, there are many items of concern involved in the problems of restoring the carpets in the home. As contractors, we would need to provide some education to the owner when called to help with a rug problem. Clearly, we do not want to replace damaged or worn carpet with carpet of equal or poorer quality. This will not eliminate the problem. We need to provide education about rug construction and composition that permits the owner sufficient data to make a sound decision.

Some of the pertinent information includes stressing the appropriate backing and secondary backing based on the floor conditions. Next we can suggest a pile suitable to avoid the problem experienced with the older carpet. We might suggest an appropriate weight for the pile yarn, which is stated in ounces per square yard. The common weights are 20 and 26 oz, ranging to 48 oz. The pile thickness, which is the height of the tufts above the backing, may be $\frac{1}{4}$ in. for commercial and kitchen carpeting, to $\frac{5}{8}$ in. or more. The last item is the pile density, which is the closeness with which the fiber tufts are positioned. We can suggest different types of cuts, which include sculptured, sheered, looped, and others.

Finally, we can recommend a different pad or cushioning material to use under the carpet. Felt hair type would be inappropriate where moisture is likely, due to its organic fiber construction. When wet by cleaning, for example, it could rot. Cellular rubber produced in sheets as foam, or sponge rubber, is the material used most often today in residential dwellings. It is available in a wide variety of densities and thicknesses. The price per square yard goes up as the density is increased and as the thickness is increased. It is resistant to decay and mildew, and is nonallergenic. However, the contractor would not recommend a dense variety where the floor contained a radiant heating system, since the pad would block much of the heat.

For our project we shall remove and replace a storm-damaged carpet that was installed wall to wall.

Statement of work and the planning effort.   After careful examination, we conclude that the carpet must be replaced. The statement of work should be: *Remove and replace the carpet in the room.* More specifically, we should state that *the pad must be replaced with a foam type $\frac{1}{2}$ in. thick.* The carpet selection is the owner's choice and we must so state: *The owner may select the carpet with the recommendation that it have a nonorganic backing and a nylon carpet fiber pile.* The workers must be pledged to perform high-quality work. The statement could be: *Carpet will be tack-stripped tightly, and any joints or splices will match the pattern and nap in the carpet.*

The planning effort is minimal, since at the first visit we can assist the owner with all decisions except for the selection of replacement carpet. If we were an exclusively carpet company, we would have an estimator make the measurements at the first visit. The owner would visit our outlet and make the carpet selection. We would schedule the installation after the financing is established or a down payment has been received.

It is possible that the carpet is in stock; however, it might have to be ordered, which will delay completion of the job. In most cases we would send two workers to the job. The decision is based on the size of the job.

Contract.   The usual contract is the fixed-price type. There should be no unusual circumstances. Nonetheless, we must make sure that the contract specifies the entire job and any movement of appliances. Some firms charge for disconnecting and reconnecting stoves and ice-maker refrigerators, and some do not. Several items must be included: (1) type, color, and pattern name of the carpet; (2) number of square yards, (3) thickness and type of pad; and (4) other charges. Normally, the price is stipulated as $XX.XX per yard installed.

Material Assessment

Direct Materials	Use/Purpose
Carpet	Number of square yards required
Pad	Number of square yards required
Tack strips	To replace damaged strips
Rug edging (if required)	Used where rug butts up to another type of flooring

Indirect Materials	Use/Purpose
Heat-sensitive tape	To splice carpet
Masking tape	To splice the foam pad

Support Materials	Use/Purpose
Carpet installation tools	For installation

Outside Contractor Support	Use/Purpose
None	

Activities Planning Chart

Activity	Time Line (Days)
	1 2 3 4 5 6 7
1. Contract preparation	I _×_ I ___ I ___ I ___ I ___ I ___ I ___ I
2. Materials and scheduling	I _×_ I ___ I ___ I ___ I ___ I ___ I ___ I
3. Removing and replacing the carpet	I ___ I _×_ I ___ I ___ I ___ I ___ I ___ I

Reconstruction

Contract preparation. Our office staff would prepare the formal contract from the information provided by the contractor or salesperson. Most of the time the salesperson from the carpet company aids the owner with carpet selection. In the case of a damaged home, the contractor would probably subcontract to the carpet company for the replacement. In that event, we would need to add the price to the overall contract for restoration.

The contract-bid price would include materials and labor and an allowance for overhead. It would probably be stated in terms of number of square yards installed.

Materials and scheduling. The materials would be supplied by the carpet company. In some cases the replacement carpet could be taken from existing inventory. But more often the carpet would be ordered and would take a few days to several weeks to obtain.

Once the carpet is in the warehouse, the job can be scheduled for installation. We would telephone the owner and set up the period for installation. On that day two installers would load up at the store or warehouse and travel to the job. They are (in our project) expected to complete the job in one day.

Removing and replacing the carpet.   Essentially, the job requires removing the old carpet, preparing to install the new carpet, installing the new carpet, and final cleanup.

As Figure 3–5 shows, the carpet is held in place with tack strips around the perimeter walls. Where it passes a door, a metal edge may exist; this is pried up to free the carpet. The small nails grip the carpet and aid in keeping it stretched.

As installers, we first remove all furniture from the room. We pry up a corner of the carpet, freeing it from the tack strip. By lifting it we easily remove it entirely. We then usually roll or fold up the carpet and carry it outside.

Next, we roll up the old pad and carry it outside as well. Since dirt usually collects on the floor during this part of the job, we would sweep or vacuum the floor.

All tack strips that are serviceable would be left in place, but those that broke loose while taking up the old carpet would be replaced with new ones. New metal edging would be used in place of the old.

The installation can now be done. First the new pad is cut and laid. Since most padding is made 6 ft wide, a splice or several splices are made. At each joint we apply a strip of masking tape to hold the pieces of padding together. The pad does not overlap onto the tack strips but usually butts against them.

Now we are ready to install the carpet. While we were preparing the floor, the carpet has had time to relax, since we unrolled it earlier. This helps us in stretching

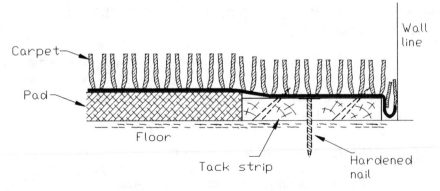

Figure 3–5   Carpet held in place with tack strips.

it during the installation. We measure and precut the carpet to the approximate size. This is usually about 6 in. wider and longer than we need. We lay the carpet on the floor and arrange it. Then working on our knees, we install it against one wall. We force it between the tack strip and baseboard and make sure that it is in contact with the tack strips.

We then work at the opposite wall and stretch the carpet to remove all wrinkles and make it tight. Next, we install the carpet on an adjacent wall, pulling it tight as well. Then we install it against the fourth wall. The final part of the job is to install it across the door opening by stretching the carpet over the metal strip and holding down the strip with light tapping on the metal.

We then clean up the trim and waste and floor with a careful vacuuming. The job is done when we load the old carpet and pad onto the truck along with our tools.

Concluding comments.   Carpets can be installed by homeowners who have some skill with tools and the agility and strength to perform the work. Carpet is heavy to carry and awkward to move into place. Kicking the knee stretcher requires considerable force. Nailing the tack strips to a wood floor is difficult, but nailing them to a concrete floor is much more difficult and requires considerable strength and skill with a hammer.

In most cases, the owner should let the contractor replace the carpet. The experienced workers know how to make splices and fit it solidly against the walls. They are also skilled in installing the metal trim across openings. They easily trim the excess around the walls as they drive the carpet between tack strip and baseboard.

In many situations, the owner can earn more wages per hour at his or her own job than the labor costs for the work.

PROJECT 6. RESTORE TERRAZZO, MARBLE, CERAMIC/CLAY, AND BRICK FLOORS

Subcategories include: understanding some of the properties pertaining to terrazzo, marble, ceramic, or clay tiles and bricks used for flooring; cleaning techniques, both common and special; cleaning chemicals; sealers; and polishing materials and techniques.

Preliminary Discussion with the Owner

Problems facing the owner.   Owners who have floors made from terrazzo, marble, ceramic, and brick sometimes find problems they'd rather not have. The worst of these problems involve damaged or cracked terrazzo, cracked marble, split ceramic tiles, and ruptured mortar joints in brick floors. Somewhat less troublesome are stained floors made from these products. Finally, there is the problem of restoring the finish to the surface.

Owners who face serious problems regarding these materials need answers about how to make restorations and what the costs will be. The least expense is involved in ignoring the problem. It will not go away, but after awhile people will rarely see it. Naturally, this depends on the severity of the problem. A single crack in a tile or section of terrazzo may remain for years. It may have been caused by stress placed on the floor during installation, or some part of the subfloor foundation may have changed with age.

When the floor becomes stained from paints, grease, chemical spills, and the like, owners face the problem of eliminating the staining with common and specially prepared solvent washes. This action must result in penetrating the flooring sufficiently to remove the stains. The final floor finish could be damaged during operation and require us to apply a new finish. The cost of these procedures is greater than ignoring the problem but less than for removal and replacement.

When the flooring becomes uneven and people catch their toes or trip over the uneven surfaces, the owner must act to make restoration. In this situation a section of the floor or the entire floor may have to be removed. If possible, the owner should learn about the flooring to talk intelligently with a contractor. For most of us this is not handyman or handywoman work. Even removing a single ceramic tile or sheet of tile can be a demanding task. When the flooring is built on top of a wooden subbase, the joists and underlayment must be substantial enough to support the added weight. If engineered correctly, this assembly will not sag or shift. Where there can be problems is where flooring has been placed over a wood-floor assembly that was not adequately prepared for the weight. Then sagging can result. Sooner or later the floor will crack.

Another equally serious problem is the improper selection of binding materials used in floor construction. Cements, improperly made, fail. This causes tiles to loosen and lift. Often, they can be restored for a modest cost. But where concrete fails, the terrazzo will probably need to be replaced. This kind of problem can cost a few dollars (a couple of hundred) to thousands of dollars.

Alternative solutions to the problem.   When we, as contractors, arrive at the house to evaluate the problems, we have a rough idea based on the discussions over the phone. We would bring a specialist with us to assist in making a fair and sound evaluation. For most floors a skilled mason can make the necessary inspection and evaluation. Some of the inspection items related to each kind of floor might include:

Flooring	Checklist item
Brick	Extent of cracked mortar joint
	Amount of abrasion to brick surfaces
	Extent of cracked or broken bricks
	Subsurface to which the brick are mortared
	Damaged subflooring
	Stained surfaces and efflorescence
Ceramic tile	Extent of cracked tiles
	Base on which the tiles were installed
	Discoloration and possible causes
	Damaged finish on tiles and the extent of damage
Clay tiles	Extent of cracked or lifted tiles
	Evidence of failed bonding cement
	Stained tiles and grout
	Damaged subflooring that caused the problem
Terrazzo	Extent of damage to sectioned-off flooring
	Evidence of decayed cement in concrete
	Damaged to surface resulting in stains
	Lack of or improperly sealed surface

Where we have to remove and replace damaged flooring we must advise the owner that the work is extensive and may be costly. Even when we assure the owner that costs will be kept to a minimum, all of the work is labor intensive. Even if we are able to use powered tools for removal operations, preparing the subsurface, installing the new floor materials, and then finishing them all require hand work. The materials, though, may not be extremely expensive unless we must replace the entire floor.

When a question about finishing the flooring is asked, we would recommend that a covering recommended by a reputable supplier be used. Then we would strictly follow the manufacturer's application instructions.

We could make quite a mess removing and replacing flooring. To avoid disturbing the rest of the house we would curtain the room to minimize dust and debris entering into these areas. We would also cover the egress passages with heavy paper to avoid damage to these floors.

For our project we will inspect a damaged floor where we will have to remove and replace some of the flooring. This will provide some idea of the efforts required by the workers.

Statement of work and the planning effort.   The first statement of work should cover the overall project, which could be to *restore the floor to its original high-quality condition.* The ramifications of this statement are far reaching, so we need to clarify the statement by narrowing it. Therefore, we can state that *the cracked sections or tiles must be removed and replaced with those of like kind, color, and texture.* This narrows the work, yet we can add *to finish the floor to a* *uniform texture or polish to blend in the replacements made.* We also need to include that *we will avoid damaging walls and other areas and clean the house where dust has accumulated from the various operations.*

The planning effort in this kind of work can be extensive, especially when restoring terrazzo. We must locate materials, equipment, and masons with the needed skills. Our planning begins with completing the estimates for the job, continues with contract preparation and negotiations, and ends with performing the work. In the actual work phase we need to plan for removing the broken materials, preparing the subsurface for new materials, and installing the new materials. Then we need to finish the surface as appropriate. Finally, we need to hire a cleaning team to clean and polish rooms and halls where dust and dirt have accumulated.

Contract.   Two types of contracts might be suitable for this project. Where the restoration is performed on a floor whose subfloor is sound and replacement materials are readily available, we can offer a fixed-price contract. But where the subfloor is part of the problem or a cause of the damaged flooring, we might need to offer a time-and-materials contract or a variation of this type of contract.

The more we can determine during the estimating phase, the better opportunity we have to offer a fixed-price contract. This will help the owner and sets certain conditions for us, the contractor. We would be able to closely identify the types and quantities of materials and can more accurately estimate the labor costs for masons and laborers.

Where shoring and other techniques of reinforcing the subfloor are required, we must either make allowance for the unknown, which drives up the cost, or take a chance that nothing unforeseen can happen to drive up the cost that we might have to absorb. Having to perform this work might require the special skills of carpenters or house movers.

The body of the contract must identify the type of contract and the specifications as described in the statements of work. The price must reflect the combined values associated with materials, labor, rental equipment, overhead, and subcontractors.

Material Assessment

Direct Materials	Use/Purpose
For terrazzo:	
Resinous topping	Epoxy and polyester with decorative chips added
Thinset, monolithic, chemically bonded	Portland cement with chips added; thinset and monolithic require a bonding agent
Divider strips	To replace the damaged ones
Epoxy or polyester bonding agent	To bond thinset and monolithic surfaces
Portland cement	Basic component

Direct Materials	Use/Purpose
Decorative chips	To make the pattern
Finishing sealer	To protect the surface
For ceramic tile:	
Sheets or tile squares	Basic flooring
Portland cement or modified cement bonding	Mixture that cements new tile to subfloor
Grout	To fill spaces between tiles
Sealer	To protect the surface
For clay tile:	
Clay tiles	Basic materials
Cement-mortar	Contains a plastic bonding agent
Grout	To fill spaces between tiles
Sealer	To protect the surface
For brick:	
Brick	Basic materials
Mortar with binders	To cement the bricks in place
Sealer	To protect the surface

Indirect Materials	Use/Purpose
Sheet plastic	To protect and curtain off other rooms
Heavy-duty paper	Taped to floors for protection
Masking tape	
Dunnage	To brace flooring where shimming must be used
Grinding stones	For use with terrazzo grinder

Support Materials	Use/Purpose
Mortar box	To mix cement
Wheelbarrow	To transport materials
Mason tools	For construction
Terrazzo grinder	To grind new surface to a polished shine
Power tools	To cut tiles and bricks to fit

Outside Contractor Support	Use/Purpose
Cleaning service	To clean the house after restoration is complete

Activities Planning Chart

Activity	Time Line (Days)
	1 2 3 4 5 6 7
1. Contract preparation	I _×_ I ___ I ___ I ___ I ___ I ___ I ___ I
2. Materials and scheduling	I _×_ I ___ I ___ I ___ I ___ I ___ I ___ I
3. Removing the old flooring	I ___ I _×_ I _×_ I ___ I ___ I ___ I ___ I
4. Installing the new flooring	I ___ I ___ I _×_ I _×_ I ___ I ___ I ___ I
5. Applying the sealant	I ___ I ___ I ___ I _×_ I ___ I ___ I ___ I

Reconstruction

Contract preparation.   In every case the office personnel will become heavily involved with this contract and its preparation. The estimator will need to make careful examinations of the old floor to identify conditions, problems to solve, and new materials to obtain. He or she will then evaluate the skills needed to make restoration. He or she will also spend time locating the replacement materials. The contract preparation can also take time to prepare, even when the estimator turns over the job description and worksheets. A subcontract must be obtained from the cleaning service company so that the pricing can be included in the general contract. Then overhead for fixed and variable costs must be computed and an allowance for profit added to arrive at the final bid/contract price.

Materials and scheduling.   Depending on the age of the floor and its materials, obtaining materials may require a few days to several weeks. The older the floor is, the more difficult it is to obtain matching materials. Although, for example, tile and brick products have remained basically the same dimensions for years, the colors vary due to different clays and fillers used. Most of these products are created in lots. All pieces within a lot are basically the same because they were made from the same batch of raw materials. Colors vary from lot to lot. This translates to problems for the owner. When it is impossible to match the flooring with a new lot, the owner either accepts a close approximation or contracts for an entire new floor. The same problem exists with a terrazzo floor. The chips of stone used in the original floor can be identified as to type; however, obtaining a matching color is difficult. All other materials, such as mortar, bonding agents, and cements, are readily available. In summary, materials acquisition may be time consuming and costly.

Scheduling the work involves several considerations. First, the materials must be located and obtained. Nothing can be done without them. Next, properly skilled workers need to be found, and these people are usually in demand, so their availability must be determined as soon as the materials have been obtained. These dates are communicated to the owner, who must decide on the final acceptable dates to have the work done. If the house is empty, no member of the owner's family need be at the site, but if the house is occupied, someone needs to be home.

In the scheduling process, we would also advise the cleaning contractor when his or her part needs to be done. Usually, a few days' notice is all that is required in this case.

Removing the old flooring.   Whether tile, brick, or terrazzo, the old materials must be removed to make room for their replacement. This is difficult, heavy work, since a lot of hammering and chipping are involved. Grinding tools may also be brought onto the job to ease the work. But even these tools require considerable physical effort. Chisels and hammers break up the pieces of the old floor that must be removed. Where sections only are removed, the workers must not chip or otherwise mark up adjacent surfaces and edges.

Ceramic Tiles.   Two types of ceramic tiles are used on floors. One is a sheet of miniatures (about 1 in. square) bonded to a fabric backing. These sheets are cemented in place and grout is added to fill the spaces between tiles. Removing this type of tile requires chipping out all small pieces one at a time and removing the cements under them.

The second type is the larger tile squares of other patterns, such as hexagon and octagon. These pieces are either cemented in place with a portland cement mortar or glued in place with a ceramic tile cement applied to the subsurface with a serrated trowel. In the first case, getting the old tiles up and smoothing the subsurface is very difficult and time consuming. However, breaking the tiles free when they are secured with a ceramic tile cement is quite simple. Most will pop free when force is applied between tile and floor. The old cement can easily be scraped away. (*Note:* Marble tile squares are treated and handled like ceramic tile.)

Terrazzo.   Over a wood subfloor, the terrazzo is usually a bonded type consisting of resinous materials and stone chips. This material is removed to the wood floor. Over concrete a thinset, monolithic, or chemically bonded topping made of cement and chips is applied. This material must be removed to the concrete slab below. Heavy machines may be required to break up and scrape away the damaged topping.

Brick.   Damaged brick is removed just like ceramic tile. Each brick is chiseled away a piece at a time until one or more have been removed. Then the chisel is used at the joint between the brick and the subfloor. The idea is to pop up bricks by cracking the mortar joint. The old mortar must be removed to the slab or subfloor before a new brick can be installed.

Cleaning.   Where the damage is only surface deep, cleaning and restoration of sealer may be the only procedure needed. In this situation we must remove the old sealer and stains with chemicals that dissolve and clean or with abrasion from a grinding machine.

Installing the new flooring.   Ceramic tile is cut to fit and cemented to the subfloor, brick is mortared to the subfloor, and terrazzo is poured in place and allowed to set. In each case the masons would lay out the materials to match the pattern of the rest of the floor. They would prepare the proper mortar or use a preprepared mixture sold in 1- and 5-gallon cans.

When a tile and brick floor is replaced, foot traffic must be restricted for 24 hours. When terrazzo is installed the tasks are much more time consuming. For example, masons must mix the portland cement mixture with marble chips and pigment if required and water is added. The mixture is poured into the area between dividers and seeded with additional chips. The added chips should be soaked prior to being added to the new mixture. Then the masons roll the area to force the water to the top, where the top is again troweled. Normally, the topping is kept wet for 7 days to ensure proper curing and to achieve almost maximum strength. Then the grinding operations can begin.

Applying the sealant.   Several manufacturers prepare sealant for these types of flooring. In every case applications must follow the maker's suggestions or directions. Many floors made from these materials possess sufficient luster that no special sealant need be used. Liquid cleaners can be used to clean the floor, and a clear water wash afterward, followed by a dry buffing, are often sufficient. There are also some don'ts: Don't use detergents, soaps, scrubbing powders, or water-soluble salts as cleaning agents; and don't allow water to dry on the surface.

Concluding comments.   In this project we have explored the problems with terrazzo, brick, and ceramic tiles. Marble floors are similar to clay tile and ceramic tile floors. We examined the problems and solutions associated with each kind of floor. Restoration work is very strenuous. Materials are heavy, and mortar is difficult to mix and transport. A lot of kneeling and bending is required.

Beyond the physical efforts, we need to recall that obtaining matching materials for color, texture, style, and pattern can be difficult or impossible. This will directly affect the cost of the restoration. It takes someone familiar with the masonry trade to locate replacement materials. This is a task more suited to the expert than to the homeowner.

CHAPTER SUMMARY

In this chapter we have examined a wide variety of floor problems and their solutions. All restoration of floors is expensive. Craftsmanship of the best quality is required. The materials selected by the owner or contractor must meet building standards and certain federal standards for durability, soundness, fire retardation, abrasion resistance, and in many cases, discoloration or staining.

We found a wide selection of causes for the problems involved in each type of flooring. Fortunately, there was at least one solution for restoration, but more often there were several suitable cures.

The data, examples, and discussions should help the owner with a unique problem. He or she can gain full insight and therefore be better at ensuring a high-quality restoration. The contractor using this information will be reminded that the owner is entitled to be advised from a fair and equitable viewpoint that establishes trust.

Any time that a floor must be restored, the routine in the house will be upset drastically for a short period. In some cases, the work disrupts the household for just a few days, sometimes for a week or more. Cleaning is usually required after every job.

4

DOORS AND DOOR UNITS

OBJECTIVES

To understand the principle of door operation

To rehang an interior door

To reset the locks and striking plates

To trim off the door bottom

To reglue a door

To remove and replace an interior door unit

To replace a custom door frame, trim, and stops

To restore a bifold door unit

To restore a pocket door to serviceable operation

To replace the finish on interior doors

OPENING COMMENTS

Conditions or circumstances that necessitate corrective action. In this chapter we examine problems with interior doors. In the past, doors and door frames were installed separately, and this is still true in some special situations.

Carpenters built frames from 1×6 fir or pine and trimmed them with either 1×4 door trim or molded door casing. After installing the door frame, called a jamb, they fit and hung the door. Following this, they installed stops and door locks. Almost no interior doors use a threshold. When there are problems with these doors, a set of conditions exists for their repair, and we examine this later.

Today, a new type of door is used. It is the unit assembly, which consists of a door and frame already assembled at the factory. The frame is usually a two-piece arrangement, as we see in Figure 4–1. The carpenter separates the halves and installs first one side and then the other to complete the installation. When something

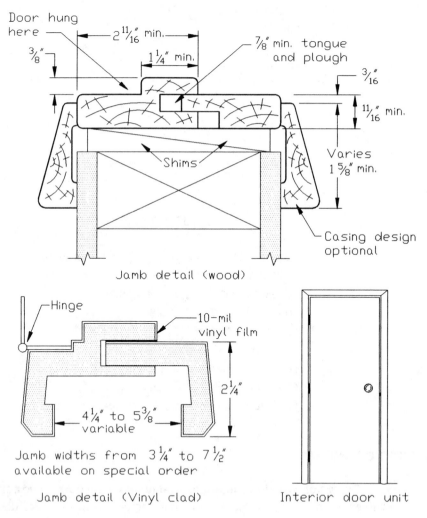

Figure 4–1 Unit door assembly.

goes wrong with this kind of door, a set of conditions that differ from those described above are involved in the repair.

Although doors generally function well for many years, there are times when they fail to close, lock, slide, hang, or swing properly, or sustain physical damage. This means that someone must perform the restoration work. Let's make a short list of the problems we might encounter.

Problem	Cause(s)
Does not close	Door warped, lock broken, hinges loose
Does not open properly	Loose hinges, bad lock, warped door
Lock sticks	Rusted, broken spring
Knob off	Retainer broken
Door hits jamb	Hinge loose, jamb moved, door sagged
Falls off track	Track loose, rollers defective or loose
Plywood peeling	Damaged by water
Panel door separating	Glue failed, no pins installed
Hits floor	Loose hinges, needs to be trimmed
Squeaks	Hinges lack lubricant
Closes by itself	Tilted door jamb
Bifolds fail to close	Alignment incorrect
Accordion door does not stay put	Jamb head not level
Dutch doors do not close	One half or the other sags
Trim or casing is loose	Insufficient nailing
Stops are loose or have moved	Improper or insufficient nailing
Striking plate loose or has moved	Loose screws, missing screws

Many of these situations can be fixed by owners, but they will need some know-how. This chapter should help in solving many problems; however, an experienced carpenter is sometimes needed.

Contractor's responsibility.   When a contractor is called to fix a door, the situation is usually serious. Most contractors realize that an owner will put up with a problem door for years rather than fix it or have it fixed. However, when the time does come for outside help, we need to provide skill and knowledge to solve the problem. As contractors, we should examine the door and provide the owner with a simple explanation of the problem. Even when the problem is complex, we do not need to provide too much detail, which in many cases may not set well with the owner.

Yet it is our responsibility to analyze the problem in sufficient detail and offer to fix it at the most reasonable cost. In many cases we should bring our tools to the job when we make an examination. Sometimes we can fix the problem without parts. This would save the owner considerable expense, since every trip adds to the cost of the job.

When extensive restoration is required, we need to provide the owner with the facts, although we may not be able to price the job during the first discussion. A severely warped door, for example, cannot be straightened and usually must be replaced. The same is true with broken locks and physically damaged interior doors and jambs. For these serious problems we would require time to determine the materials needed and estimate the labor involved.

Homeowner's expectations.   Even though we, as contractors, proceed fairly well with solving the problem, the owner expects a good-quality, quick, and reasonable job. If he or she could have fixed it, no discussion would be required. So provide a simple answer or explanation of the work and materials involved.

Scope of projects.   We shall examine six problems concerning doors: rehanging a door, repairing and refinishing a door, removing and replacing a door unit, restoring a customized door and frame, restoring bifold door operation, and solving problems with a pocket door.

PROJECT 1. REHANG AN INTERIOR DOOR

Subcategories include: trimming off the bottom of the door; resetting the hinges; ensuring proper clearances between door and frame; resetting the striking plate; and compensating for warp.

Preliminary Discussion with the Owner

Problems facing the owner.   The owner can be faced with several problems that rehanging the door can cure. These include the door hitting the jamb, scraping on the floor, or failing to stay closed, and a generally poor fit. In Figure 4–2 we can see that the correct gap between door and jamb should be about $\frac{1}{8}$ in. or slightly more. The gap between floor and door bottom should be not less than $\frac{1}{2}$ in. In most cases this is sufficient to permit the return of air to the heating and air-conditioning system. If these parameters differ significantly, the door needs to be refit or rehung.

When the door fails to latch, the cause can be a warped door, a loose or missing striking plate in the door jamb, a broken door lockset, or a poorly set stop. If

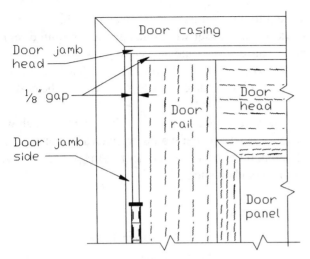

Figure 4–2 Gap between door and jamb.

these conditions exist, the door's hinges, stops, or lockset need work or replacement. Finally, a door may have hinges whose screws have pulled loose.

Alternative solutions to the problem.   The alternatives for these conditions include moving the hinges to make the front edge of the door align with the jamb, refastening the striking plate, replacing the lockset, and either moving the jamb or trimming the door to fit. In the worst case we would have to replace the entire door, install new stops, or replace the lockset. Finally, we can reinstall the hinges by taking appropriate action to ensure that the screws are firmly anchored.

Statement of work and the planning effort.   We must *restore the door to proper working order*. We must *replace broken parts of the door, hinges, lock, or stops*. We must also perform high-quality work so that the following standards are achieved:

1. Maintain $\frac{1}{8}$ in. of clearance between the jamb and door on the top and front.
2. Make sure that the door does not bind on the hinge side.
3. Ensure that the hinges are anchored soundly.
4. Install the lockset properly.
5. Provide proper clearance between the stop and the door when the door is closed.
6. Ensure that the clearance under the door is even at $\frac{1}{2}$ in.

For this job the planning effort is very simple. We, as contractors, would bring a toolbox to the job. Rather than make a formal estimate we would evaluate the work and make the restoration on the spot. This concept would be applicable for every problem identified except for replacing the door. In all probability, we would allocate 2 hours for the work. If the lockset were damaged and required replacement, we would take longer because of the time needed to get a new lock.

For planning purposes we would take a bill with us rather than have the office make a bill. However, as office policy, some contractors always bill the customer.

Contract.   For this project we would make an on-site contract which would be handwritten. In almost every case the owner would be given a verbal estimate of the job's cost after the evaluation. If there were agreement on the price, work would begin and the final bill would be paid on site.

Material Assessment

Direct Materials	Use/Purpose
Glue and plugs	To fill screw holes that have become stripped
4d finish nails	To reposition stops
8d casing nails	To fasten a frame that has moved
Wood screws	To replace lost or missing screws
Wood putty	To fill nail holes and mortises where hinges or striking plates were moved

Indirect Materials	Use/Purpose
Sandpaper	To sand off wood putty

Support Materials	Use/Purpose
Carpenter tools	To make repairs

Outside Contractor Support	Use/Purpose
Owner	To refinish a door

Activities Planning Chart

Activity	Time Line (Days)						
	1	2	3	4	5	6	7
1. Contractor evaluation	I _×_ I ___ I ___ I ___ I ___ I ___ I ___ I
2. Door restoration	I _×_ I ___ I ___ I ___ I ___ I ___ I ___ I

Reconstruction

Contractor evaluation.   The contractor would require knowledge of the percentage or allocation of overhead to apply to the job. In this case the allocation would be added to the hourly rate. In this way, he or she can easily provide an on-site estimate and later finalize the bill. Upon returning to the office, the office manager would record the job and associated costs and income, and would break down the income to the various accounts.

Door restoration.   Everything wrong with the way the door hangs, fits, and closes must be corrected. We will treat each possible problem as a separate item.

Does Not Close.   The door is warped and the lock plunger does not catch in the striking plate. When this happens, we must move the upper or lower hinges or both to compensate for the warp. When the warp is out at the top, we move the lower hinge out first. This moves the top front side of the door in toward the stops. If this is enough, all we do is move the stops to complete the job.

Before reinstalling the hinge, we need to shape wood plugs for filling the old screw holes. Then we dip each plug into glue and drive it into the hole. We trim off the excess with a saw or wood chisel.

The door may not close because of a broken or loose hinge. When trying to close the door, the edge strikes the frame; force or a lifting action is required to get it closed. If the hinge is loose—for example, the screws have worked loose—we must remove the rest of the screws from the hinge and plug the holes before replacing them. Driving longer ones into the jamb will not accomplish the desired results. As Figure 4–3 shows, there is usually an air gap between the $\frac{3}{4}$-in. jamb and the stud opening.

If the hinge is actually broken (a very usual situation), it must be replaced. Sometimes a hinge freezes due to lack of lubricant. This situation can be fixed on site with sandpaper and light oil.

Does Not Open Properly.   Loose hinges, a bad lock, improperly set stops, or a warped door are the likely causes when a door does not open properly. We have already addressed hinges. A bad lock may be either a broken locking mechanism or a change in the way the lock works. If we detect a broken piece inside the lock assembly, we are forced to replace the lock. However, if we discover rust or an area of binding, excessive looseness, or the like, we can make on-site repairs. The lock needs to be cleaned and lightly oiled. The cylinder must move freely in and out. The handles must turn easily in each direction. When turned to its fullest, the cylinder must fully retract. To ensure this, we check the travel of the cylinder. Sometimes the 1-in. hole is not deep enough, and the rear of the cylinder strikes the wood at the back of the hole.

Another problem with locks involves handle installation. Although they are machined accurately, carpenters or owners sometimes install them with a twist. The plates do not sit flat against the door stile. This causes the cylinder to bind and restricts its travel.

If the door stops are separate pieces instead of molded into the frame, we can

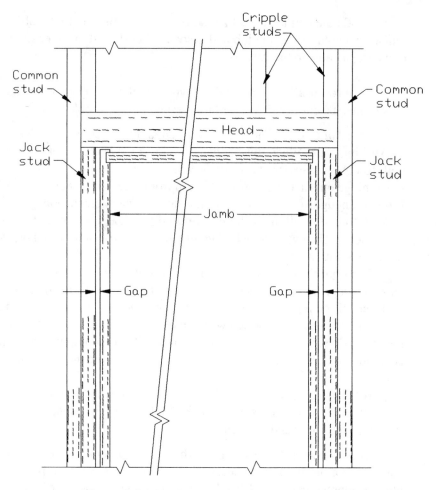

Figure 4–3 Gap between door jamb and jack stud.

take them off and reposition them. We would probably remove the front stop first and try the door. If it closes and looks good, we would renail the stop to accommodate the closed position. By "looks good" we mean that the gap on top and along the front are correct and that the door is flush with the jamb at the lock.

Knob Is Off.   Knobs work loose for several reasons. Repeated slamming of a door loosens the retaining screws that hold the lockset in place. This provides more freedom of the knobs to wiggle. By tightening the two screws behind the handle or knob, a lot of play is removed. If the handle falls off, the cause may be that it slipped over the retainer or that the retainer has broken. First try to reinstall the knob or handle. Push the retainer in while slipping the knob over it. Make sure that the retainer is aligned over the square retainer slot.

Door Hits Jamb.   Hinges are loose, the jamb has moved, or the door has sagged. We have discussed loose hinges. The jamb can move. Nails hold the jamb in place. In earlier days when jambs were made on site from pieces of wood, they seldom moved after installation. They were fit to the door frame opening with blocks or shingles as shown in Figure 4–4. The only plausible way for these jambs to move would be a sagging floor or physical damage to the jamb. In these situations we must remove the trim and reinstall the jamb by adjusting the blocks behind the jamb.

Today, when interior door units are used, nails are seldom driven through the jamb. The two-piece jamb is usually nailed in place through the attached casing. In effect, the jambs are freestanding. Although this arrangement is very reliable,

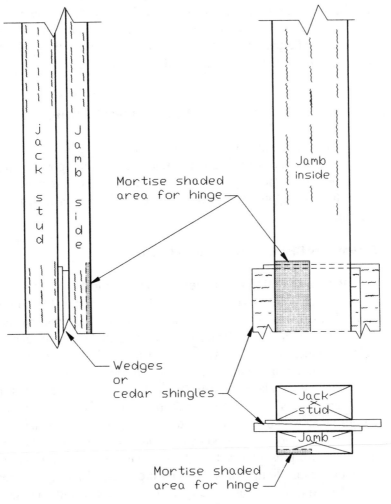

Figure 4–4   Blocking used to make jamb rigid.

sometimes the units are installed incorrectly. When this happens the door hits the jamb and often will not lock properly, as well. The best cure is to remove the unit and reinstall it.

If these corrective measures fail to solve the problem, we are left with trimming the door's width with a plane. First we bevel the inside edge of the door to provide clearance for it to swing closed without hitting the jamb. Then we dress it throughout its full length to achieve a $\frac{1}{8}$-in. clearance top to bottom. This technique is also used at the top of a door.

Concluding comments.   Calling a carpenter or contractor to the home to restore an ordinary door can result in a modest expense. There would be a flat rate plus materials involved. However, a well-trained and experienced carpenter would solve the problem for a great many years. Amortized over the owner's lifetime, the cost would be pennies a year. On the other hand, an owner with some skills in carpentry could perform these repairs if he or she had the tools. The supplies are readily available at hardware and builder's supply outlets.

PROJECT 2. REGLUE AND REFINISH AN INTERIOR DOOR

Subcategories include: principles of panel and nonpanel door construction; mortise-and-tenon door construction; preparation of the door for gluing; gluing and clamping tasks; types of glue to use; paint and varnish removal; painting and staining techniques; applying clear finish materials; and tools and chemicals used in the operations.

Preliminary Discussion with the Owner

Problems facing the owner.   Interior doors are made using two basic construction techniques: stile and rail, which have inset panels, and flush doors (commonly known as hollow core and solid core). Let's deal with the panel door first.

Panel doors have vertical stiles and horizontal rails. The panels are also called lights, and there might be any number, from as few as one to as many as twelve. The more common varieties are the four-panel and six-panel colonial types. When wood panels are replaced with glass as in French doors, more lights are appropriate.

Panel doors are made using mortise-and-tenon construction. Many include dowels along with the mortise and tenons. Figure 4–5 shows a view of such a joint. Since the tolerances employed by doormakers are very tight, these doors are often not glued, just pressed together. Rather than glue, metal pins are used to bind the tenon on the rails to the stiles. The pins are recessed and filled with putty.

With time and wear these joints become loose and door sag results. Some-

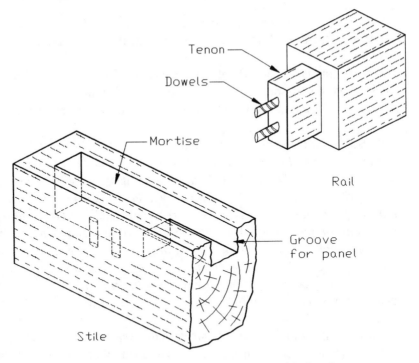

Figure 4–5   Mortise-and-tenon joint with dowels.

times a violent storm can cause physical damage to a door that makes it move out of square. In either event, our problem is that the door must either be replaced or squared and rejoined.

The flush door is either hollow core or solid core. This means that the plywood outer panel is glued to the core with interior glue. Interior glues cannot resist water or dampness without delamination, resulting in peeling. The most-interior ply will delaminate from the core. Our problem is reduced to two alternatives: replace the damaged door and reglue. Regluing requires application of glue and the proper clamping tools.

Alternative solutions to the problem.   From the contractor's viewpoint, the problem of replacing or repairing a panel door depends on whether or not the door is unique to the architecture to the house. From time to time and from manufacturer to manufacturer, the dimensions of stiles and rails differ slightly. As long as the door is the only one in the room, slight dimensional differences will not be noticeable. But where there are other doors in the room, a match must be maintained. Where this is the situation, the best solution is to restore the panel door.

When the contractor must make a decision about a delaminated or damaged flush door, he or she will usually replace the delaminated door. If the damage to a hollow-core door is a severe puncture, the same solution will probably be used. Sometimes the cost of labor is far greater then the cost of buying a new door and hanging it.

If rotting is associated with the damage to either kind of door, the contractor could make repairs or recommend a new door. Labor could be expensive while making repairs compared with the hours spent hanging a new door.

Statement of work and the planning effort. For this type of problem we need to state that *the door will be restored or replaced to its original condition of reliability and appearance.* Where the door is the panel or light type, workers will *use appropriate techniques and tools to replace damaged parts and apply glue and pins to ensure door integrity and squareness.* In this job *the owner will finish the door at his or her expense.* If we add specifics, they would include: *fitting the door and maintaining a $\frac{1}{8}$-in. clearance along the top and front edge will be assured;* and *the door travel and locking mechanisms will operate smoothly.*

For the planning effort, we will make an initial inspection of the job and gather details. Then we must prepare an estimate of costs and a description of the job. Materials and labor costs must be determined by the estimator or contractor. Then a meeting with the owner to arrive at the final okay and to schedule time to do the work must be set. Since a carpenter will do all the work, no subcontractors will be involved.

One aspect of the job may delay the development of a contract/bid and restoration. If the door must be replaced and an exact replica made, a special order would have to be made with a door company. This could delay restoration for 6 to 8 weeks.

Contract. Except for the very unusual circumstance, a fixed-price contract is appropriate for this work. The contractor can determine every aspect of the job during the inspection phase and can determine the materials and labor required for the job.

Material Assessment

Direct Materials	Use/Purpose
Replacement door	If required
Glue, dowels, pins	For panel door restoration
Sandpaper	To smooth or sand joints
Wood putty	To fill blemishes and dents

Indirect Materials	Use/Purpose
Wood blocks and strips	Used between door and clamps to prevent marking up door

Support Materials	**Use/Purpose**
Bar clamps	To pull door together
Carpenter tools	For construction
C-clamps	To clamp loose plywood on flush doors

Outside Contractor Support	**Use/Purpose**
Owner	To refinish the door

Activities Planning Chart

Activity	Time Line (Days)						
	1	2	3	4	5	6	7
1. Contract preparation	I _×_ I	___ I	___ I	___ I	___ I	___ I	___ I
2. Materials and scheduling	I _×_ I	___ I	___ I	___ I	___ I	___ I	___ I
3. Restoration	I ___ I	_×_ I	___ I	___ I	___ I	___ I	___ I

Reconstruction

Contract preparation.   The office personnel take the notes from the first inspection, make the necessary estimates, and prepare the contract/bid. All of the considerations mentioned earlier are taken into account and all statements of work are added as required. Then labor figures are prepared, and overhead and profit factors are applied.

Materials and scheduling.   For the panel door repairs, acquiring materials is a simple matter of picking up a few items from a hardware store. Ordering a new door requires a specific set of specifications. These include the actual door thickness, height, and width; the dimensions of the stiles, rails, and panels; and their design. To assure an exact replication of the design in the panel we might have to send the door to the plant for them to extract the original panels and insert them into the new door.

To replace a flush door, the carpenter would pick up a new one on the way to the job. In all likelihood, the old hinges and lockset would be serviceable and work well in the new door. If the old door could be reglued and made serviceable, the carpenter would pick up glue and clamps to make the repairs.

Restoration.   On a panel door, the carpenter would drive the pins through and remove them to enable disassembling the stiles from the rails. He or she would use wood blocks to separate the joints carefully. Once apart, the joints are cleaned of old glue, if any; dirt that has entered the joint; and broken dowels or tenon materials. Then new dowels are cut and the gluing process can begin. Glue is spread along the four sides of the mortise. None needs to be added to the edges of the rails since some from the mortise usually escapes and covers the edges.

After all mortise and dowel holes have glue, the rails and panels are set in place and the opposite stile is installed. The long bar clamps are used to bring the joints together and keep them under pressure until the glue sets. During this part of the job we use the framing square to make sure that the door is perfectly square. Finally, we drive two pins into each joint and countersink them. After the glue sets, we sand the door and fill the nail holes with wood putty.

On a flush door, repairing the delaminated plywood from the core requires squirting glue between the parts and then clamping the plywood to the core. For this operation we use C-clamps and strips of wood. The strips should be 2×4s so that pressure distributed along the full line of freshly glued area is present. Excess glue should be wiped away to avoid extensive sanding later.

Concluding comments. It is possible to save a door that has damage from deteriorated joints or delamination. If there is good reason for doing so and the cost is not prohibitive, the original architecture is preserved. However, there are times when the only sensible solution is to replace the door. In this situation an exact replacement may need to be custom made or a suitable substitute can be purchased.

PROJECT 3. REMOVE AND REPLACE AN INTERIOR DOOR UNIT

Subcategories include: principles of interior door assembly construction; remove and replacement techniques; alignment of spacing between door and jamb; blocking techniques; and nailing techniques.

Preliminary Discussion with the Owner

Problems facing the owner. The interior door unit we discuss here consists of a split jamb and door. The door is prehung at the factory. Some, but not all, come with a lockset already installed. The installation follows a standard procedure:

1. Separate the two halves of the jamb while leaving the door hinged in place.
2. Insert the half with the door into the wall opening. The door casing should be flat against the wallboard.
3. Using 6d casing or finish nails, drive the nails partway through the casing, first on the hinge side, from top to bottom. *Do not drive the nails home.*
4. Install the other half of the jamb assembly from the other room by sliding it into place in the groove. Tack-nail the casing to the framing.

5. Adjust the frame for the $\frac{1}{8}$-in. clearance on the top and front edge of the door by moving the jamb left or right.

6. Drive all nails home and set them when the door unit has been properly set.

7. Install the lockset, as required.

The seven steps above constitute the activities involved in installing a new door unit. Taking the old door unit out may provide a clue to the practical problems of weight and size, as well as stress. The only associated problem is selecting, purchasing, and transporting the new door unit from the supply house to the home.

Alternative solutions to the problem.   In this situation, the alternative is to have a carpenter perform the work. The carpenter takes care of everything. Further, a painter will take care of finishing the door unit to match the others in the house.

Statement of work and the planning effort.   This job is simple and straightforward. The work is described as *remove and replace the interior unit*. The quality of work should include: *The standards for fit must be maintained, the door must close and open properly, and the lockset must function free of any binding.* The workmanship may also state: *During installation, carpenters will not make hammer marks or other marks that affect the surface of the wood. Nails must be set and filled.*

As for the planning effort, we would need to make an inspection of the old unit, determine its size and casing style, and determine if the owner would perform the finishing tasks. Then our office personnel can estimate the job and prepare the bid.

After the contract is signed, we would assign a carpenter, who would pick up the new door unit on the way. This job will require less than a day to complete. It could be fit into an afternoon or when a larger job is delayed.

Contract.   A fixed-price contract is the best for this job. There are no unknowns. The body of the contract would have the statements of work as well as a description of the door unit. This description may include the size, such as 2'8" by 6'8" LH (LH means "left-hand swing") interior hollow core.

Material Assessment

Direct Materials	Use/Purpose
Interior door unit	To replace the old one
6d casing or finish nails	To nail casing to wall
Wood putty	To fill nail holes

Indirect Materials	Use/Purpose
Shims	To put support behind hinges and lock area between jamb and studs

Support Materials	Use/Purpose
Carpenter tools	For construction

Outside Contractor Support	Use/Purpose
Owner or painter	To finish the door and frame

Activities Planning Chart

Activity	Time Line (Days)
	1 2 3 4 5 6 7
1. Contract preparation	I _x_ I ___ I ___ I ___ I ___ I ___ I ___ I
2. Materials and scheduling	I _x_ I ___ I ___ I ___ I ___ I ___ I ___ I
3. Removing and replacing the door	I ___ I _x_ I ___ I ___ I ___ I ___ I ___ I
4. Finishing the door and frame	I ___ I _x_ I _x_ I ___ I ___ I ___ I ___ I

Reconstruction

Contract preparation. Due to the simplicity of the job, the main effort by office personnel is to locate the appropriate replacement unit, prepare the bid and contract, and schedule the carpenter. Once the estimator finds the appropriate door unit, he or she can price it and then add the labor and overhead costs.

Materials and scheduling. Unless there is an unusual dimension to the unit, locating one of the same type and size of casing should not be difficult. Many builder's supply houses carry ample stock in a wide variety of sizes. They also carry LH- and RH-swing versions. However, if they are out of stock, deliveries can usually be made to the supplier within 2 to 3 days.

If the owner decides to locate the new unit, he or she can encounter the same situation. Further, the owner can have the door delivered to the home. Some places do this at no cost, but most cover their labor and transportation costs by charging a delivery fee.

Unless problems arise, the carpenter will require 2 to 3 hours or less to remove and replace the unit.

Removing and replacing the door. We will not repeat the seven steps listed earlier but will discuss where problems can arise. For example, we stated that the half with the door attached needs to be installed first. This is to use the door as a guide in aligning the jamb and casing. We usually set the jamb on the floor and work from the back hinge side. By moving the jamb and casing left or right, we can adjust the gap or spacing between the door top and the jamb. This area must be $\frac{1}{8}$ in. and even from front to back. Next, we adjust the position of the front piece of jamb and casing for even spacing top to bottom by moving the pieces in and out while driving nails. With this half tack nailed, we should be able to open and close the door properly. For the unit to operate properly, the other half of the jamb does not need to be installed.

When installing the other half of the jamb with its casing, we must be careful to avoid moving or twisting the first half. Any pressure we place on the first half causes the unit to change its operation.

Once everything fits well and the door closes properly, we drive the nails home and set the heads. We usually prepare a wood putty from powder. Some carpenters now use spackling paste. It works fine for doors that are to be painted but does not work well when stain is to be applied.

Concluding comments.   Of all the projects dealing with doors, replacement is the one that many homeowners perform. Whereas a carpenter can remove and replace a unit without help, the owner may require assistance. A unit is large and may be difficult to handle because of the two separate pieces and the fact that the door is hinged.

When a carpenter does the work, he or she usually assumes responsibility for every part of the job, which saves the owner considerable time and expense. Since the job requires less than a day to complete, many contractors will not be interested, but when they are, they will usually fit the job in where they can. This requires that the owner make the time to fit the carpenter's schedule.

PROJECT 4. REPLACE A CUSTOM DOOR FRAME, TRIM, AND STOPS

Subcategories include: removing the old door frame and trim; constructing a new door jamb; installing the new jamb; trimming both sides; hanging the door; installing the stops; and installing the lockset.

Preliminary Discussion with the Owner

Problems facing the owner.   The owner of a house that was built with custom door jambs or on-site-built jambs has a door unit with a custom-fitted door. The carpenter started with the basic pieces shown in Figure 4–6, which include the jamb, made from three pieces—a head and two sides; six pieces of casing or door trim for each side; and three pieces of door stops. Every piece must be planned for, marked,

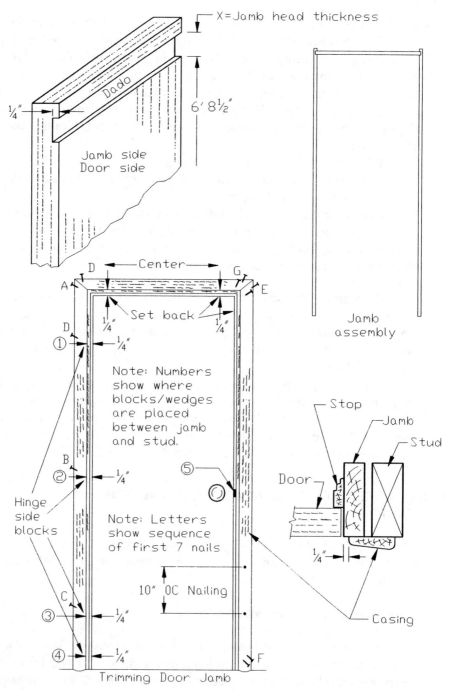

X = Jamb head thickness

Dado

¼″

6′ 8½″

Jamb side
Door side

Jamb
assembly

D ← Center → G
A
Set back
¼″   ¼″
E

D
① ¼″

Note: Numbers
show where
blocks/wedges
are placed
between jamb
and stud.

B
② ¼″   ⑤

Hinge
side
blocks

Note: Letters
show sequence
of first 7 nails

Stop
Jamb
Stud

Door

10″ OC Nailing

C
③ ¼″

¼″

④ ¼″   F

Casing

Trimming Door Jamb

Door jamb and trimmed door frame

Figure 4–6 Basic pieces of a custom-made jamb with trim and stops.

cut, and assembled into the opening. In addition, the owner must make sure that the frame is just large enough to permit an accurate and perfect fit of the door.

The owner must know how to fit the door into the opening and how to mortise the hinges in place on the door as well as on the frame. The door needs a lockset and the owner must accurately bore holes into the door for this. Also included in this task is the skill required to cut and fit the door stops and striking plate. These tasks are advanced carpentry skills and require a lot of knowledge and practical experience.

Alternative solutions to the problem. It is possible to use a pre-manufactured door unit *if* the casing matches the old casing, but this is seldom true. The owner can purchase the materials and custom fit them to complete the job if he or she has advanced carpentry skills, or the owner can call a finish carpenter to have the work done. Not every carpenter has the required background and experience to perform this skilled work, so the owner may have to shop around.

If style and character of the door must be maintained, an exact replica of door casings, door stops, and even the door itself must be found or made. Generally, the old lock and hinges can be reused. However, with very old doors, a mortise lockset was used that required drilling a mortise about 4 in. long into the edge of the door. Before that time the lock assembly was flush mounted on the inside of the door and a hole was drilled for the key and knob.

Statement of work and the planning effort. The basic statement of work must be *to restore the door frame and door to its original condition by replacing the damaged parts.* The specifications should also state that *all designs, shapes, and characteristics of the door trim must be replicated and fit to baseboard and jamb.* We should also state that *the door must be fit accurately into the jamb and the lockset appropriately.* Where there is a need to finish the door with either stain and varnish or paint, we need to specify this: *The door and frame will be finished to match the other doors* (or *the painting scheme presently employed*).

The planning effort is begun by evaluating the problem and determining the extent of work to be done. We must take stock of the conditions of the old frame and door and of the lock and hinges. We must carefully preserve pieces of the trim and stops to use as patterns for making the new pieces. We must also preserve parts of the door as well as taking all measurements needed in having a new door manufactured. We must also take down information pertaining to the finish materials needed to complete restoration.

After gathering the basic information, our planning focuses on obtaining estimates, locating materials, and finding a cabinet shop that can make the trim and door. Then we need to locate a painter who can match the finish needed on the door and frame. We would need to work very closely with these subcontractors to obtain cost figures and determine production schedules.

Contract.   If we, as contractor, were permitted the appropriate time to obtain replacement materials at the best cost possible, we could provide a fixed-price contract for this restoration. This type of contract would let the owner know exactly how expensive the job would be. But if he or she had to have the work done as quickly as possible, the cabinet shop owner, the painter, and we would need to work on a cost-plus basis. This means that we would use a time-and-materials contract, with no opportunity to lock in either labor or material costs.

The body of the contract would contain the specifications derived from the statements of work from the painter, cabinetmaker, and from us. It is also possible that on contract signing, we would require a deposit on the work.

Material Assessment

Direct Materials	Use/Purpose
Door jamb	To replace destroyed jamb
Door stops	To replace damaged stops
Door trim or casings	To replace damaged casings
8d common nails	To nail jamb together
8d finish nails	To nail jamb in place in the opening and casing to jamb and wall
4d finish nails	To nail stops in place
Wood putty	To fill nail holes
Primer or stain	To finish door
Varnish or paint	To finish door

Indirect Materials	Use/Purpose
Sandpaper	For smoothing operations
Wood shingles or wedges	To position jamb during installation
Cleaning solvent	To clean locks and handles
Lubricant	To oil lock assembly

Support Materials	Use/Purpose
Carpenter tools	For construction
Sawhorses	To assemble jamb and prepare door
Door jack	To position door while planning edges and installing hinges
Power tools	To ease cutting and driving screws

Outside Contractor Support	Use/Purpose
Cabinetmaker	To prepare casings, stops, and new door
Painter	To finish the new work to match the decor of the house

Activities Planning Chart

Activity	Time Line (Days)						
	1	2	3	4	5	6	7
1. Contract preparation	×						
2. Materials and scheduling	×						
3. Cabinetmaker preparing materials		×	×	×			
4. Building and installing the jamb					×		
5. Trimming out the door jamb					×		
6. Installing the new door					×		
7. Finishing the new door						×	×

Reconstruction

Contract preparation.   Due to the needs of the job, we must prepare a contract that incorporates our efforts and materials as well as those of the subcontractors. Our office personnel must contact these contractors and have them obtain the specifications and samples of materials. From these samples they can prepare their bids. On small jobs of this kind, we would probably turn to our usual sources and accept their bids as best and final. If the job were extensive, for example, if every door in the house had to be restored, we might seek several bids.

Once the bids are in and our estimates have been made on the job worksheet, our office personnel will prepare the contract/bid for presentation to the owner. The owner may require time to consider the offer or may accept it immediately.

Materials and scheduling.   The jamb is made from clear pine or fir unless a hardwood jamb was used originally. The other wood products are made by the cabinetmaker. The painting or staining system materials are provided by the painter. These should be readily available.

The scheduling would follow this sequence:

1. Obtain a signed and approved contract.
2. Notify the cabinetmaker to begin work and obtain a projected completion date.
3. Notify the painter that he or she has won the contract and the earliest date expected to finish the door and frame.
4. Schedule the carpenter to install the frame and door based on the completion date projected by the cabinetmaker.
5. The painter completes the work.
6. The contractor meets with the owner for a final inspection and payment.

Building and installing the jamb.   We pick up material for the jamb from a lumberyard. If the walls are the modern variety with drywall covering, this material is already prepared to the correct width. If the walls are plastered, we must trim a 1×8 to the necessary width and dress the sawed edge. Figure 4–7 shows this detail.

Next we must make a dado in each side piece for the head. As shown in Figure 4–7, we position the bottom of the dado 6 ft $8\frac{5}{8}$ in. up from the bottom. This allows for $\frac{1}{2}$ in. of clearance between the door and the floor and $\frac{1}{8}$ in. of clearance between the top of door and the jamb. The dado must be wide enough to insert the head jamb piece and about $\frac{1}{4}$ to $\frac{3}{8}$ in. deep. If the opening is high enough, we can let some of the jamb sides extend above the dado.

After nailing the three pieces together, we install the jamb in the opening and use shims or wood shingles at strategic points. These are the locations where the hinges are to be installed and where the lock is to be installed. At all times we maintain proper separation and alignment. Figure 4–7 provides many of the details. Verify each of the items in the following checklist:

1. Jamb side separation is equal to the door width plus $\frac{1}{4}$ in.
2. Jamb separation is uniform from floor to head.
3. The jamb edge is even with the wall's outer surface.
4. The angle between the head and the jamb side is an accurate 90 degrees.
5. The blocks anchoring the jamb are behind the hinge and lock areas.
6. The blocks are at floor level.
7. All nails driven through the jamb into the studs are set.

Installing the door casings or trim and fitting the stops.   There are so many varieties of trim and casings that we cannot cover them all. However, there

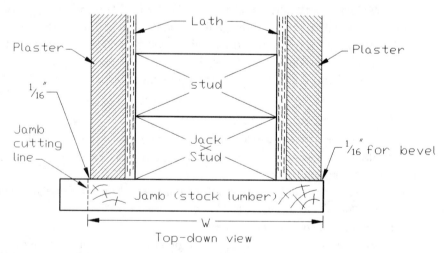

Figure 4–7   Defining jamb width for custom-made jamb.

are two basic treatments and we will cover both. The simpler of the two requires three pieces of trim or casing: one for the head (horizontal) and one for each side (vertical). A simple 45-degree miter is used to join the side and top trim. When these miters are cut, the experienced carpenter always undercuts the joining pieces. This allows for irregularities between the wall and jamb and ensures a tight joint at the face. The second treatment requires several more pieces of trim than the three basic pieces. Figure 4–8 shows an example of this treatment. In each corner a square piece with some decorative embossing is installed. At the floor another

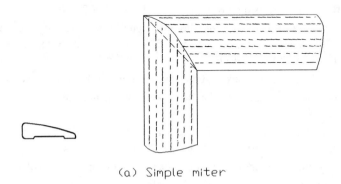

(a) Simple miter

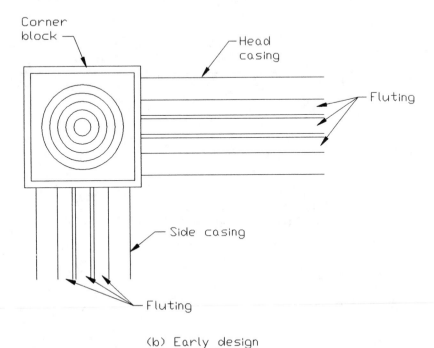

(b) Early design

Figure 4–8   Corner treatment for casings.

piece is installed, which has some decorative design. Between these pieces straight pieces, with fluting in some cases, are cut and fitted. In this arrangement there is no need for miters.

Simple Three-Piece Trim.   Installing the simple three-piece trim is done as follows:

1. Set the combination square for $\frac{1}{4}$ in. and scribe a line along the inside edge of the jamb. See Figure 4–9.
2. Square off and cut the end off a piece of trim and stand it up along side the mark on the jamb. (If it is over 8 ft long, cut it to 7 ft 2 or 3 in.)
3. Mark the trim at the point where the pencil lines intersect at the head and side. This is the shortest point. Lay the piece down and make a 45-degree line up and away. See the detail in Figure 4–9.
4. Cut the piece and tack-nail it in place on the jamb with 4d or 6d finish nails.
5. Repeat steps 2, 3, and 4 for the opposite vertical piece but do not tack-nail it in place yet.
6. Mark the end of a piece for the head and cut a miter. Try it for fit against the other miter. Make adjustments with a block plane, if necessary.
7. Measure and mark the other end of the head trim and cut a 45-degree miter.
8. Tack-nail the side and top trim in place. If necessary, adjust the second joint with a

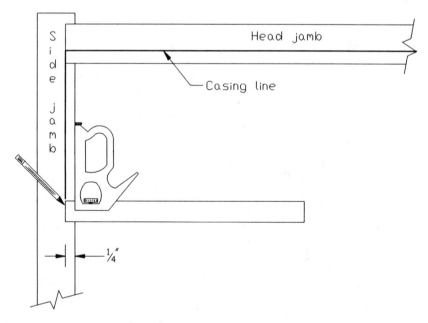

Figure 4–9   Marking jamb for trim.

block plane. Then drive and set all nails. Then using 8d nails, drive several along the outer edge of the trim into the studs behind the wall and set them.

9. Repeat the steps above on the other side of the door.

Multiple-Piece Door Trim.   Hopefully, the top corner pieces and baseboard-level pieces can be salvaged from the damaged door. If they cannot, new ones must be made. We would copy the pattern from the other doors and either have them made in a wood shop or set up tools on site to do the work. Where the other pieces of trim also have a design, we need to make new pieces to match.

With the four baseboard-level pieces available, we can begin the trimming operation. We would first make a pencil line along the jamb as in a simple trimming operation. Then to make sure that we do not split these custom-made pieces, we drill pilot holes for the nails. The drill bit needs to be the diameter of the nail's shaft. The flared head will do most of the holding. Then we can nail all four pieces in place.

Next, we prepare and install the four vertical pieces. Since in most cases the fluting runs from end to end, this is a simple task. We measure from the top of the baseboard piece to the line intersect point on the jamb or the bottom of the head and transcribe this to the trim. (*Note:* In some installations the corner blocks actually intersect at the corner of the jamb's side and head, and sometimes the block is in line with the door trim.) A square cut is all that is needed for both ends. These four pieces should be tack-nailed in place to allow for adjustment later, if needed.

Next, the two head pieces are cut to the same reference as the side trim pieces, but at the head, and tack nailed. Then we set the four corner blocks in place and try for fit. Since the block is a perfect square and the design is perfectly centered, we will make no adjustments to these pieces. All adjustments for a perfect fit between block and trim must be made to the end of the trim bucking up to the block. When the block fits well, we predrill pilot holes for the nails, nail the block in place, and set the nails. Then we can drive all nails home and set them. This finishes the door trim.

Installing the Door Stops.   Three pieces make up a set of door stops. The head piece is square cut and tacked in place when the door is closed and in place. Each side piece is individually measured, mitered, coped, and tacked in place. The coping is shown in Figure 4–10. Experienced carpenters never use 45-degree miter joints when installing stops because the joints tend to move and open up. When a coped joint is used, any movement in the jamb width, for example, will never be seen.

Installing the new door.   Given the price of a new door, even a new hollow-core door, the task of fitting and hanging a door must be left to an experienced person, whether carpenter or homeowner. With that said, let's define how we proceed.

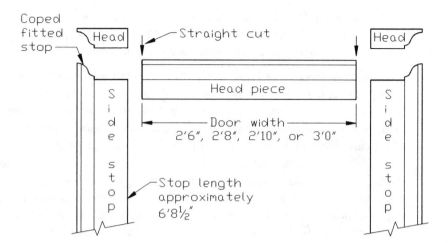

Figure 4–10 Fitting door stops.

1. Lay the door on a workbench or across a pair of sawhorses and trim off the dog ears (ends of the stiles).

2. Set the door into the opening and with a flat bar slipped under it, raise it up to check the fit.

   a. It must fit evenly across the head.

   b. The edge to receive the hinges must fit snugly against the jamb.

   c. There should be about a $\frac{1}{4}$ in. gap between the front edge of the door and the jamb.

   If any of these conditions are not met, make the correction with a large plane or power saw and plane if required.

3. Mark the position of the hinges. We would use the same measurements as on the other doors, usually 6 to 7 in. down from the top and 11 in. up from the bottom. If there is a center hinge, it will be centered between the two outside hinges.

4. Lay out and mortise each hinge on the door. See Figure 4–11 for the details. Then drill pilot holes and drive the screws in place.

5. On the jamb where the hinges will go, measure the position of the top hinge as equal to the distance down from the top of the door plus $\frac{1}{8}$ in. to allow for clearance.

6. Use the hinge to mark the shape of the hinge on the jamb, and mortise the space. Drill pilot holes and install one screw through the hinge.

7. Hang the door on the hinge and mark the position of the lower hinge. Remove the door and mortise and set the lower hinge in place.

8. Try the door operation after hanging it on the hinges. It must not bind along the back, and it must close in the front. It must maintain a $\frac{1}{8}$-in. gap along the top.

   a. Set the hinge in deeper if the front hits.

   b. Shim behind the hinge if the door binds.

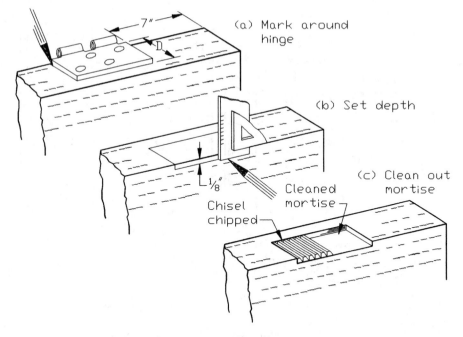

(a) Mark around hinge

(b) Set depth

(c) Clean out mortise

Cleaned mortise

Chisel chipped

Cleaned mortise

Figure 4–11   Installing mortise hinge on door.

c. Set the hinge in deeper or shim the lower hinge if the head is too low or too tight.
d. Bevel the front edge of the door if more clearance is needed and the back is not bonding.

Setting the lock.   Like hanging a door, setting a lock is an exacting task that allows for *no* error. Only an experienced person should attempt to install a lock. There are many varieties, from the old mortise locks to the modern cylinder types. There are simple locks and complex ones. Some are passage locks and others have locking capabilities. Each manufacturer usually includes a template in the lockset box. This tool is invaluable in aligning the points where holes must be drilled. Some companies prepare lockset tools that include drill bits and hole saws along with a chisel to make all holes and to chisel out areas for plates. Figure 4–12 shows the steps used to install a simple passage lock.

Most locks are installed 38 in. up from the floor. Once the lockset is in place in the door and works without binding, the striking plate must be installed in the jamb. This task requires careful positioning and marking. Then a mortise must be made to set the striking plate flush with the jamb. After this, the center hole must be drilled or chiseled out. The most difficult part of the operation to set the plate to the proper position front to back:

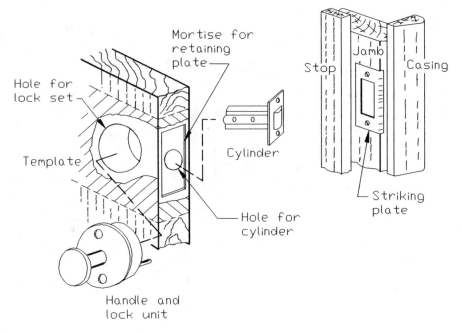

Figure 4-12   Installing the lockset.

1. If too far back, the door will not close.
2. If too far forward, the door will rattle.
3. There will be about $\frac{1}{16}$ in. of clearance between the stops and the door when the plate is properly installed.
4. The hole must be deep enough to allow for full-depth plunger travel.

Finishing the new door.   The painter is called to the job early to identify the type of finish needed for the new door and frame. Whether the door is painted, or stained and varnished, the color must match the old door. The painter must purchase the materials and later, after the door is installed, perform the work.

For a painting system, the holes are first filled and sanded. Then a prime coat and two top coats are applied. Modern latex systems provide excellent coverage and are readily available in hundreds of colors.

When the door is to be stained and varnished, transparent stains are usually preferred to the heavy-bodied types. The former permits the grain to show through. After staining, sanding smooths the wood. Then several thin coats of varnish or other finish are applied. Varnish is not available in a wide variety of types. Spar varnish is seldom used today; polyurethane varnishes are used more widely. They are easier to apply, simpler to control, and dry more quickly. As a rule they are also waterproof or at least water and moisture resistant. Each coat is applied no more than 1.5 mils thick, and sanded lightly when dry. Three top coats usually improve the quality of the job, but most often only two top coats are applied.

Concluding comments.   The tasks we have described in this project are very difficult to perform even for the experienced carpenter. Each requires extensive knowledge of joinery, use of a wide variety of power and hand tools, and a host of other "tricks of the trade." Due to the high cost of the materials, the owner who elects to have someone perform the work should shop around to find a person with many years of experience performing this work.

We have described the entire process in ample detail to identify the full scope of the project. With this detail the owner can ask the correct questions and know when a contractor can or cannot do a high-quality job.

Contractors who expect to perform this type of work can also make use of the information and help the owner by explaining why the project is costly.

PROJECT 5. REHANG BIFOLD CLOSET DOORS

Subcategories include: replacing the door guides; refitting the doors; relocating the adjustable guides for proper door action; refastening the hinges; and reinstalling door pulls.

Preliminary Discussion with the Owner

Problems facing the owner.   There are not very many parts to a bifold closet door unit. They consist of the two doors that are hinged with solid pin hinges, pulls or knobs, a track for the guides on the doors to fit into, a roller guide on the leading edge of each door, a clamp and pin guide to hold the rear door in place under the track, a floor assembly with a pin in the bottom of the rear door, and a piece of metal that acts to guide the lower edges of the front or leading door. The problems that owners have with these units are:

1. Knobs strip and fall off.
2. Rollers freeze and break.
3. Rear clamp and pin assemblies work loose and cause the door to fall out or bind.
4. The bottom pin works loose and splits the door.
5. The floor bracket works loose or changes position and the door swings improperly.
6. The track becomes loose because carpenters failed to use all the screws required.

7. When the doors are closed, they do not stay closed.

8. When two units are in the same opening, they do not align when closed.

For each problem there is a cure that can restore the unit to proper operation. Sometimes, owners can do the work since very few tools are needed. Sometimes the problem is more serious and the services of a carpenter are needed.

Alternative solutions to the problem.   Where parts are broken or missing, they can be obtained and replaced even if they have to be special ordered. This is usually a cheaper solution than replacing the unit(s). Doors that are out of alignment can be reset to work properly by adjusting the clamps and shifting the doors. This is done first; as a last resort the door can be trimmed. A split stile or worn screw hole can be filled with glue, plugged, and allowed to dry. Afterward, the parts can be reinstalled, although sometimes the door may need to be replaced.

Statement of work and the planning effort.   Regardless of the number of bifold doors needing work, the statement of work is the same: *Restore the bifold door unit to perfect operating condition.* If there was damage to parts or wood, we would specify that *replacement parts and repairs should be considered before opting for replacement of the entire unit.* Further, we would state that *the head gap, side gaps, and space between door edges must be uniform.* This means that all doors are at the same height when referenced to the trim in front of the track. The space between doors when they are closed should be about $\frac{1}{8}$ in. to no more than $\frac{1}{4}$ in. throughout the vertical plane. The gap between the frame and the rear edge of the doors may not be exactly the same floor to head, but the gap should be distributed about equally on both doors in a double bifold door installation. Finally, we should state that *all doors must clear the carpet or floor by $\frac{1}{2}$ in.* Fortunately, there is a lifting screw that we can use to meet this requirement.

The planning effort for the contractor is usually very simple. To keep costs as low as possible, he or she would try to accomplish the job in a single trip to the owner's house. Accounting would probably be done after the work was done rather than before. Any replacement parts would be purchased as required on the day of repair.

Contract.   A carpenter called to restore bifold doors will probably charge a flat rate for labor and bill for the parts needed. The flat rate could be for an hour, a half a day, or a day, depending on the person. This may not sound very appealing to the owner, especially when the carpenter charges $30 per hour or more. However, small jobs of this type are not sought after by most carpenters, since their costs are great and are seldom recovered from the fees collected. The carpenter would probably discuss pricing over the phone and bring a contract/bill to the job when he or she arrives to perform the work.

The alternative to this description is when the owner plans to have all door units restored at the same time. In this case the carpenter or contractor would proceed in a more formal way. The result could be a fixed-price contract.

Material Assessment

Direct Materials	Use/Purpose
Bifold hardware	To replace damaged, broken, or lost hardware
Pulls or knobs	To replace lost pulls or knobs

Indirect Materials	Use/Purpose
Glue and plugs	To repair damaged stiles
Lubricant	To lubricate frozen parts

Support Materials	Use/Purpose
Carpentry tools	For construction
Sawhorses	As a workbench to make repairs on doors

Outside Contractor Support	Use/Purpose
None	

Activities Planning Chart

Activity	Time Line (Days)
	1 2 3 4 5 6 7
1. Contract preparation and scheduling	| _×_ | ___ | ___ | ___ | ___ | ___ | ___ |
2. Making repairs	| _×_ | ___ | ___ | ___ | ___ | ___ | ___ |

Reconstruction

Contract preparation and scheduling.   Due to the nature of the job and its size, very little office management and administration will be done. A simple invoice listing replacement parts and a flat fee for labor can be completed by the contractor on the job site after the bifold doors have been restored to proper operation. Replacement parts can be bought at several places locally and should only require the carpenter to travel a short way.

This job would be scheduled as a "fill-in." Larger jobs would take precedence. This means that the owner would have to be willing to make arrangements with only a few hours' notification.

Making repairs. As we described earlier, repairs of split stiles or separated doors requires gluing and clamping. Sometimes screws are also used to reinforce the split area. If we can use screws, we can proceed to reinstall the hardware even though the glue has not dried.

To fit the doors properly in the frame, we use the adjustments available on every bifold door. The pin in the bottom of the door has a hex nut fit over a shaft with screw/bolt-like threads. We use a wrench and raise and lower the door with it. The top slide assembly rides back and forth in the track. When we loosen the locking screw, the bar can slide from the end of the track to the middle. The hole in the bar houses the pin that is inserted in the top of the door. By sliding the bar one way or the other we adjust the relative position of the door to frame and bifold door to bifold door in the case of a double unit. Once the door is in place, we tighten the screw.

We make the alignment of the doors by using these two mechanisms. In the case of a pair of bifold doors, as is customarily used in closets, the four adjustment mechanisms are used to position the doors in the opening.

When we have a knob that does not stay on, we usually replace it with a new one of like kind because the knob will generally have stripped threads.

Concluding comments. Generally, the homeowner can restore bifold doors to operate acceptably. The quality or precision of the job may not match that of an experienced carpenter, but the doors will operate. But when the doors are split and the owner does not want the cost of full replacement with associated painting, a carpenter needs to do the work. A good-quality restoration is one that includes properly fitted and operating doors.

PROJECT 6. RESTORE OPERATION TO A POCKET DOOR

Subcategories include: removing the door; reestablishing the head track; adjusting the track for proper door travel; replacing damaged trim and casing; and catastrophic replacement activities.

Preliminary Discussion with the Owner

Problems facing the owner. Pocket doors are still designed into new homes, but not often. They were used frequently in homes built before and after the turn of the twentieth century. They are extremely convenient because they take no wall space. No allowance is made for door swing since there is none.

For the door to operate, there must be a track. Refer to Figure 4–13. In some

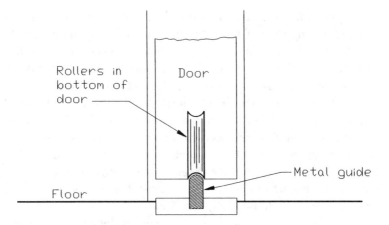

Figure 4–13   Track and pocket door (end view).

installations the track is in the floor and the wheels are inserted in the bottom of the door or attached to the bottom of the door. In other installations the track is mounted to the head jamb of the frame and wheels are fastened to the top face of the door (very similar to sliding closet doors). As a rule, the doors do not travel completely back into the pocket in the wall, but travel only to a point just before the door knob strikes the jamb.

With this description, we can now identify problems the owner might have. These include:

1. Frozen or broken wheels that restrict travel.
2. Damaged track that causes the door to stick.
3. Bent wheel brackets that cause the door to scratch along the jamb and ruin the finish and door.
4. Improperly aligned wheels or track that cause the door to be aligned against the jamb improperly when open or closed.
5. Damaged locking assembly of knobs that makes it hard or impossible to open or close the door.
6. Damaged door stiles or rails.
7. Damaged finish from causes cited above.

The owner with carpentry skills can often restore the door unit to its original condition for operation and appearance. Replacement parts can be ordered with the help of a hardware store person. The finish can be stripped and reapplied, and the door can be realigned in its track. However, when the owner has no skills or knowledge of carpentry and finishing, a contractor needs to do the work.

Alternative solutions to the problem.   The most radical alternatives include removing and replacing the entire assembly, including the door, with one that matches the old unit. Another is to replace the damaged tracks, preserving all other materials. The third is to rehabilitate the old hardware and make it serviceable.

If we, as contractors, had to find a replacement unit, it might take some time to locate a matching kind. In addition to finding the door unit, the labor required to remove and replace the old unit would be expensive. The owner needs to be apprised of this. Finding replacement hardware would be simpler to do, and the cost of removing and replacing it would be cheaper. In terms of the seven problems listed above, it would be best to replace the hardware if conditions 1, 2, 3 (unless the brackets can be straightened), or 5 exist. It would be best to rehabilitate the door or hardware if conditions 3, 4, 6, or 7 exist.

In this project we will restore a pocket door that has most of the problems listed, except that the door lock unit is serviceable although it does not latch into the striking plate.

Statement of work and the planning effort.   When the door jumped the track and the owner could not put it back on track, we were called to the job. Evidence showed the problems stated above; thus we *contracted to make repairs and restore the door to its original operating condition and appearance.* Specifically, we agreed to *replace damaged hardware, realign the track and door travel, align the striking plate, and refinish the door.*

For our planning effort, we made notes about the door, its hardware, and the problems we had to solve. The carpenter assigned to the work would perform all the repairs and alignments and would repair the door. The painter would refinish the door and frame disturbed during the repair. Our office personnel would prepare the contract and secure a bid/contract from the painter.

Contract.   If we are able to obtain replacement parts locally, we can prepare the contract/bid without delay. Given this circumstance we can prepare a fixed-price contract. The body of the contract could contain the following information.

For the fixed price specified below, we agree to restore the pocket door to its original conditions of operation and appearance. We will take every precaution to avoid damage to adjacent walls and floors and will remove all construction materials upon completion of the work.

The owner must have someone present while the work is being performed.

Full payment is due on completion of the job.

Total price: $xxx.xx

Material Assessment

Direct Materials	**Use/Purpose**
Finishing materials	To paint or stain and add polyurethane varnish
Hardware	For rollers and track
Trim and nails	For door casing, as required

Indirect Materials	**Use/Purpose**
Sandpaper	Belts and sheets to sand the door
Glue and filler	To make repairs to the door
Vinyl sheeting	To protect floors while painting
Paint stripper	To remove finish from door

Support Materials	**Use/Purpose**
Carpentry tools	For construction
Painter tools	To paint door and trim
Stepladder	To ease work
Pair of sawhorses	To act as workbench to work on door

Outside Contractor Support	**Use/Purpose**
Painter	To perform the painting work

Activities Planning Chart

Activity	Time Line (Days)						
	1	2	3	4	5	6	7
1. Contract preparation	×						
2. Materials and Scheduling	×						
3. Restoring the pocket door		×	×				
4. Refinishing the door and casing			×	×			

Reconstruction

Contract preparation. Due to the nature of the job, the office personnel will have very limited involvement. Their main effort is to coordinate with the painter to obtain a bid/contract and have the estimator locate replacement hardware for the parts we determined should be replaced. The office personnel would use the worksheet to finalize the contact price by adding the painter's bid, an allowance for overhead, and an allowance for profit.

Materials and scheduling. As the activity chart shows, we will schedule the job and obtain materials on the same day if the contract can be signed. If, on the other hand, there is a delay before signing, we would postpone everything until then. Nevertheless, once the contract is signed, we would have the owner agree to have the required 3 days to perform the work. This means that the owner would have someone at home while the workers are present.

Restoring the pocket door.   The carpenters would proceed in the following way:

1. Remove the door from the track and pocket.
2. Reestablish the track's original position and secure it there.
3. Remove the wheels on the door. Either restore them to serviceable condition or replace them with new ones.
4. Make repairs to the door where separations, scars, and splits were identified. This includes stripping the finish off the door.
5. Clean and lubricate the lockset.
6. Remove damaged door casings.
7. Reinstall the door wheels and place the door on the track.
8. Make adjustments to ensure accurate, free door travel.
9. Reseat the striking plate and put filler in if required.
10. Install new door casings, as required.

Refinishing the door and casing.   The painter has the job of refinishing the door and new casing if any is installed. He or she would probably want to paint or stain and varnish the door before it was reinstalled. However, this would interrupt the carpenter and delay his or her efforts, thus adding cost to the job. So unless removal was quite simple, the painter would probably ask the carpenter to remove the door from the track prior to leaving the job.

To finish the door appropriately, it needs to be out of the opening. This is understandable since there is always a small amount of door that is inaccessible to the painter.

With the door out of the frame, the painter also has more freedom to refinish the casing and door frame. When the painter is through, the carpenter or contractor will reinstall the door and verify its operation.

Concluding comments.   To some homeowners, solving the problem of a defective pocket door would be impossible and a contractor would be the only person capable of making restoration. To those handy with tools and mechanics, the job would be one to attempt. Then if things went bad, the contractor would take over.

Pocket doors may be single, where there is only one door, or in pairs, where there is a pocket on each side for a door. In the two-door configuration, the doors must close in the center exactly right. All of the work is classified as finish, which means that there is no room for mistakes. Quality must be incorporated in every aspect of the restoration.

CHAPTER SUMMARY

In this chapter we have examined just about every problem that can happen to every type of interior door. We have looked at the causes that lead up to calling for experienced help, and discussed those jobs that can be done by homeowners with some skill with tools.

We have provided ample data to educate the owner and contractor on the problems and solutions involved in restoring interior doors. The data in the statement of work and contract sections should be followed to ensure high-quality work. The activities chart indicates the amount of time for work to be done but does not indicate delays between events that might occur. Rather, it assumes the best possible time frame. Finally, the owner and contractor can reach mutual accord on work required in this area of the home if they use the guidance provided here.

5

INTERIOR TRIM

OBJECTIVES

To replace the baseboards and shoe molding
To reinstall windowsills, aprons, trim, and stops
To replace ceiling moldings
To replace chair rail moldings

OPENING COMMENTS

Conditions or circumstances that necessitate corrective action. Under normal wear and tear, interior trim lasts a long time with little care except for occasional painting. However, there are numerous conditions that can cause decay and damage to the trim in a house, some of the most common being water damage, which is especially true around windows, and physical damage, especially around door openings and other types of passageways. Damage to baseboards and shoe molding comes from furniture and the vacuum cleaner. More serious causes of trim failure are fire, flooding, earthquakes, hurricanes, and tornadoes.

Owners tend to delay any trim restoration for a long time except for painting. But when the point of action is reached, owners must either perform the work themselves or contract to have the work done.

Contractor's responsibility.   As contractors, we need to make the owner aware of the technical aspects of installing trim so that they can develop an appreciation of the costs associated with restoration. We would also make it clear that trim is customarily expensive, due to the machining necessary in its manufacture.

Let's discuss the technical aspects of trim installation. A carpenter must know how to fit every piece of trim, whether it is a simple shoe molding to the complex crown molding used with a ceiling. Sawing techniques such as mitering and coping are widely used. Most of the work is done with hand tools. Compound miters are employed in many cases. In a high-quality job the only need for putty or spackling is to fill the nail-head holes after the nails have been countersunk. Every other joint between two pieces of trim must be fit without filler. Therefore, a practiced finish carpenter must do the work. Most rough carpenters or novice carpenters lack the skill to handle this level of accuracy.

Having discussed these needs with the owner, we move on to the types of trim used throughout the house that require restoration (or replacement). Windows have different requirements depending on the type installed. All wood windows have windowsills, aprons under the sills, casing above the sill and across the head, and stops where casings are installed.

Over the years, a wide variety of shapes and dimensions of baseboard have been installed. Some are built up from several pieces, including molding, and some are very plain. Others are shaped to shed dust and dirt readily. Their height ranges from $3\frac{1}{4}$ to almost 12 in. The very wide baseboard is frequently used in homes with high ceilings. Along with the baseboard is the shoe molding. Where floors are made of strip oak or fir, pegged, or covered with vinyl, shoe molding is installed over the flooring and against the baseboard to cover the gap between the flooring and the baseboard. Shoe is not used in carpeted rooms.

Ceiling wall corners employ a wide variety of moldings. Some are the simple quarter-round, which is functional but lacking in aesthetics. The simple 2-in. cove is better, since it gives the ceiling a nicer appearance. As we get into the more ornate uses of trim, we find bed and crown moldings, which are used alone or in combination. Much additional skill and work is needed to build these ornate moldings. The mitering and coping requirements escalate along with the complexity of the design.

Chair molding may also be a single piece of trim about $3\frac{1}{2}$ in. wide or may be 6 in. wide, made from stock lumber and moldings. Either kind requires of mitering and coping skill to make perfect joints. Lateral runs should have as few splices as possible. This means that both ends of the trim must be cut to fit exactly with no margin for error. Since this molding is so visible, experienced finish carpenters are required to achieve the necessary level of quality.

Homeowner's expectations.   If the owner has moderately damaged trim, he or she would expect a simple solution to any problems and a very inexpensive to modest cost. He or she might attempt to restore the trim to its original condition using fillers and paint, for example. He or she might even attempt to replace a broken or rotted piece of trim to avoid the expense of a carpenter. But when the damage is severe and complex joinery is required, the realistic owner knows that materials and labor will be expensive.

Scope of projects.   There are four projects in this chapter dealing with trim: (1) replacing baseboards and shoe molding: (2) restoring window trim, (3) restoring ceiling moldings, and (4) restoring chair railing. Although we are treating these as separate jobs to give clarity and definition to their requirements and complexity, we can readily expect that these jobs would be a subset of a larger overall restoration. But with this detailed information, the owner can appreciate the work required of carpenters and painters. The contractor using this information would be able to support decisions used and costs incurred. Certainly, the person drawing up the contract would be able to define clearly the work and quality expected.

PROJECT 1. REPLACE BASEBOARDS AND SHOE MOLDING

Subcategories include: removing baseboards and shoe molding; fitting and cutting baseboards; fitting and cutting shoe molding; treatment of built-up baseboards; descriptions of standard and custom baseboards; and reinstallation of baseboards and shoe molding.

Preliminary Discussion with the Owner

Problems facing the owner.   The owner who has split, rotted, or otherwise damaged baseboard and shoe molding must have it restored. The old materials will be removed and replaced and then finished.

Aside from the work needed to make the restoration, each room in which work is required work must be upset. Furniture and wall hangings must be removed, or moved to the center of the room and covered. The room will remain in this condition for more than a day. In fact, if the painter is delayed after the carpenter has finished, it could remain so for quite a while. If the job is a small one, just one room, getting a carpenter to do the work could also be difficult and might require spending more for labor than desired.

Alternative solutions to the problem.   One option is for the owner or a friend to perform the work. This certainly is an alternative. The disruption to the room or rooms is not diminished, but labor costs are reduced significantly, thus reducing the total cost. In addition, delays waiting for the carpenter and painter are eliminated.

With regard to matching the original architecture piece for piece, we could substitute types or species of wood, but not their design or dimensions. In this regard we have no alternative. Due to the fact that lumber and trim have different (mostly smaller) dimensions today, we have to decide which is better: to have baseboard materials and shoe custom made in the shop, or to remove and replace an entire room's baseboard and shoe with materials of today's dimensions. In this situation a trade-off may be required, and the following questions must be answered:

1. Will the wall above the baseboard require touch-up or refinishing because the modern baseboard is smaller?
2. Will the thinner baseboard and shoe molding cause a line to show on the floor where the old joints used to be?
3. Will wall-to-wall carpet fit as well against the thinner baseboard?

These questions are posed to create a series of thoughts that explore the ramifications of making substitutes.

Statement of work and the planning effort.   In our project we will restore the baseboard and shoe in a den with a wood floor. Thus our initial statement of work is to *remove and restore the baseboard and shoe in the room.* The baseboard could be one of several kinds and we would be obligated to *make the new materials match the old materials in size and shape.* To add quality to the work, we need to state that *all joints and miters must fit well without the use of fillers.* When the carpenters are done, the painter must *finish the replacement materials in the same manner and colors as the original.* Finally, we need to guarantee our work with a statement: *We guarantee no damage to walls or floors as a result of our activities. Any problems with walls or floors identified before the job begins must be noted to avoid misunderstandings.*

The planning effort for this job involves contract development, materials acquisition, and subcontractor support. Our office personnel will locate materials or have them made, solicit a bid from the painter, and prepare all paperwork. We will need to plan a time for the work to be done.

Contract.   In almost all cases where the contractor replaces or otherwise restores trim, a fixed-price contract can be used. The materials can be estimated accurately, even allowing 10 percent for waste. Labor costs can also be calculated accurately, even making allowances for furniture that might have to be moved. The contract statement should include references to every statement of work.

Material Assessment

Direct Materials	Use/Purpose
Baseboard	For replacement
Shoe molding	For replacement
Nails	Finish nails

Indirect Materials	Use/Purpose
None	

Support Materials	Use/Purpose
Miter box	To cut miters
Carpentry tools	For construction
Painting tools	To finish baseboard and shoe

Outside Contractor Support	Use/Purpose
Painter	To finish baseboards and shoe

Activities Planning Chart

Activity	Time Line (Days)
	1 2 3 4 5 6 7
1. Contract preparation and scheduling	I _x_ I ___ I ___ I ___ I ___ I ___ I ___ I
2. Removing and replacing the baseboard and shoe	I ___ I _x_ I _x_ I ___ I ___ I ___ I ___ I
3. Finishing the baseboard and shoe	I ___ I ___ I ___ I _x_ I _x_ I ___ I ___ I

Reconstruction

Contract preparation and scheduling. The inspection and data-gathering effort of the contractor or estimator established the number of linear feet of baseboard and shoe molding required to replace the trim damaged. He or she also determined what old materials can be reclaimed for reuse. In this effort a decision is made based on the probability that the old materials could be removed with little or no damage.

Upon return to the office, the estimator would prepare a job worksheet to arrive at the costs. He or she would also contact a painter and provide specifications for finishing the wood. With the subcontractor's bid/contract in hand and added to the building contractor's costs, the office person types a final bid/contract for the contractor, who will present it to the owner.

   After agreement as to the price and details of the work effort, the contractor and owner must agree to the time for work to take place. Once again, the contractor will customarily ask for someone to be home while workers are present. From the activities list, we see that the carpenters will take 2 days and the painter will also take 2 days. These times are rough estimates. For example, a carpenter can remove the baseboard and shoe molding from all four walls in a room in less than 2 hours—"if": if the old materials are not to be reused, if the walls are to be repainted, if the new flooring is not already in place, if the baseboard is above the flooring, and so on. But longer is required to save the old materials, prevent damage to walls or flooring, and leave the carpeting undisturbed—to mention just a few reasons for added time.

   Time is also extended when the baseboard is built up or includes trim. Multiple pieces are fit individually, and this takes time. We shall obtain more understanding about this later. The painter will need a day to prime or stain the wood and another day to apply the top coats.

   Removing and replacing the baseboard and shoe.   Next, we describe the removal and reinstallation of various types of baseboard to understand the carpenter's role and the skill needed. Three types are described: dustless, 1×6, and built-up and built-up with molding and are shown as section drawings in Figures 5–1, 5–2, and 5–3.

   Dustless.   Figure 5–1 shows the section of a dustless baseboard with shoe molding. The major character of this baseboard is its steep curved surface, which lends itself to allowing dust to roll off rather than collect. The baseboard is less than $\frac{3}{4}$ in. thick with a cavity back and $3\frac{1}{2}$ in. high. Although there are specifications for

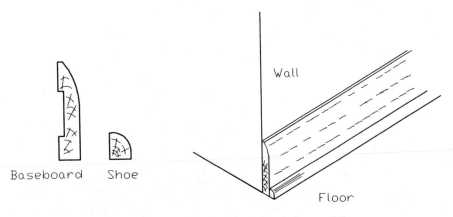

Baseboard   Shoe

Wall

Floor

Figure 5–1   Dustless baseboard and shoe molding.

this type, there are variations between runs at the mill or between mills. Matching these can be a problem. To make outside corner joints a simple miter is used. But to make inside corner pieces fit well, the carpenter uses a coping technique.

Most carpenters rarely set the molding directly on the floor. Rather, they keep it off the floor about the thickness of a wooden ruler blade or 6d finish nail. Using this technique, they are able to ensure a straight line along the top and remove any variations in splices and at corners by making the top exact.

The shoe molding is added over the baseboard in rooms requiring it. Shoe is removed with a flat bar or wood chisel and hammer. The same tools are used to remove the baseboard; however, the carpenter uses a piece of thin plywood to prevent marking up the wall. Most of the time it is not possible to tell which piece has the coped mitered edge. So the work begins away from a corner to reduce the chance for splits and breakage.

One-by-Six. Figure 5–2 shows a 1×6 baseboard with a cavity back. Normally, the top leading edge is rounded off, but only slightly. This baseboard can range from a full $\frac{25}{32}$ in. to less than $\frac{3}{4}$ in. thick and from $5\frac{5}{8}$ in. to $5\frac{7}{16}$ in. high. Matching can be a problem. Carpenters use the miter cut on outside corners and butt joints on the inside corners even though there is a small roundness that creates a gap. If the rounded edge is prominent, the carpenter will use a coped miter joint instead. The same technique is used to remove the old baseboard.

Built-up Baseboard. A typical built-up baseboard is shown in Figure 5–3. At the root of any baseboard is a 1×6, 1×8, or 1×10. The 1×6 and 1×8 are generally used where the wall height is 8 ft. The 1×8 or 1×10 would be used for a wall height greater than 8 ft. On top of the 1-in.-wide piece the carpenter places some form of molding: a bed molding, quarter-round, or several different types in combination. Sometimes the molding overhangs the baseboard; other times it is recessed or held back. The shoe may also be custom made to a height greater than $\frac{3}{4}$ in.

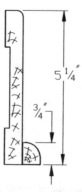

Figure 5–2 1×6 baseboard with rounded edge and shoe.

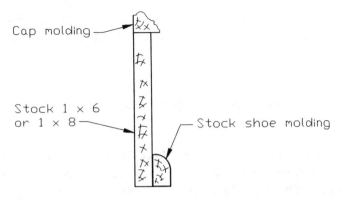

Figure 5–3   Built-up baseboard and shoe.

Removing the built-up baseboard and shoe is more time consuming since each piece must be taken off separately. Since the moldings are added last, they are the first to be removed. Once again a chisel is used to pry the material loose and to give the hammer claws a point to grab. We must prevent marks not only on the wall but also on the top edge of the baseboard. Once we know the angle at which the nails were driven through the molding, we can use the best alternative to free all moldings. When removing the baseboard, we must use exceptional care. The boards have probably been in place a long time and are very prone to splitting.

Installing or reinstalling built-up baseboard is much more time intensive because of the variety of pieces to install and the need for many more coped miter joints. In terms of time, carpenters can spend twice as long completing a room with built-up baseboard compared with other types.

Finishing the baseboard and shoe.   The painter must apply the finishing materials in a very restricted area. He or she must control the applications to avoid the wall surface and floor. Because of the need to "cut in" the paint or stain and varnish, considerable time is required. Experienced painters seldom tape the wall or floor; they are very adapt at controlling a paintbrush. Those who are less skilled will apply masking tape prior to applying the finish materials.

In new construction, the painter would finish the baseboard before the carpets and tile floors are installed. But in restoration, the floors are usually in place. This means that the baseboard may not get finished all the way to the floor, but it will be finished far enough to preclude seeing raw wood.

Concluding comments.   Restoring baseboards and shoe moldings is classified as finish work. The carpenter and painter must perform high-quality work, joints must fit accurately without fillers, and no damage to walls or floors must result from their work.

Although it is distinctly possible that this work can be required as a separate job, in all likelihood it will be a part of a larger job resulting from rot or physical damage.

PROJECT 2. REINSTALL WINDOWSILLS, APRONS, CASINGS, TRIM, AND STOPS

Subcategories include: fitting windowsills to window and opening; shaping aprons; fitting trim between window and wall; adding casings; adding stops; and techniques of mitering and self-returns on aprons.

Preliminary Discussion with the Owner

Problems facing the owner.   Because of the variety of windows installed in homes, the methods used by carpenters to finish them range widely. Sometimes the methods used cause problems for the owner. Other causes are weather and wear and tear or abuse. Let's cite a few problems that owners can face. Windowsills take a lot of abuse, especially where the sill is used to sit on or as a resting place for objects. They also tend to rot due to continued exposure to rain and snow and to other wetness. The trim around the window is abused near the top by installation and removal of curtain and drapery hangers. Window stops become damaged over time as windows are opened and closed.

A real problem facing the owner is finding a carpenter who would be willing to do restoration work on just one window. An owner with some skills can perform the work, however. Where there are a host of trim problems, as there are in all the projects in this chapter, the owner can probably locate a carpenter to do the work.

Another problem an owner faces is obtaining matching trim for a window. In very old homes and some modern expensive homes, custom designs were used. If these have to be replaced, the contractor may require the services of a cabinetmaker to make replicas of the casings, apron, and sill.

Alternative solutions to the problem.   If the architecture must be maintained when, for example, only one or two windows are affected, the choices are to do the work yourself or have it done. The owner can also have the woodwork made elsewhere and perform the finish work himself or herself.

If all the windows in the house require work, the owner may opt for a change in architectural style and have the contractor prepare a bid accordingly. In this situation, the changes need to be subtle versus drastic, since the change may significantly alter the character of the house.

Statement of work and the planning effort.   For our project we shall plan to restore a double- or single-hung wood window. The following information can then be applied to any number of windows and a wide variety of styles. The basic statement of work begins: *Restore the trim on the damaged window to its original condition.* Specifically, *eliminate the cause for damage if weather or insect damaged, remove and replace all damaged materials, and finish trim to match the other woodwork.* Finally: *The quality of the work is guaranteed and there must be no damage to adjacent walls.*

The planning effort requires an original on-site call and examination. Then we would either plan to buy the replacement trim or have special trim prepared for the job. The office would prepare the bid/contract. We would need to schedule a carpenter and painter if the owner did not want to finish the new wood.

Contract.   We would offer a fixed-price contract. There are no hidden problems that we can encounter, regardless of the type of window. We have the skills and knowledge to solve all problems. The body of the contract should contain the statements of work along with the price and any conditions, such as payment on completion or within 30 days.

Material Assessment

Direct Materials	Use/Purpose
Casing	Used on three sides and for apron
Windowsill	Standard type or flat board
Stops	As required for wood widows
Finish nails	4d, 6d, and 8d
Wood putty	To fill nail holes

Indirect Materials	Use/Purpose
Sandpaper	For smoothing joints

Support Materials	Use/Purpose
Carpentry tools	For construction
Miter box	To make miters
Painting tools	To finish the trim

Outside Contractor Support	Use/Purpose
Painter	As required

Activities Planning Chart

Activity	Time Line (Days)						
	1	2	3	4	5	6	7
1. Contract preparation	I _×_ I	___ I	___ I	___ I	___ I	___ I	___ I
2. Materials and scheduling	I _×_ I	___ I	___ I	___ I	___ I	___ I	___ I
3. Restoring the window trim	I ___ I	_×_ I	___ I	___ I	___ I	___ I	___ I
4. Painting the trim	I ___ I	_×_ I	_×_ I	___ I	___ I	___ I	___ I

Reconstruction

Contract preparation.   The actual time for the carpenter to restore a window will be less than a day. He or she will remove the trim from the window in less than 30 minutes (even when trying to preserve all pieces) and replace the trim in an hour or less. This means that up to five or six windows can be restored in a day. Our contract must consider time for picking up new materials, travel time, and actual work time. The costs will be charged at the daily rate if less than a day's work is used. The office personnel will prepare the contract on this basis.

Materials and scheduling.   If standard sill, casing, and stop materials are to be replaced, these will be readily available. If the trim is on an old window, stock materials such as 1 × 6, corner blocks, and specially shaped pieces will need to be produced by the carpenter or cabinetmaker.

Scheduling the job is the responsibility of the office, and the assignment will be given to a skilled carpenter. Someone from the owner's family will need to be home unless the house is empty.

Restoring the window trim.   In Figure 5–4 we see several detail drawings. One is for the wood or vinyl-clad wood window. Another is for the aluminum or other metal window. Each requires a different approach to trimming. Although both are shown, only trimming the wood window is described, since it requires all the pieces and skills to complete the work.

There is always a set sequence used to trim the window.

1. Fit and install the windowsill.
2. Fit and install the apron below the sill.
3. Fit and tack-nail the vertical casing pieces.
4. Fit and install the head casing.
5. Finish installing the vertical casing pieces.
6. Fit and tack-nail the head stop.
7. Fit and nail the vertical stops.
8. Finish installing the head stop.
9. Set all nails and fill with wood putty.

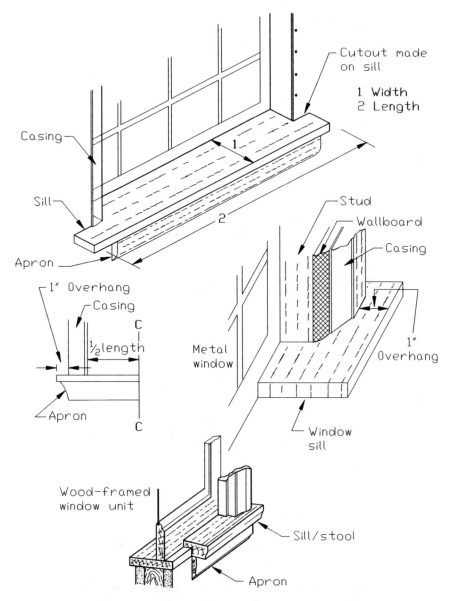

Figure 5–4   Window trim: details for (a) wood (b) aluminum.

From this list it appears quite simple to perform these skills. Let's examine each more closely to identify the decisons the carpenter must make so that each piece will fit. Notice from the details shown in Figure 5–4 that the sill is specially designed to fit over the window frame sill, which is sloped. To fit accurately three points must accurately fit. Point A requires that the shoulder on the cutout in the sill fit against the wall. Point B requires that the sill permit the lower sash to pass the

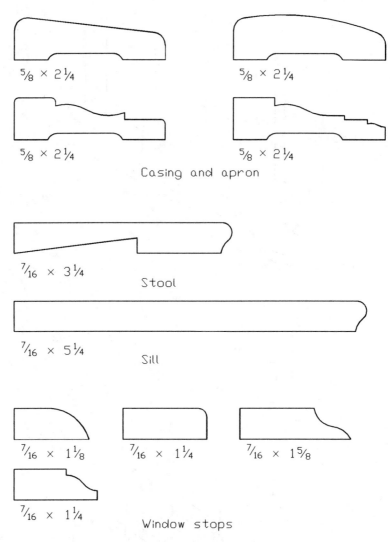

$\frac{5}{8} \times 2\frac{1}{4}$ $\frac{5}{8} \times 2\frac{1}{4}$

$\frac{5}{8} \times 2\frac{1}{4}$ $\frac{5}{8} \times 2\frac{1}{4}$

Casing and apron

$\frac{7}{16} \times 3\frac{1}{4}$

Stool

$\frac{7}{16} \times 5\frac{1}{4}$

Sill

$\frac{7}{16} \times 1\frac{1}{8}$ $\frac{7}{16} \times 1\frac{1}{4}$ $\frac{7}{16} \times 1\frac{5}{8}$

$\frac{7}{16} \times 1\frac{1}{4}$

Window stops

Figure 5–4   (*continued*)

edge of the sill while allowing about $\frac{1}{16}$ in. of clearance. Point C requires that the ears on each end of the sill extend beyond the casing about $\frac{3}{4}$ in. after the end is shaped to match the front edge of the sill. Subpar or poor-quality work results if any one or all three of the points are not performed. When the sill is hand-cut as indicated above, the carpenter nails it in place with three to four 8d finish nails.

Casing is used to make the apron. The shape of the casing must be cut into the ends of the apron with a coping saw. The length of the apron is equal to the total width from the outer edge of vertical casings. This translates to $\frac{3}{4}$ in. in from each end of the sill. When cut and shaped, this piece is nailed snugly under the sill. Quality work ensures perfect center alignment and minimal pressure on the sill (no lifting of the sill).

Three pieces of casing close in the sides and head. Whereas casings on a door jamb are held back from the edge about $\frac{3}{16}$ to $\frac{1}{4}$ in., casings on windows are usually held even with the window frame. So each piece of trim must fit accurately in the joint, on the sill, and flush with the window frame. The reason why tack nailing is used is to permit easy removal to hand-plane joints for a perfect fit.

The head stop is easily fit and tacked in place, since it simply requires square cuts on each end (no miters). The side pieces are measured, mitered, and coped to fit against the head. Since there is a left and a right piece, a pair must be made. The final position is against the lower sash and the sash must be raised and lowered to ensure smooth, even travel and no excess clearances that will later result in rattle.

In finishing an aluminum window, drywallers usually return the drywall to the window on the sides and head. The carpenter follows and installs a simple sill made from 1 × 6 pine or fir with or without ears. Below this he or she cuts, shapes, and nails in place an apron to finish the job.

Concluding comments.   The job of restoring the window trim is all finish work that requires skill and knowledge. The joints must fit exactly right, the design must be correct, and the materials used must be proper for the job.

The time required for the carpenter to remove and restore the trim is relatively short, so the costs can be equalized only if several windows require restoration at a single time. Otherwise, flat rates are applied.

PROJECT 3. REPLACE CEILING MOLDINGS

Subcategories include: treatment of simple cove molding; installation of bed and crown molding; rebuilding built-up ceiling moldings; moldings down from the ceiling; and mitering techniques.

Preliminary Discussion with the Owner

Problems facing the owner.   Problems with baseboards and window trim pale by comparison with problems involving ceiling moldings. Of all the interior trim that carpenters install, ceiling trim is the most difficult. Almost every type of molding used to finish off the joint between ceiling and the wall requires a compound miter joint and coping. Add to these skills the fact that the carpenter must think upside down. This means that every piece of molding installed in the miter box is placed upside down—the longest point in the cut molding is against the wall and the shortest cut is against the ceiling. This is very technical work and usually requires a carpenter skilled in finish work.

In addition to the problems of cutting and fitting, the ceiling molding may also be constructed of multiple moldings and other lumber. This built-up molding, as it is called, is actually constructed as a series of individual steps. Figure 5–5 provides a cross section of just one of numerous possibilities.

The problem of restoring damaged ceiling molding involves considerable expense. Moldings of the type used can cost more than $1 per foot. The entire job is labor intensive since each piece must be individually cut, fit, installed, and finished.

Besides the molding at the ceiling–wall joint, many homes have other molding installed about 8 to 12 in. below the ceiling. This molding is smaller and provides the appearance of interior cornices made from built-up plaster which were so

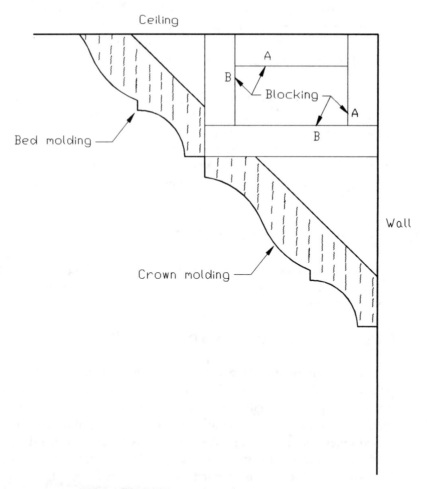

Figure 5–5   Cross section of built-up ceiling trim.

common in the late nineteenth and early twentieth centuries. This lower piece of molding has a coped miter in the corners and a common miter for splices between corners. (For this book, we equate this molding to chair rail molding made from a single piece.)

Even though the work of installation is performed at the ceiling, one carpenter can do the work. Two carpenters make the work go faster and is simpler, but only one carpenter is needed.

Alternative solutions to the problem.   If we, as contractors, must maintain architectural integrity, the choices are very limited. We can locate replacement moldings if the work was done very recently. If it was done earlier, we would need to have special tools made for the shaper to match the exact contours of the old molding. To accomplish this we would subcontract the work to a cabinet shop or commercial molding manufacturer.

The other alternative is to approximate the shape of the molding with modern materials that closely resemble the original. If we adopted this solution, the owner would need to agree to have all the old molding removed from the walls and all new molding installed. Because of the changes in shape and size, there may be added work to restore the walls. Or to avoid added work and costs on the walls and ceiling, we would need to add more design and materials to cover all earlier marks.

Whether an owner or carpenter performs the work depends on the skill of, and cost to, the owner. Only an experienced woodworker/carpenter owner should attempt this work. No mistakes, no fillers, and no excuses will ever cover poor workmanship. The owner who insists on performing the work but lacks experience can practice with small pieces of molding until the skill of using the coping saw and making miters fit is acquired.

Statement of work and the planning effort.   For our project we shall assume that the house has built-up ceiling molding that incorporates a base and two different moldings: crown and cove. In addition, a small molding is installed about 8 in. down from the ceiling. Given this, we establish our first statement of work: *New ceiling molding approximating the original destroyed materials will be installed at the ceiling.* To clarify this, we add: *Specifically, the trim consists of a built-up molding at the ceiling and a smaller molding about 8 in. down.* We need to include a statement pertaining to the quality, such as: *All joints will fit without use of fillers. All nails will be countersunk and filled with wood putty.* We also need to identify the need to avoid damage to wall and ceiling: *no damage to either ceiling or wall shall result from removing and replacing the trim.* Our final statement specifies the need for finishing: *The replaced materials must be finished to match the other trim in the rooms.*

The planning effort begins with determining how many rooms or how many feet of trim must be restored. These data provide two elements for planning: it provides us with a materials requirement and suggests how many labor hours we would need to complete the job of restoring the wood. Coupled to this is the time required for painting.

Since we are approximating the original materials to avoid tooling and special orders, we can plan to pick up materials from local suppliers. The painter can also mix the paint, so no special requirements exist.

The work involves accessibility, which means that furniture, paintings, and the like must be removed from the room to make way for the workers. This should be done on the day the carpenter arrives. Someone needs to be home if the house is occupied.

The office personnel can readily prepare the job worksheet and obtain an estimate from a painter. They will prepare the contracts and plan for the work after contract signing.

Contract.   From what we know about our generic project and the materials and skills needed, we can offer the owner a fixed-price contract. All materials are known and we can easily determine the labor and overhead costs from office information or our database. In this job the body should state:

For the fixed price stated below, we agree to restore the ceiling trim in the hallway and the following rooms: great room, dining room, master bedroom, and library. We agree to approximate the original design and position of the trim at the ceiling. We further guarantee no damage to walls and ceiling. The painting will match the door and window trim color. The carpentry and painting will include no fillers for joints, fillers in nail holes, and no runs or off colors in painting.

Total price $XXX.XX

This price is good for 60 days. Payment will be as follows; 25 percent on contract signing and the balance within 20 days after job completion.

Material Assessment

Direct Materials	Use/Purpose
Crown molding	Part of built-up trim
Cove molding	Part of built-up trim
Lumber	Base for moldings
10d or 12d common nails	To fasten lumber in place
6d and 8d finish nails	To fasten moldings in place
Wall molding	Picture frame molding
Latex painting system	Interior system

Indirect Materials	Use/Purpose
Vinyl sheet goods	To protect carpets and furnishings

Support Materials	**Use/Purpose**
Carpentry tools	For construction
Painting tools	To paint trim
Stepladders	To access the ceiling
Sawhorses and bench planks	To provide a work surface
Miter box	To cut miters in moldings

Outside Contractor Support	**Use/Purpose**
Painter	To complete the finishing work

Activities Planning Chart

Activity	Time Line (Days)						
	1	2	3	4	5	6	7
1. Contract preparation	❘ _×_ ❘	___ ❘	___ ❘	___ ❘	___ ❘	___ ❘	___ ❘
2. Materials and scheduling	❘ _×_ ❘	___ ❘	___ ❘	___ ❘	___ ❘	___ ❘	___ ❘
3. Removing the damaged trim	❘ ___ ❘	_×_ ❘	_×_ ❘	___ ❘	___ ❘	___ ❘	___ ❘
4. Installing the new trim	❘ ___ ❘	_×_ ❘	_×_ ❘	_×_ ❘	___ ❘	___ ❘	___ ❘
5. Painting the new trim	❘ ___ ❘	___ ❘	___ ❘	_×_ ❘	_×_ ❘	___ ❘	___ ❘

Reconstruction

Contract preparation; materials and scheduling.   Preparing the contract for this job is straightforward. The estimator provides the painter with specifications for the job and obtains a bid/estimate. He or she includes the price on the worksheet with the estimates from suppliers of lumber and moldings. As we see from the activities list, the job requires a total of 3 days for removal and replacement for the hall and three rooms. The labor rates are applied against the time, and overhead and allowance for profit is added.

The office person loads the job/estimate into the database for companies that have computers, or into an accounting ledger. He or she types the contract, and the contractor presents it to the owner.

After contract signing, a carpenter is assigned to the job and the dates are coordinated with the owner. The materials will be picked up on the day that work begins, to avoid extra costs.

Removing the damaged trim.   Removing the old trim from the ceiling and wall may seem simple but great damage can result if done incorrectly. To minimize damage to walls and ceilings and avoid costly repairs that would be borne by the contractor, we must do the following:

1. Score the ceiling and wall with a utility knife. At the point where the molding touches the ceiling, we score the paint. At the point where the moldings touch the wall, we score the paint or wallpaper.

2. Beginning in the approximate middle of the wall (corner to corner), we carefully drive a chisel or flat bar behind the molding and then slip a piece of $\frac{1}{4}$-in. plywood between the ceiling or wall and the chisel. With an even pressure, we pry the molding loose.

3. Once an opening is made, we use the claw of the hammer to free more of the molding. We proceed toward the corner using the chisel and hammer until the molding is free.

4. Some nails come free with the molding and others pull through. Those that come with the molding must be removed immediately after the molding is free from the wall to avoid a hazard. Those that pull through must either be driven home or be removed with a hammer and a block of wood.

When the job is done there are no visible marks from tools on the wall or ceiling. There will be lines where the scoring was done. These will be covered with the new trim.

Installing the new trim.   For our project we are reconstructing the built-up molding and adding new picture frame molding. Let's describe first the actions the carpenter makes to form the built-up molding. Figure 5–5 shows some of the details.

The lumber is ripped, smoothed, and cut to fit against the wall. It may be either a solid piece or built-up as shown. In our situation we use four pieces. We nail the filler piece to the wall and ceiling as a foundation. These need to be made from spruce or soft pine (not yellow pine) to simplify construction.

Next we nail pieces A and B together and then onto the wall. If the wall's length is over 16 ft, we are forced to make a splice. The splice on the bottom piece, A, must be offset from the one on B to strengthen the base.

In almost every case the carpenters would build the base entirely around the room before installing molding. We would use butt joints in the corners since they will be covered anyway.

Next we install the moldings. The crown goes from wall to base, and the bed cove goes from ceiling to base. If we let $\frac{1}{4}$ to $\frac{3}{8}$ in. of the base show, we use the combination square and pencil to make a pencil line for a reference on both the face and underside of the base. These two lines will make the job of nailing molding

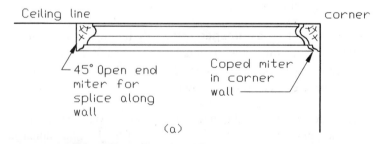

Figure 5–6 Details of ceiling molding installation.

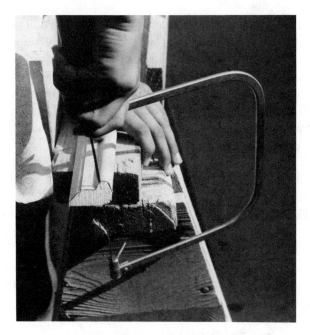

Figure 5–6   (*continued*)

much easier. As we spoke of earlier, the cuts of the molding for corners begin with a miter at 45 degrees. Then the coping saw is used to make the pieces fit. (Figure 5–6) The first piece is installed with butt joints at the corners.

To ensure that we install the picture frame molding straight, we mark the wall and snap a chalk line from corner to corner. The line is at the top edge of the molding rather than the bottom. In this way its residue is hidden from view. The same mitering and coping techniques are used while installing the molding.

The carpenter would clean up the job after completing the work.

Painting the new trim.   The latex system of painting was covered in Chapter 1. Recall that we use a prime base coat followed by two top coats, each 1.5 mils thick. An experienced painter would probably not need to use masking tape to keep paint off the ceiling or wall. He or she will "cut in" the paint with a brush and a steady hand. Because of the quick-drying properties of latex paints, the prime and first top coat can be applied in less than a day. The final coat would be applied the following day, as our activity chart shows. Cleanup of the job is also the painter's responsibility.

Concluding comments.   Whether the ceiling–wall joint molding or trim is simple quarter-round or of complex built-up type as depicted in this chapter, the only acceptable method for making an inside corner is with a miter box cut first and finished with a coping saw. Mitered 45-degree cuts will never work, although they should. Wood, even moldings, shrink and the walls are almost never exactly a 90-degree corner or straight. The joint always fails unless coped. So if the owner cannot make such joints, an experienced finish carpenter must do the work.

Replacing trim at the ceiling is high-quality finish work and requires expensive moldings. Waste must be held to a minimum. The experienced carpenter can avoid waste. The experienced owner can also save waste as well as labor by performing the job himself or herself.

If the owner elects to paint the trim and is not very experienced at cutting in, he or she must rely on masking tape to establish safe lines so as to avoid painting the ceiling and wall.

Finally, this is work that must not be rushed. Each joint must be cut and fit accurately before proceeding to the next. Lines must be absolutely straight. Quality cannot be sacrificed for price or time.

As we stated in the introduction to this chapter and in this project, the homeowner with chair molding problems can adapt the solutions used to restore picture frame molding, to restoring chair rails.

1. Chalk lines are snapped from corner to corner.
2. Corners are fit with miter and coping.
3. The first piece is installed with a butt joint into the corner.
4. Built-up chair rails are a 1 × 4 or 5 with molding above and below. The procedures above apply, as do the procedures for installing built-up baseboards.

CHAPTER SUMMARY

In this chapter we examined the trim used inside a house. We discussed problems with baseboards and shoe, window trim, and ceiling trim. In every case the projects required a great deal of skill in tools and techniques. Hand tools needed to be used with great care to avoid damage to walls and ceilings. Power tools were limited to ripping actions and some very limited cross-cut operations. Miters and coping were all made with hand tools.

We examined simple baseboard, window trim, and ceiling trim as well as complex adaptations that used multiple pieces to achieve the desired appearance. In every case quality of joint and straightness were key points. Painting also required good-quality materials and workmanship.

The owner should always determine the better of two alternatives for restoring the trim: Do it yourself and reduce cash outlay, or have the work done and earn more in wages than the cost of restoration.

6

ELECTRICAL SERVICE
AND LIGHTING

OBJECTIVES

To remove and replace a defective receptacle

To remove and replace a defective switch

To replace a circuit breaker

To replace a ceiling or wall lighting fixture

To remove and replace an over-the-stove vent and light unit

To remove and replace a fluorescent fixture ballast

To remove and replace a door bell, chime, or switch

To understand the principles of electricity

To understand the problems with defective wiring or components

OPENING COMMENTS

Conditions or circumstances that necessitate corrective action. The modern home runs on electricity. Almost all of the time we can take for granted that our needs will be met with lights and appliances, heating and air-conditioning systems, and other products. But there are times when the electric service is interrupted and we experience discomfort. The problems range widely and the solutions to them require immediate action by qualified personnel.

Some of the conditions and circumstances that cause owners to take corrective actions include overloaded circuits, decayed insulation around old wire, cut conductors, damaged circuit boxes, burned outlets and switches, corroded terminals and wire, inoperative electrical fixtures, and open transformers.

Contractor's responsibility.   As contractors we need to solve the electrical problems for the owner. We have to apply our knowledge and skill to the problem and restore the service efficiently. We have to provide some explanation to the owner regarding the problem that he or she faces. This should not, as a rule, include technical details about electron flow or the principles of series and resistor circuits, distribution plans, and the like. However, we should show the owner what the source of the problem is and try to provide some explanation of why the damage occurred, unless, of course, it was natural damage from a storm or storm related.

Beyond this, it is our responsibility to be fair when estimating and submitting final bills for work done. This means that we need to cover direct and indirect costs, overhead costs, and allowance for profits.

Finally, we must convince the owner that the charges are reasonable. He or she must have confidence that the work will be performed according to accepted code guidelines that ensure a safe electrical circuit, and efficiently by using as little time as possible.

Homeowner's expectations.   The owner expects a high-quality job, performed quickly, at the most reasonable cost possible. Beyond this he or she does not want too many details about electricity, but rather, would just as soon have the work done without much discussion.

Scope of projects.   In this chapter we solve problems with wall outlets and switches, ceiling and wall fixtures, range hoods, circuit breaker boxes, and bell or chime systems.

PROJECT 1. RESTORE ELECTRICAL SERVICE
TO RECEPTACLES, SWITCHES, AND FIXTURES

Subcategories include: rewiring; circuit breaker replacement; changing duplex receptacles; changing switches; removing and reinstalling light fixtures; principles of wiring; principles of electricity; safety precautions to take; voltage checking and testing techniques; principles of two-way, three-way, and four-way switches; wiring schemes and schematics; wire stripping tools and techniques; wire nut uses; and removal and replacement techniques.

Preliminary Discussion with the Owner

Problems facing the owner.   The problem the owner has with electrical service may be simple or extensive. It may have caused a short circuit, which we explain later, or a fire before burning open. The problems range from the simple worn-out wall switch to a damaged wire in the wall leading to the circuit breaker on one end to an outlet or fixture at the other end. Physical damage from storms that tear homes apart creates severe damage to electrical service throughout the house or a part of it.

In each of these conditions the owner is faced, more or less, with the threat of personal physical pain if he or she attempts to make repairs. There is more threat when he or she has no knowledge of the potential threat or proper actions to take to eliminate the threat. There is less threat when there is knowledge sufficient to remove the power at the circuit breaker or fuse box.

The owner is also faced with the choice of making repairs or having the work done. Many change a switch or wall receptacle, remove and replace a ceiling or wall fixture, replace blown fuses, and replace light bulbs themselves. Most do not restore circuits because of the difficulty of the work and the lack of knowledge of electricity. In most cases this reasoning is sound. However, our society is very conscious of the need to protect its citizens. So building codes are in place in every community that lets licensed electricians perform restoration to circuits, and the building inspector inspects the completed work to ensure that it meets building codes. This concern carries over to the homeowner's insurance. Although the damage may be paid for by the insurance company, they will probably not pay the second time if the restoration was not performed and inspected by the proper personnel.

Alternative solutions to the problem.   In this area the replacement parts have been improved over time. There are more safety features included, better installation techniques devised, and the life expectancies are increased. All of these are transparent to the owner when replacing the damaged component or wiring.

Switches and receptacles are swapped one for one using like kind. Circuit breakers are replaced based on the voltage and amperage ratings. Here we have no choice but to replace a 20-ampere breaker with another 20-ampere breaker, for example. We cannot increase the amperage without proper diagnosis of the service first. The size of the wire in the wall is a major determining factor on the line's amperage rating. If we must replace the wire from the distribution box to all outlets, we can install heavier wire and thus select a circuit breaker of higher amperage.

We can also change the fixtures for different styles, shapes, and number of bulbs. We can also convert a fluorescent fixture to incandescent, or vice versa. Or we can reverse the logic and install energy-saving fixtures, thus reducing the electric bill.

Finally, we can select from several alternatives to determine costs. The insurance company's adjuster will provide a cost, or the owner can work with a contractor directly to arrive at the restoration costs, or solicit bids from several contractors. The fact that a homeowner's policy has a deductible clause may be a major or minor consideration in selecting the best way to pay for the work.

Statement of work and the planning effort.   In this project we assume that the home has sustained severe damage to a section of a fairly old home that was wired with Romex wire. The distribution box has circuit breakers. For our project the lightning burned two circuits that had several outlets, switches, and fixtures. Our first statement of work must be *to restore the two damaged circuits*. To this very general statement we add that *all new 12–2 with ground wire will be used in the restoration*. We are also expected to *replace all damaged switch boxes, receptacles and boxes, and junction boxes as required*. These are in the walls and ceiling. We must also *replace the damaged receptacles and switches, light fixtures, and damaged parts in the distribution box. The owner will have the opportunity to select some of the replacement parts, including fixtures within a specified price ceiling, and colors of switches, receptacles, and their covers*. We must also address safety: *All materials and work will conform to electrical codes and be inspected upon completion*.

The planning effort for the electrician includes determining the extent of the damage. He or she or the estimator from the company, or the appraiser from the insurance company, must provide a definition of the work. From this we can plan for the replacement materials as well as labor costs. We must take immediate emergency measures to prevent use of the service. We must plan for how many electricians are required, to obtain replacement parts and components, to obtain a local building permit, to prepare a bid/contract, to schedule workers, and to work directly with the insurance company.

Contract.   Because we have to lay new wire into covered walls, we must add labor costs that would not be added if the walls were not covered. Even so, we can figure the base costs and add the additional costs to arrive at a fixed-price contract. If there were any really unusual conditions that prevented us from making this assessment, we would have to revert to a time-and-materials contract.

The body of the contract should contain the statements of work or a very close approximation of them. We need to include the scope of the work, the quality of the job, licenses required, inspections required, and method of payment. In the area of payment the body could stipulate that the insurance company will pay the contractor. In this arrangement, both the owner and contractor sign the check and the contractor retains the check for services performed.

Material Assessment

Direct Materials	Use/Purpose
Wire	12-gauge solid wire
Boxes	Receptacle, junction, and switch
Wire nuts	For mechanical connections
Circuit breakers	To replace damaged ones
Distribution panel	To replace damaged one
Common bus	To replace damaged one
Receptacles and switches	To replace damaged ones
Covers	To replace old and damaged ones
Fixtures	To replace destroyed ones

Indirect Materials	Use/Purpose
Mason line	To thread cable through wall

Support Materials	Use/Purpose
Voltmeter	To measure voltage and current
Electrician's tools	For construction
Stepladder	To reach ceiling fixtures

Outside Contractor Support	Use/Purpose
None	

Activities Planning Chart

Activity	Time Line (Days)						
	1	2	3	4	5	6	7
1. Contract preparation	_×_						
2. Materials and scheduling	_×_						
3. Replacing damaged wiring		_×_	_×_				
4. Replacing damaged distribution box and circuit breakers		_×_	_×_				
5. Replacing receptacles, switches, and fixtures			_×_	_×_			

Reconstruction

Contract preparation.   The office manager, estimator, and contractor will work together to arrive at the final bid/contract price for the restoration. We also figure in the cost of the building permit. Several sources of prices will be used to assimilate the labor costs, and several calls to the local electrical supply house will establish the cost of materials. Since, in the statement of work, we agreed to set a limit on the amount the owner can spend for fixtures and covers, we include this in the contract. If he or she exceeds the limit, we will add the amount to the price to arrive at the total cost.

Materials and scheduling.   After contract signing, the owner must go to the electrical supply house and pick out the fixtures. We will pick them up along with the bill of materials called in ahead of time.

We see from the activity chart that our best estimate is to schedule 3 days on site for the restoration work. If we send two electricians, the time will be less, possibly even less than one-half. This does not alter the price but does reduce the time spent on the owner's premises.

Principles of electricity and current flow.   Electrical circuits operate on the principle of alternating current (ac) and parallel circuit design. Figure 6–1 shows both principles in a schematic drawing. The source of energy (the circle with the sine wave inside) represents the voltage applied to the circuit. Notice that one half of the wave is above the reference line and one half is below. This is the shape of the ac waveform. Two wires are connected to the power source and are connected to the receptacle's top and bottom. As long as nothing is plugged into the receptacle, the voltage is just a potential force. However, when we plug in a lamp and turn it on, current flows through the light bulb and because of its resistance (filament), heat is generated and the bulb glows. The heat is a transformation of amperage to heat energy. The current flows back and forth through the filament 60 times per second (call 1 hertz). This happens for two reasons: (1) the circuit is

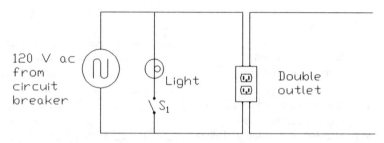

Figure 6–1   Circuit designed for ac uses.

complete (there is a complete path for the current to flow), and (2) there is resistance in the filament. If the resistance were absent, we would have a short circuit and maximum current would flow for a very short time until the circuit breaker's thermal couple heated and opened the circuit.

A switch acts like a circuit breaker of sorts, but it does not have a circuit breaker thermal couple. In fact, it should have no resistance since its use is to close a circuit or open it. On closing the circuit it actually shorts across the conductors, causing a very small arc of current, even though we never see it. The switch that draws current because it has resistance is the dimmer type. It is designed to reduce the voltage to the lamp, causing the light bulb to draw less current and glow less. Switches are made for various purposes. Some are single-throw, toggle types; others are three-way and four-way. These are illustrated in Figure 6–2. Notice the wiring technique. We will use some of these illustrations again.

Rewiring the service and installing the new distribution panel.   Part of our generic project is to replace damaged circuits, including the distribution panel. In Figure 6–3 we show a circuit breaker panel and box of the work to be done. We would remove and replace the distribution box as follows:

1. Turn off the main power to the house.
2. Remove the cover that contains the door.
3. Examine the box and remove the circuit breakers.
4. Remove the wires from the common terminal or bar.
5. Remove the normally hot leads.
6. Remove the panel.

Then we would install the new panel in reverse order, but we need to replace the damaged circuits with new cable, boxes, outlets, and switches. Our job in replacing the cabling follows a relatively straightforward routine. We can start at the distribution box and lay cable through the attic to the wall that contains the receptacles and switches. In our problem there are three wall outlets and one ceiling light connected to the circuit. Normally, we would run the cable down between the studs and after connecting to the first outlet, we would run parallel to the floor to the other outlets. Then we would run cable to the switch and ceiling light. But since we have covered walls, we need to parallel the connections in the attic by using a junction box. So we drop a new line from the junction box down through the wall each place there is a wall outlet and wall switch.

The job sounds very simple, but we know that it is much more difficult. The area of work is very confining and we must drill holes through double plates first. Then we use a pilot line to access the box in the wall or area where the new box will be installed. We finally fish the new cable down the wall and out the wall.

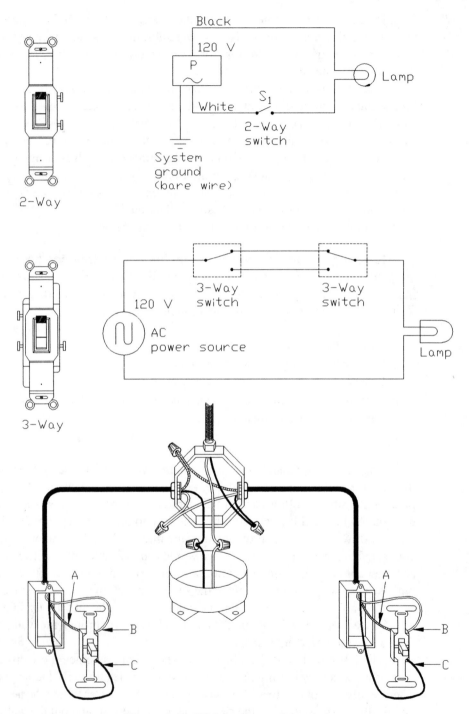

Figure 6–2   Wiring schemes for switches.

Circuit
breaker

Returns

Figure 6–3   Circuit breaker panel with cover removed.

Here's what we have done. We have the cables in place from distribution box or panel to the junction box. We have individual cables to each outlet and switch and from switch to ceiling light. Next we continue with installing the new boxes and other hardware.

Installing the new fixtures, receptacles, and switches.   The receptacles require two wires to operate. Each modern receptacle has screws that can be used to secure the wire wrapped around the post of the screw, or the lead from the wire can be inserted into the small hole in the back of the receptacle. The green screw is used for the bare ground lead in the cable. Then we secure the receptacle to the box with screws provided and install the cover.

Installing the switch is similar but slightly different. We can secure the wires with the screws or insert them into the switch. But where we placed a black lead on one side of the receptacle and the white on the other to maintain a parallel connection, we must use a series connection on switches. However, the cable has only a black-and-white lead. So we connect one wire to each side and assume that both are white. Up in the attic we connect the fixture to the switch and power source as

Figure 6–3 shows. Once the wiring is done at the wall, we can install the switch in the box and place the cover over it.

The new fixture needs to be wired to the new cabling. We usually feed the cable from the source and switch to the box in the ceiling and let some hang through. Then working from downstairs, we make the connections by using wire nuts. The lamp must hang from the box. To do this all fixture makers provide several pieces of hardware to connect to the box in the ceiling and then the fixture is held in place with bolts inserted through the lamp into the hardware.

Most of these tasks are used to replace the fluorescent light fixture, too. However, these lights contain a ballast, which is a form of transformer that permits ionization of the neon gas in the tube at a low voltage. The ballast has several wires, and these must be connected as directed by the documentation provided by the vendor. If the ballast were the item replaced rather then a new fixture being installed, we would carefully mark the wires and their connections prior to removing the old, damaged one. This way we are assured of making the right connections when installing the new ballast.

Finally, we feed the cable into the distribution box and secure the ground lead, return lead, and power lead. The power lead is connected to the circuit breaker and the circuit breaker is installed.

Performing the power checks.   Now that the circuit is installed, we can reapply power and make the necessary voltage checks. For this we use a multimeter. Sometimes a specially made tool with a lamp on one end and two wires on the other end is used for testing. Each circuit in the house is checked. The multimeter is set to "AC" and the reading must be between 105 and 120 volts. The lamp must light when the pigtails are inserted into each receptacle. The wall switch must turn the ceiling lamp on and off. The local building inspector makes the final test and okays the job.

Concluding comments.   What every owner faces when there is an electrical problem is how to prevent damage from fires and personal safety. He or she must avoid direct contact with unprotected wires and with damaged or shorted wires or fixtures. Only qualified personnel should make repairs and replace damaged materials. Besides the chance for electrocution, the work of installing replacement cable is physically stressful. Quarters are cramped, full of insulation, and frequently are very warm. The effort usually requires crawling around on hands and knees or belly to drill holes and pass cable.

Since the work is labor intensive, we can expect to pay a modest-to-expensive price for the restoration. We are also reminded that to replace a single receptacle can be expensive when the electrician demands a flat rate for a service call.

PROJECT 2. REMOVE AND REPLACE AN OVER-THE-STOVE VENT UNIT

Subcategories include: purpose and design of the unit; fan assembly; light assembly; hood construction; removal techniques; safety; and installation and wiring techniques.

Preliminary Discussion with the Owner

Problems facing the owner.   Almost every over-the-stove hood has electrical wiring. The fan operates by electricity and the light operates by electricity. Some of the units contain charcoal that absorbs smoke and cooking vapors. Others have access to a vent pipe much like a stove pipe.

Several things usually happen to the unit that require the owner's attention. These include burned bulbs, damaged or frozen fan motors, excessive buildup of grease, yellowed or scorched hood paint, frozen vent flap blocking the vent to the pipe, a fire in the unit, contaminated charcoal, and damaged wiring leading to the unit.

Sometimes the defective unit can be restored, and sometimes it must be replaced. Except for replacing the bulb and generally cleaning the hood, the unit must be taken down and worked on or replaced. The owner is faced with removing the unit and at the same time disconnecting the wiring. For safety reasons the power must be removed. Yet due to the weight and position of the unit, removing it may require two people. Disconnecting the wires from the cable is done before the screws holding the unit in place are loosened.

Once the unit is down and can be examined, the owner or electrician makes a critical examination to determine which solution is most desirable. If a new unit is purchased, and the owner installs the unit, there will be variations in screw placement and maybe ports for wiring and connecting to the stove pipe. Nothing is very simple.

Alternative solutions to the problem.   There are two basic alternatives to the problem of restoring or replacing the range hood: replace the unit, or restore the unit. In replacing the unit there are two alternatives: replace the old one with a like-kind one, or replace the old unit with a different type or model. What would help us decide to replace the old unit? Since the fan and light fixture are the two parts most likely to fail, we would need to buy new ones. This may prove to be quite difficult. Although some electric supply stores carry subassemblies, they may not fit as purchased and might require modification before installation. The metal flap may be rusted open or shut. We can break it free, sand the posts free of rust, and lubricate it during reinstallation.

But if we decide that the old unit is beyond restoration and purchase a new one, we must be concerned with matching the old one for size, color, model, and type. On the other hand, we can replace a vent type with a charcoal type much more easily then the other way around. We can close off the stove pipe much more simply than we cut a hole in the ceiling and install a pipe.

Statement of work and the planning effort.   In our generic project we will replace the old, damaged range hood. Therefore, the statement of work is: *Replace the damaged old range hood with a new one of like kind.* We should also state that *care must be used to prevent damage to stove and cabinets.* We should also *examine the wiring for damage and replace if damaged.*

This is a small job that requires less than a day to complete. Therefore, we, as contractors, should attempt to arrive at a contract price at the time we arrive at the owner's house. To do this we would ask the owner for the length of the old hood and its type and color. A simple call to the electric supply store provides us with the price and we assign a flat-rate charge for labor and overhead.

Contract.   Unless we find unusual conditions, we inspect the job site, we can offer a fixed-price contract. We should bring one with us or if necessary complete the pricing on site before work begins. The body of the contract should already state the conditions and specifications. The body could be very simple:

For the fixed price shown below, we agree to remove and replace the range hood with one that is the same kind, color, and has the same features. We will inspect the wiring to verify its good quality, but should it require replacing, the materials and time will be added to the price.

Total price to be paid upon completion of the job is $XXX.XX.

Material Assessment

Direct Materials	Use/Purpose
Range hood	Replacement hood
Wire nuts	To secure wire ends

Indirect Materials	Use/Purpose
Electric tape	Optional in place of wire nuts

Support Materials	Use/Purpose
Electrician's toolkit	For construction
Stepladder	As required

Outside Contractor Support   **Use/Purpose**

None

Activities Planning Chart

Activity	Time Line (Days)
	1 2 3 4 5 6 7
1. Contract preparation and materials acquisition	I _×_ I ___ I ___ I ___ I ___ I ___ I ___ I
2. Removing and replacing the hood	I ___ I _×_ I ___ I ___ I ___ I ___ I ___ I

Reconstruction

Contract preparation and material acquisition. This is a small job but still requires the accumulation of prices and estimates of time to remove and replace the hood. There is a need to apply overhead and profit percentages even though they are very small. Our office personnel prepares the contract in standard form as suggested above. The estimator will prescribe the exact model, so its price can be included. He or she also applies a table of time for the job and may elect to use the $\frac{1}{2}$ day flat rate versus the hourly rate. If the inspection revealed damaged wire, the contract would stipulate the need to install new wire from the fan/hood unit to the junction box or all the way back to the distribution panel. The contractor contacts the owner and presents the bid/contract price for agreement and the go-ahead.

The materials would be ordered and the electrician would pick them up on the day the work is done, or the materials would be delivered to the office with other materials for another job. The only major purchase is the hood. Wire, wire nuts, screws, and the like are usually normal items available at the contractor's shop or in the electrician's truck.

Removing and replacing the hood. Figure 6–4 illustrates the hood and the relative position with respect to the bottom of the wall unit. Let's list the tasks as we would perform them, and then, if needed, we can discuss one or two points.

1. Remove the power from the unit and check for "0" volts with a voltmeter. Then move the stove out of the way. If electric, simply disconnect the power cord. If gas, shut off the gas at the line and disconnect the flexible hose.
2. Remove the screen and light bulb.

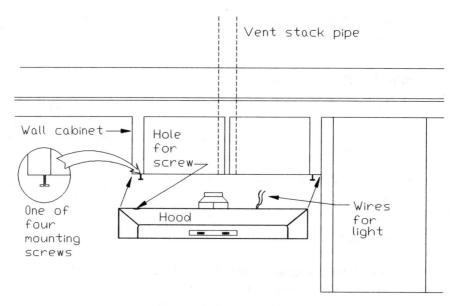

Figure 6–4 Range hood.

3. Remove the screw holding the cover plate and the plate, thus revealing the wiring.

4. Remove the wire nuts and separate the wires. If they were taped with electric tape, remove this.

5. Look up under the hood and locate the four screws that hold the hood up to the wall cabinet. Loosen all four screws about $\frac{1}{2}$ in.

6. Look inside the wall cabinet above the hood and ensure that the stove pipe is not screwed to the flange on the hood. If there is a screw or two, remove them. These should be $\frac{3}{4}$ in. sheet metal screws.

7. Slide the hood forward, away from the wall, and lower the hood. This may take some effort since the flange is usually connected to the hood.

These steps complete the removal actions. We must always practice safety. First, we ensured that the power was removed from the circuit at the circuit breaker box. Then we moved the stove, to remove the chance for strain and added stress. This also eliminated accidental damage to the stove should we have lost control and dropped the hood.

The actual removal of the hood unit can be difficult under the best of conditions because of the flange that connects to the stove pipe. Sometimes we have to remove all four screws holding the hood because the hood will not move forward enough.

Now to the task of installing the new hood.

1. Set the old hood on a work surface and remove the stove pipe flange. Be sure to mark the front with a marker. Also note the exact position. The new one must be placed at exactly the same place on the new hood.

2. Remove the new hood from the box and prepare it for the stove pipe flange. This requires knocking out or cutting out a hole for the flange.

3. Remove the cover plate to access the wiring inside the hood.

4. If a template is provided for positioning the hood under the wall cabinet, tack it up and mark the points where screws should be started.

5. Remove the template and start the four screws. If no template was provided, use the top of the hood as a reference and mark the holes based on the measurements taken.

6. Slide the hood into the hole in the cabinet and over the screw heads. Tighten the screws.

7. Connect the stove pipe to the flange on the hood.

8. Wire the hood to the source wiring by connecting black to black, white to white, and grounding the case. Install the bulb and check for proper operation of both the lamp and fan. If they work, replace the cover over the wiring.

9. Reinstall the stove and test for proper operation.

In this installation we need some strength to lift and position the unit into place. That is why we install the screws partially. The metal cutouts for the screws are teardrop-shaped to permit the head of the screw to pass through.

Regarding the stove pipe, we might have to prop it up to keep it from sliding down through the hole between the time we remove the old hood and when we install the new one. Since the pipe may extend all the way through the roof, we use caution when doing this. In cases where the pipe extends only into the attic, moving it up does not cause problems.

Concluding comments.   Removing and replacing the hood over the stove is a common job. It can be done by one person; however, a helper makes work easier. If the job is contracted, the owner can expect a fair price but must expect to pay a flat rate because the job takes less than half a day. The price also includes overhead costs, which include contract preparation, estimating costs, transportation costs, and others, as well as a small amount for profit.

If we, as owners, were to replace the unit ourselves, our first and most important concern would be safety. We would need absolute assurance that the power is removed from the circuit powering the hood fan and lamp. We could solicit the help of a family member with the dismantling and installing tasks to lessen chances for personal injury.

PROJECT 3. REPAIR ENTRY BELL OR CHIME SYSTEM

Subcategories include: principles of bell and chimes operation; wiring diagrams; transformer action; removal procedures; reinstallation procedures; and testing techniques.

Preliminary Discussion with the Owner

Problems facing the owner.   The most obvious problem with the door bell or chime is that it does not work. Repeating pushing on the button will not make it better. Since the bell is a circuit with several components as shown in Figure 6–5, we can trace the problem to several likely causes. The switch terminals may have corroded due to moisture accumulations, and may have opened. The transformer may have opened in the primary or secondary, or one of its terminals may have corroded and opened. The power wire leading to the transformer may have been disconnected by some force, or inadvertently. The small wire leading from the transformer to the pushbutton may have been cut or ruptured. The pushbutton itself may be inoperable. Finally, the bell or chime may have corroded or been damaged.

These are the physical things that can go wrong with the bell. Any one of the things mentioned will cause the problem. A series of troubleshooting steps must be followed to isolate the trouble and restore the circuit. The owner must have the knowledge and some skill to perform the troubleshooting. He or she must be able to recognize defective or corroded contacts, be able to test the transformer for shorts or opens, detect inoperative pushbutton switches with a meter, and trace wiring for breaks. This entails climbing around in the attic, removing and replacing the pushbutton switch, and checking the bell or chimes.

Alternative solutions to the problem.   There is always the alternative of calling an electrician to restore the bell to full operation. He or she has the know-how to fault-isolate the problem efficiently and accurately. Then he or she can make the repairs accordingly. Beyond this, the owner might be required to chose a

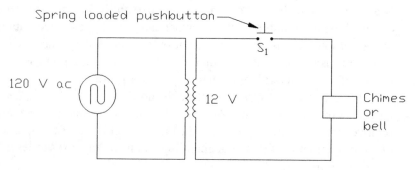

Figure 6–5   Bell or chime circuit.

different pushbutton switch because an exact match cannot be located. If the bell or chimes are defective, an exact match might not be available, and a substitution might need to be chosen. Beyond this, the electrician makes the decisions about replacement materials since none are seen.

Statement of work and the planning effort. For this project a single statement of work can suffice. It would state: *Restore the bell to operable condition.* But we can also add a small amount of detail to clarify the work to be done. This might be *to replace defective parts to the bell or its circuitry as required.* Added detail would become cumbersome.

For the planning effort we, as contractors, would make an inspection. After locating the cause, we would need to obtain cost figures for parts and labor and compile the contract. In this job the actual work would be done in a few minutes to several hours, depending on the problem and its location. We would probably plan to establish the contract price after the inspection, using cost figures from memory, but it is possible that we might require the owner to pick out a new chime or bell from a supplier we suggest.

Contract. We would assume all the costs for the job. Even if the owner were required to pick out a new chime or bell, the cost would be included in the contract price. Since we can describe the problem and the solution with the owner, it simplifies our contract wording somewhat. In this job we opt for a fixed-price contract. The body could be as simple as the following:

We agree to restore the bell system for the price stated in our discussions and indicated below. Costs for all materials selected by the owner and those provided by this contractor are included in the price.

The owner agrees to pay in full upon completion of the job.

Total cost for labor and materials: $XX.XX.

Material Assessment

Direct Materials	Use/Purpose
Pushbutton switch	To activate the bell or chime
Bell or chime	To create the sound when activated
Transformer	Step-down transformer required for the bell circuitry
Wire	12-gauge power and 18-gauge bell circuit
Wire nuts and tape	To make connections as required
Solder	Optional substitute for tape and wire nuts

Indirect Materials	Use/Purpose
Junction box	To splice power wire, if required

Support Materials	Use/Purpose
Electrician toolbox	For construction
Multimeter	To measure voltage, resistance, and current
Ladder	To reach chime or bell or get into attic

Outside Contractor Support	Use/Purpose
None	

Activities Planning Chart

Activity	Time Line (Days)
	1 2 3 4 5 6 7
1. Contract preparation and materials acquisition	⊢ _ × _ ⎮ ____ ⎮ ____ ⎮ ____ ⎮ ____ ⎮ ____ ⎮ ____ ⎮
2. Bell restoration	⎮ ____ ⎮ _ × _ ⎮ ____ ⎮ ____ ⎮ ____ ⎮ ____ ⎮ ____ ⎮

Reconstruction

Contract preparation and materials acquisition. As we stated above, there is nothing special about this job. Yet we must make the appropriate assessment, obtain the materials, and allocate the costs. For this our office personnel perform their jobs and enter the job into the database. However small, certain percentages of the contract price are allocated to indirect and direct overhead and to profit. Other costs are allocated to labor for the electrician and account in part for weekly wages earned.

Since the amounts of materials are small, many can be taken from stock. But if the chime or bell must be replaced, its cost must be obtained from the supplier.

Bell restoration. Let's take the project a step at a time and describe the work associated with removing and replacing different parts.

Pushbutton switch. Our check of the switch is done by disconnecting it from the two wires (called leads). Since a switch is a planned break in the circuit that has 12 volts, we can make a test which proves that switch was good or bad.

1. The switch is bad if by simply touching the bare ends of the leads together, we hear the bell ring.
2. The switch may be good if the bell does not ring when the ends of the leads are shorted.

3. The switch is good if when the multimeter is set to "OHMS" and its two leads are placed across the two terminals it reads "OPEN" (infinity) without pressing the button and "ZERO OHMS" when the button is depressed. Any other conditions indicate a bad switch.

4. If the switch is bad and the crossed wires do not result in the bell ringing, we have multiple problems.

5. If the switch is the only problem, replace it with a new one. This often requires soldering.

Transformer.   A transformer isolates one voltage level from another and changes the secondary voltages. Since there are two separate windings, the voltage and current from the primary couple to the secondary using electrical fields of current, without physical contact. The bell transformer reduces the primary voltage of 120 volts (V) ac to 12 V ac, which is sufficient to operate relays and cause vibration type devises to work.

A power surge can destroy the transformer. It can burn wires or melt insulation from wires, which results is in a short first, then an open. It does not matter if the primary or secondary are shorted or open or if there is a short between primary and secondary windings. The results are the same—the transformer is destroyed and must be replaced.

We can verify this with the voltmeter measuring the primary voltage at 120 V ac (actual voltage may range from 105 to 125 V ac). We can measure the secondary voltage at 12 VAC while attempting to activate the circuit, and if either are missing, the transformer could be bad.

But we need one more test to make sure of our decision. If the bell circuit or relay was shorted, the transformer would not have a load and a false reading would be obtained from the voltmeter.

Removing and replacing the transformer is not difficult. Most are in a box with connector posts clearly marked for primary and secondary. We would simply replace the wires from one to the other.

Bell and Relay Components.   Since both the bell and relay that operates the bell are mechanical/electrical devices, they can be damaged from excessive current, corrosion, and physical harm. If we have, through a process of elimination, arrived at examining the unit on the wall which houses the bell or chimes and relay that operates the bell, we must remove it from the wall or at least take the cover off. We can test the relay by listening for the click when someone pushes the button at the door. If it clicks and the bell does not ring, we look at the bell and its wires, if any. There may also be a very small circuit board with components that collectively make the bell operate. If these show signs of burning, we might be safe in assuming it's damaged and inoperable.

If the relay does not click, we can measure the voltage at its terminals to make sure that the voltage is present when the button is pressed. If it is absent, the problem is between the transformer and relay. If it is present but there is no reaction, the relay could be bad.

Depending on the bell or chime's original cost and years of service, we have arrived at the source of the problem. We then make the decision to have repairs made, buy a new unit, or select a combination of both decisions to restore the bell system.

Concluding comments.   If all parts of the bell system were located in a central place, finding the problem and isolating it would be simple. However, some parts are at the door or doors, some are in walls, some are in the attic, and some are in the house on a wall. We must know some things about circuits and how to measure voltage. We must cause transformer action to measure the secondary, and we might need to install new wiring and parts. Some homeowners can do all these things; others need the assistance of an electrician.

Due to the short duration of the job, homeowners must expect to pay either a half-day's wages plus materials or a flat-rate labor fee plus parts to have the job done. As contractors, we might be reluctant to perform the work due to the small expected potential for profit. Yet we can cover some fixed costs by performing the work. In some cases we could even forgo profit for the sake of goodwill. This assumes that the small job at a modest or minimal price can be the key factor to more extensive follow-on work or word-of-mouth advertising.

CHAPTER SUMMARY

In this chapter we have examined the types of problems that homeowners face when nature creates damage to electrical services. We have learned that electricity is very dangerous and can cause serious injury and death. Extreme care must be used when working on circuits. Proper tools such as meters and light probes must be used to verify the presence and absence of voltage and current.

Beyond safety considerations, we must know and understand how electric circuits operate and the methods that make components function. We must know about current loads to select proper-size amperage circuit breakers and the right-gauge wire to carry the current safely.

Next, we need to know what the electrical codes are and how to apply them. Electricians must know these and apply them. Inspectors must also determine that the codes are carried out properly when the work is done.

7

PLUMBING

OBJECTIVES

To remove and replace a damaged commode unit

To replace defective faucet assemblies in sinks and tubs

To replace damaged waste lines under sinks

To replace a hot-water heater

To clear lines of waste materials

To understand the principles of potable water systems

To replace the damaged or defective garbage disposal

To replace or repair an under-the-counter dishwasher

To restore an ice maker to full operation

OPENING COMMENTS

Conditions or circumstances that necessitate corrective action. There are two basic circumstances or conditions that owners face with regard to plumbing. One is an annoying problem that an owner would put up with for a long, long time. The other requires immediate attention. We usually put up with dripping faucets, faucets that are hard to turn off, commodes that run just a little bit, shower heads that don't spray water evenly or drip, and tubs, sinks, and lavatories that drain slowly. However, there is that time when something must be done, and this means that we are going to do the work or hire a specialist such as a plumber or sewer pipe cleaner to fix our problems. Problems that require immediate attention are those that have water running out of control, which include ruptured pipes and constantly running commodes. Other problems that require immediate attention deal with drainage systems, which can be either simple ones such as a stopped-up sink, tub, or commode; or those that deal with sewer lines and septic tanks and fields.

Contractor's responsibility.   When we are called to a home to solve any of the problems indicated above, we have the responsibility of restoring the plumbing to a serviceable condition. Sometimes the solutions are simple and we have the parts in our truck to make repairs. Sometimes, we need to take emergency steps to stop further damage to the property or to restore liveability to the house. Then we would return to the house later and make permanent repairs.

In any of these situations, we would be fair and demonstrate integrity when dealing with the owner. If our company employs more than one plumber, we probably would be able to handle many customers who have problems. But if we were a one-person operation, it would be much more difficult, since we would look to the larger jobs for the bulk of our income. So we would need to satisfy these customer's needs according to our capacity.

Let's describe our responsibilities according to the various types of problems the owner faces.

1. *Faucet and valve problems.* We need to examine the faucet and determine from our experience and knowledge the type of internal structure, the age, and the likelihood of repairing it. Some are washerless, some have washers, and some have O-rings. Some are mixer types, some are separate types, some are shower/tub types, and some are cutoff types. If we can repair the faucet, it will probably be cheaper than replacing it. Most of the time it is cheaper to replace the valve than try to repair one, since valves are relatively inexpensive.

When we replace the faucet or valve, we must open water lines and make new connections when installing the replacement one. In almost every case this is no problem for us. However, when the owner attempts the work, there could be problems in making the new connections and ensuring that there are no leaks. We have ample experience ensuring that flared and pressure copper connections are completed properly. We know how and when to use tape to seal the pipe joint and when to use pipe joint compounds. We know through experience how to disconnect and reconnect nuts and the like without causing damage to pipes and other connections. If the owner has such experience, he or she can perform these tasks as well.

2. *Piping and waste lines.* Since we can be called to a 50-year-old home with galvanized piping and chrome or to a modern home with plastic piping, we must be able to solve the problem in terms of the owner's peculiar circumstances. Yet in many cases, maintaining architectural integrity with piping and waste lines may not be essential. Therefore, we can substitute modern plastic piping and waste lines for galvanized and polished chrome. We may also suggest that a modern water control unit be used in the commode versus the old mechanical metal types. So there are some alternatives that we can suggest which could save material and labor costs.

3. *Water heaters.* One pipe fills the water heater, but several pipes distribute the hot water from the heater. Electricity powers heating elements in some types of water heaters, while flames from gas do the job in other types. In homes with solar energy water heaters, there are two tanks and a combination of electrical and mechanical devices that control the flow of water and supplemental heating. Plumbers can make repairs to defective piping, can swap-out an old unit for a new one and reconnect all lines, and can replace the gas burner or electric heating unit in the heater. But if there is a significant buildup of chemicals along the walls of the tank and in the piping in the heater, repairs would cure only the immediate problem of inadequate operability. The best solution would be replacing the unit.

4. *Sewer lines and septic problems.* Stopped-up sewer lines and a defective septic tank or drain fields are serious problems that require immediate attention. The owner may call a specialist who cleans sewer lines with a snake. This person may or may not be a plumber, but they have the tools to open clogged lines or detect when the line has collapsed. When dealing with a clogged or inoperable septic system, the contractor must have considerable knowledge of the principles of this system. If we are called to help restore operations, we may need to subcontract the work to someone who is more expert. There are cleaning service companies who have the trucks and pumps to clean the tanks. Others can measure the bacteria count in tanks and tell if the levels are proper for proper operation. Still other types of personnel might be required where field drains need to be dug up and replaced.

5. *Appliances.* There are three appliances that the contractor may be required to repair or remove and replace: the commode, made of vitreous china and with mechanically operating parts; the garbage disposal unit under the sink; and the ice maker in the freezer compartment of the refrigerator. We have to make sure that we can repair the unit economically or show that the repairs would be a costly solution.

Sometimes, we are an agent for an appliance center who sells the replacement units. Sometimes, the owner prefers that we obtain the parts and make all restoration. In the first case the owner pays the outlet or center and the outlet pays us. Where we provide all support for repairs and replacement parts, the owner pays our company.

When emergencies occur, the owner wants quick, effective service. We must resist any attempt to overcharge due to the emergency. However, we can justify flat-rate costs, and we should use these accordingly since many jobs take less than a day or half a day.

Homeowner's expectations.   From these brief descriptions we see that the contractor or specialist called by the owner to fix the problem has to have a wide range of understanding in all aspects of systems that transport potable water and those that remove waste from the services in the home. We need to discuss the problems openly with the customer, yet avoid long detailed explanations that tend to give the impression that we are trying to run up the bill.

The owner expects immediate relief from the catastrophic problem and is forced to accept the added cost for emergency repairs. Yet the owner will shop around for the best price and availability or response time. In cases where the problem has been around for quite a while, they will shop for the best price and may also be confronted with response time. But in this case response time may not be very important. In every case they expect quality work. To most this means: Fix the problem correctly the first time so that it does not need repairs for a long time, if ever again.

Scope of projects.   We examine four types of problems in this chapter: removing and replacing the commode and water closet, repairing and replacing components on sinks and bath tubs, refurbishing or replacing the water heater, and restoring the sewer waste lines.

PROJECT 1. REMOVE AND REPLACE A COMMODE AND WATER CLOSET UNIT

Subcategories include: the components that make up a water closet; techniques in installing water closets; removing and replacing the defective water controls in the water tank; removing and replacing the commode; replacing the seat; and testing the system.

Preliminary Discussion with the Owner

Problems facing the owner.   A constantly running water closet or a slowly emptying or stopped-up commode mean trouble and expense. A cracked or split commode or water closet is a very expensive item to replace (see Figure 7–1).

There are several types of residential water closets. One is the floor-mounted tank with vitreous china (ceramic) closet, bowl, valved closet supply control, and set with cover. In this type the bowl anchors to the floor and the closet bolts to the bowl. Another type is the wall-hung vitreous china closet with elongated bowl, valved closet supply, and seat with cover. A third type is a one-piece, floor-mounted vitreous china closet with elongated bowl and toilet seat and includes a valved closet supply. As we can see by the three descriptions, there are several different approaches that need to be taken if any of the china parts must be disturbed or replaced. In some of the very early homes the tank was elevated about 5 ft

Water tank with controls

Water inlet valves

Bowl with cover

Figure 7–1   Commode.

above the floor because water pressure was relatively low and the force of falling water was required to flush the commode (bowl). Today, designers have made improvements in bowl design so that the normal surface air pressure and gravity is ample to flush the bowl. Thus the tank is located just behind and above the bowl.

There are several mechanical parts in the water closet, the tank that holds the water used for flushing, that fail.

1. Valved closet supply or water-level regulator (Figure 7–2), which is a unit designed to permit water to fill the tank and stop the water at a predetermined level. These units are adjustable, thus can be set to points that stop overflow and minimize the use of water. The parts that fail are the regulator-valve itself and sometimes the ball float, if there is one.

Figure 7–2   Valved closet supply: two-piece floor model.

2. Stopper unit (Figure 7–3), which operates from the lever that causes the flushing action. When the tank is empty, a flap falls down to close off the entry into the commode. The parts that fail are the flap, and lever arm, and the chain that connects the two.

The china parts can be broken, too, when heavy objects strike them a downward or glancing blow: for example, a deflected hammer blow or a falling joist. They are easily cracked when repairs have to be made. A common problem is cracking the tank where it bolts to the bowl. There are special washers used between bolt and china and other soft washers between china parts, so excessive torque on the tightened bolts can crack either the bowl or the bottom of the tank. *Major problem and cost!* The area on the bowl most likely to be cracked is at the two ports where the unit sits on the floor. These ports permit passage of the anchor bolts that hold the bowl in place. When tightening the nut too tightly, the china cracks; thus the bowl cannot be firmly anchored. *Major problem and cost!* Only enough tension to hold the bowl in place without movement is required for satisfactory installation.

Another problem facing the owner can be an inlet water pipe or fitting leak. The supply water pipe fits into the bottom of the tank and is held in place with a pressure washer and nut in almost every case. Most units today are made of plastic nuts. Some supply pipes are chromed metal which are malleable, and some are flexible hose types. One end connects to the gate or shutoff valve and the other end connects to the tank. Leaks occur at either end. Sometimes the gate valve fails due

**Water level
control unit**

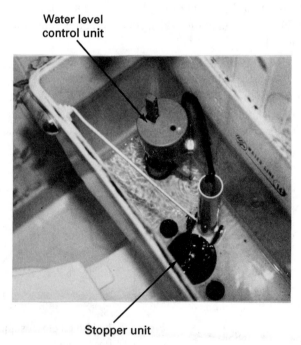

Stopper unit

Figure 7–3 Stopper unit inside tank.

to an extended open position and accumulation of chemicals. This means that we need to change it for a new one. These problems are severe but not as costly as replacing china.

Another problem facing the owner is the stopped-up bowl. When a plumber's helper—a plunger—cannot clear the bowl, the owner must determine if the sewer line is the problem or if the commode is blocked. Here detective work sometimes saves time and money. By questioning the people who very recently used the bathroom, the cause of the problem can be located. For example, a missing sock or other apparel could have fallen into the commode and be flushed down, only to stick. Other items that cause blockage are hairpins, barrettes, hygiene devices, washcloths, pocket items, and the like. Even excessive use of toilet tissue can sometimes cause blockage. If we are able to pinpoint the item, we can usually rule out a stopped-up or blocked sewer pipe, since the pipe is 4 in. across and not likely to be blocked by an object that can get past the bends in the bowl. If our detective work eliminates the possibility, we need to determine if the blockage is in the sewer pipe. Some homes have sewer lines with an access port with cover. We remove the cover and run water through the line to test its operation. No water backup, no apparent problem. The problem is in the bowl. If the water in the line is slow or backs up, we need the line cleaned with a snake. If the snake cannot get through, we probably have a collapsed line. This means digging the line up and replacing part or all of it. *Major problem and cost! Note:* This line connects the commode to the city sewer line or septic tank.

Alternative solutions to the problem.   We must restore the commode to operational order without causing further damage to either the unit or surrounding wall and floor. Depending where the problem exists, we can use several alternatives.

Problem	Alternative
Running commode	Replace control valve with modern type or use an exact replacement
Inoperative tank discharge	Replace flap, reconnect or install a new chain, replace the old arm
Leak at inlet pipe	Tighten nuts, replace washers, replace gate valve, replace connecting line, replace pressure connectors, reflare the pipe ends
Leak between tank and bowl	Tighten nuts, replace soft washers and grommets, reposition tank
Loose bowl (it moves)	Tighten lock-down nuts
Loose or broken seat or cover	Replace with new one or tighten nuts
Cracked china	Replace tank or bowl
Blocked bowl	Remove bowl and clean out, try plumber's helper; use a thin flexible snake

| Blocked or slowly draining sewer line | Snake the line clear, replace the line where damaged |
| Constantly running tank | Adjust the water level, decrease input water pressure with gate valve, replace the valved closet supply (control valve assembly) |

Statement of work and the planning effort.   For our project we shall be called to the house to unstop a commode that the owner could not clear using a plumber's helper or snake. Our basic statement of work is to *make the commode operational.* More specifically, we must *isolate the problem to the sewer lines or commode, then make repairs.* We may find a very old system whose parts are likely to rupture, crack, or otherwise be damaged during repairs. Therefore, we should stipulate that *in the event that parts of the commode are old and not reusable, the new parts will be installed with costs and labor charges added to the cost of the job.* The owner may not readily trust an unknown, so we can modify the last statement to *show and explain the damaged parts that must be replaced.* Finally, *we guarantee our work against leaks for one year.*

For this job our planning includes inspection of the problem commode, testing and examination of the sewer line from house to city connection or septic tank, estimating the cost of restoration, preparation of the bill, and time to complete the work. Since the owner considers this problem catastrophic, we are expected to react quickly. Therefore, we must plan to complete all the work on one service call.

Contract.   As a plumbing contractor we have had many similar problems; therefore, we have a basis for establishing flat rates for the various possibilities we encounter at the job site. Rather than make several visits and determine costs, we take a standard-form contract with us and fill it out after the work is done. However, the owner may first request an estimate. To satisfy this we provide an estimate type of contract which includes a flat rate for labor and a list of material prices. We perform the inspection and determine the problem to the commode. Thus, in fact, we provide a time-and-materials contract. It could read as follows:

There is a flat rate for the labor of	$XX.XX
The following materials are estimated:	
Water closet valve	
Stopper unit	
Wax ring	
Miscellaneous materials	
Gate valve	
Total materials	XX.XX
Total estimate for restoration	$XXX.XX

In this situation we substitute actual coats plus markup for estimated prices and add the local percentage for tax to the entire job. Profit is included in the flat labor rate.

Material Assessment

Direct Materials	Use/Purpose
Wax ring	To seal the bowl to the sewer pipe in the floor
Closet valve assembly	As regulator for water inlet and control
Stopper unit	To activate the flushing action
Soft washers and O-ring	If required, used between tank and bowl
Bolts and nuts	If required, to replace anchor bolts that hold down the bowl
Water line and connecting nuts and washers	If required because of damage
Gate valve (shutoff valve)	If required because old one is corroded open

Indirect Materials	Use/Purpose
Paper towels	For cleanup
Trash bags	To gather old wax and other debris

Support Materials	Use/Purpose
Plumber's toolbox	For construction
Snake	To test or clear line
Shovel	(Optional) To access line for snake use
Ladder	(Optional) To climb on roof to access sewer line with snake

Outside Contractor Support	Use/Purpose
None	

Activities Planning Chart

Activity	Time Line (Days)
	1 2 3 4 5 6 7
1. Inspection and contract	I _×_ I ___ I ___ I ___ I ___ I ___ I ___ I
2. Materials acquisition	I _×_ I ___ I ___ I ___ I ___ I ___ I ___ I
3. Restoration	I _×_ I ___ I ___ I ___ I ___ I ___ I ___ I

Reconstruction

Inspection and contract.   At the office an employee takes the call and asks enough questions to localize the problem to the commode and sewer line. We identify the probable costs associated with each problem from our data files or database in the computer. From our price listings we select the most probable parts required for each job. Then we use our charts to select the flat rate to charge. Allocation for fixed costs and profit are charged as part of labor, and variable costs are an additive to materials for this job. That way we can provide on-site estimates and final costs.

The on-site inspection entails only labor and fits within the time allocated in the flat rate.

Materials acquisition.   Due to the variety of parts that may be required, we can bring some but not all types. Once we are on site or after we have removed the commode and cleared the obstruction, we can drive to the supply house for parts, if required.

Restoration.   For the restoration we must disassemble the commode, clear out the obstacle, and reinstall the commode. Here is the list of tasks:

1. Shut off the water using the valve below the tank or at the house inlet pipe.
2. Flush the toilet and sponge out the rest of the water in the tank.
3. Loosen the water inlet pipe under the tank. Refer to Figure 7–1 for this valve and pipe.
4. On a two-part system, remove the two nuts holding the tank to the bowl and lift off the tank.
5. Pop the china covers off the screw/bolts on each side of the bowl.
6. Remove the nuts and lift the bowl off the floor. Use caution to avoid cracking and spilling the water remaining in the bowl.
7. Scrape the old wax ring off the floor and clean up the area under the bowl.
8. Up-end the bowl and locate and remove the obstruction if in the bowl or clear the sewer line under the bowl.
9. Test that the line is clear by running water into it.
10. Test that the bowl is clear by running water through it.
11. Install the new wax ring over the open sewer pipe.
12. Set the bowl over the ring and bolt to the floor. Use extreme caution to avoid cracking the china. Use putty to hold the china covers over the nuts.
13. Install the washers and set the the tank onto the bowl and fasten—but not overtightly.
14. Connect the water line.
15. If required, remove and replace the assemblies in the tank before connecting the water pipe to tank.
16. If required, replace the gate valve.
17. Turn on the water and test for the following:
     a. No leaks at the water connections.
     b. No leaks between tank and bowl (additional tightening of nuts might be required).

    c. Water level is set to mark on tank when filled. Adjust float if too low or too high.
    d. Flush the toilet and test for no water leaks on the floor.
    e. Flush toilet and check for rapid flushing action.

If there are no problems, clean up the surrounding areas. Prepare the bill with final costs and present it for payment.

    Concluding comments.   This project appears to be very straightforward from start to finish. All plumbing is this way. But owners can make the job cost more than necessary if they lack the basic knowledge, tools, and skills to perform the work. Owners can crack the china very easily by mishandling the pieces—they are heavy and awkward, can strip nuts and bolts, and can misalign and cross-thread nuts when reinstalling bolts and pipes. The plumber's cost will be more than self-help, but the work should be guaranteed. A plumber takes responsibility for the entire job and will only charge for parts that were unusable or damaged because of a prior condition. If the plumber cracks the china parts, he or she would normally absorb the cost of replacement.

PROJECT 2. REMOVE, RESTORE OR REPLACE FAUCETS AND WASTE LINE COMPONENTS

Subcategories include: types of faucets and components in the faucets; replacing washers; removing and reinstalling faucets; installing new mixer faucets; components in the wastewater line system; dishwasher waste lines; removing and replacing the trap and connecting pipes between sink and sewer lines; checking the vent pipe for problems and testing the system for leaks.

Preliminary Discussion with the Owner

    Problems facing the owner.   The owner has a faucet that does not fully or partially shutoff, drips water all day and night, does not turn on, has corroded or lost its sheen, and has a direction faucet that is so loose it leaks and sprays water in certain positions. The owner has either a single faucet or a mixer with a problem (see Figure 7–4). He or she may have a leak in the water line connectors under the sink that are connected to the faucet. There may also be a leak in the waste lines under the sink (see Figure 7–5) or behind the tub. The trap may be filled with waste products and debris and slow the drainage of the sink or tub. The trap may have rotted through and leaks. The connections to the garbage disposal may begin to leak. The connections and lines to the dishwasher may have begun to leak. The drain hose to the dishwasher may have a leak at the clamp. Finally, the sewer lines leading from the sink or tub may be clogged.

Figure 7–4 Mixer faucet.

The owner may try to solve the problem using self-help. Let's examine this in terms of what the owner must know and do. The owner must have the correct tools to remove and replace the defective part or clean out the clogs. This translates to plumber's wrenches, cutting tools, flaring tools, soldering tools, and tanks to provide the high temperatures needed, to mention the more common ones. He or she also requires a knowledge of plumbing and how parts are measured and assembled. Although most faucets and pipes are standardized according to plumbing and in-

Trap

Trap

Figure 7–5 Waste system under sink.

dustry standards, older homes may use larger pipes and different types. He or she must also be quite agile. Most of the work is performed on one's back or side with arms raised above the head or when in a sitting position with arms reaching far outward. If the owner lacks all or some of these skills there will be a steep learning curve to master the tasks. There could be considerable cost in purchasing the proper tools. There is also a real chance for fire damage if torches are used to sweat new joints. Finally, the owner must be able to use a snake, which sometimes calls for climbing on the roof to get access to the vent pipe protruding through the roof.

On the other hand, the services of a plumber may be the best alternative. However, we understand that these tradesmen are in high demand and therefore are sometimes difficult to obtain. But most are licensed, skilled, and efficient at their work. Therefore, once they are on the job they usually pinpoint the problem quickly and correct it.

Alternative solutions to the problem.   There are alternatives to these problems in many cases. The first is that the owner can resolve the problems systematically. He or she can, with several good-quality wrenches, remove a trap and clean it out if that is the problem. He or she can easily remove older-type faucets with a wrench and screwdriver and take the unit to the local hardware store, where a washer kit can be purchased, or have the hardware salesperson perform the work. He or she can make a variety of inspections to pinpoint the problem of a leak and can decide what parts need replacing. Once these are removed, a trip to the hardware store can sometimes result in obtaining suitable replacement parts. And when the pipes are clogged a specialist company that cleans clogged lines can frequently respond more quickly than a plumber.

In addition to who will perform the work, we can also solve problems in other ways. Old parts beyond repair need to be replaced. They can be replaced with a like-kind device or one of a different type or style. Plastic pipes and flexible pipes can be used where old pipes were made from galvanized metal, copper, or chromed-white metal. These require somewhat different connecting techniques which may require gluing the pieces together. New rubber hoses can be purchased by the foot and clamps are easily installed. Sometimes the old hose is long enough to trim past the damage and be reconnected.

Statement of work and the planning effort.   For our project we will restore a sink that has the following problems: (1) slow drainage, (2) dripping faucet for a mixer-type faucet, and (3) a leaky drainage system. Our general statement of work states that *we will restore the sink's plumbing to like-new condition.* Specifically, *we will replace the defective washers/O-rings in faucets unless the seats are damaged, then we will replace the faucet; clean and replace damaged drain parts;*

and unclog the lines. If faucets need to be replaced, *we will permit the owner to make the selection, if desired.*

Although we can define much of the work that needs to be done over the telephone, we need an on-site inspection to better estimate the work involved. To minimize cost to the owner, we would expect to make repairs immediately after the inspection and provide the owner with a rough estimate of costs. We would plan to have the owner go to a plumbing supply outlet that we would choose, to pick out a new faucet if required. That way we can proceed with the other repairs and complete the job sooner. If this is not possible, we would have to use an alternative plan to pick out the new faucet. We can take cost data with us or partially prepare a bill for services at the office. Then plan to complete the bill on-site and present it for payment.

Contract. For this contract we would probably use a modified fixed-price type. After an inspection, we will have the information pertaining to labor costs. We will also have a fairly good understanding of the parts needed to be replaced. The major item that would alter the total price would be the selection of a new mixer faucet, since the prices range from slightly less than $20 to well over $100. Based on the statements of work, we would prepare a list of jobs to accomplish, which might be nothing more than bullet statements. For example, they might look like this:

The work required to restore the plumbing in the sink includes the following steps:

1. Repair or replace the mixer faucet.
2. Unclog the drain system.
3. Replace corroded parts in the drain system.
4. Test all connections for leaks.

Cost of the new mixer faucet $_____.____.

Total cost, labor and materials $XXX.XX.

Material Assessment

Direct Materials	Use/Purpose
Mixer faucet	Required if seats on the old one are damaged
Washers or O-rings	To replace old ones if seats are okay
New trap and connecting pipe	To replace corroded old parts (plastic)
Clamps	(Optional) if required for hoses
Shutoff valves	If required because old ones are inoperable

Indirect Materials	**Use/Purpose**
Plumber's tape	To make joints watertight
Plumber's pipe compound	To make joints watertight
Paper towels	For cleanup
Plastic bags	To store refuse from clogged drains and old parts

Support Materials	**Use/Purpose**
Plumber's tools	For construction
Trouble light	To provide light under the sink
Snake	To clean the sewer line
Torch	(Optional) If soldering is required

Outside Contractor Support	**Use/Purpose**
None	

Activities Planning Chart

Activity	Time Line (Days)						
	1	2	3	4	5	6	7
1. Contract preparation	I _×_ I _×_ I ___ I ___ I ___ I ___ I ___ I
2. Materials and scheduling	I _×_ I ___ I ___ I ___ I ___ I ___ I ___ I
3. Restoration	I ___ I _×_ I ___ I ___ I ___ I ___ I ___ I

Reconstruction

Contract preparation. Because of the nature of the job, its short time frame, and the limited amount of work, the office personnel perform several parts of the documentation on different days. On the first day they obtain information from the owner about the problem and log the potential job into the database. They perform routine roles assigning a job number, determining when and who will be assigned to the job if more than one plumber is employed, and arrange with the owner to have someone home during the day the plumber arrives. They may make preliminary entries onto a job worksheet regarding parts they know need to be replaced. They would allow room for unknowns. The estimator would probably predict the labor costs at either an hourly rate or a flat rate. Then a contract/bid form would be prepared for the plumber to complete at the job.

The second part of the office responsibility is to record the decisions made by the plumber while he or she was on-site. This would be an accounting of actual materials used, the purchase of a new mixer from the supply house (charged to the company), and the actual time spent. The ledgers would be posted accordingly.

Materials and scheduling.   Most plumbers carry a wide variety of replacement parts, including washers, O-rings, connecting pipes in plastic and chrome, hose and hose clamps, and other types of connectors. Since the sink is clogged, the person would carry a snake as well. The plumber would also know where to send the owner for a new mixer; therefore, the owner would not be obligated to the plumbing supply house for the mixer.

The office schedules the job. The plumber receives the assignment and performs the work during the time allotted.

Restoration.   Given the three basic problems to solve—restore or replace the mixer, replace the damaged drain system, and unclog the lines—where is the logical point to begin?

We could clear the drain pipes first, then test the rest of the line for blockage. We could replace the faucet washers first, but if the seats are damaged, we would have no water to test a cleared line. We could remove and replace the drain system, but if the line is not clear, we might need to remove the drain system to access part of the sewer line.

Our best solution is to remove the old drain system, which includes the trap and pipes from trap to sink and sewer. Then we can run a snake into the line from under the sink. After this we can install the new drain system parts and complete inspections of hoses and connectors while under the sink. Now with water, we can ascertain that the drainage system is clear to the sewer.

That work done, we shut off the water under the sink and remove the faucet handles to access the valve seats. We then make an inspection to determine if the mixer needs replacing. If the seats are smooth and intact, we replace the washer or O-ring and reassemble. If the valve stem is corroded, we need to replace it. This may require a trip to the supply store. If the mixer needs replacing, we can continue working on the faucet assembly while the owner goes to the store for the new unit if he or she desires to select it; or we can order one to have it delivered; or we can drive the owner to the store to pick one out. While the new unit is being obtained, we remove the old unit by removing the nuts that retain it, and disconnect the water lines. We clean the sink surface since there is always a buildup of soap and food around and under the edge of the mixer.

When the mixer is obtained, the gasket is placed exactly in position and the unit is placed over the openings in the sink and onto the pipes. The water line nuts are installed first, but not tightened; the mixer nuts are installed next. (Note that the mixer nuts must be slid over the water pipes before the unit is set in place.) If a spray hose is connected to the mixer, it is installed next. Finally, all nuts are tightened: (1) mixer nuts, (2) water line nuts, and (3) hose nut.

Now we test the sink and faucet for leaks and proper operation. Using a mentally memorized checklist, we ensure that the faucets operate smoothly, no water drips from the stem, no water leaks around the mixer body, all pipes are dry under the sink, and the line is clear. To test for a clear line, fill the sink. Remove the stopper and listen for a surging sound as the last of the water swirls into the drain.

Concluding comments.   The job of restoring a sink that has problems requires the correct tools, an understanding of the parts of the sink and drain systems, and a certain amount of skill working in very uncomfortable positions. Many owners routinely do the work successfully, but many require the skill and knowledge of the plumber.

Because the job we described usually takes less than a full day, the labor costs may be stated in terms of a flat rate versus an hourly rate. Owners have very little choice in this area since a variety of indirect costs are incurred by the plumber when completing these small jobs.

PROJECT 3. REPLACE OR REFURBISH HOT-WATER HEATER

Subcategories include: testing the water heater; principles of heating with gas or electricity; heater components; removing and reinstalling tasks.

Preliminary Discussion with the Owner

Problems facing the owner.   Homes with potable water heaters enjoy hot water while bathing and performing various household chores. When the water turns cold in the shower, we have a clear sign that we have used all the hot water available in the tank. The cause may be the simple result of too much demand in too short a period of time, in which case we simply let the water heat up. But when the water heater does not respond, we have a problem. If the heater is gas feed, why doesn't it ignite? If the heater is electric fed, why doesn't the heating element heat? This is the first of a series of problems we may face.

Another problem we face is a pressure valve leak. All heaters are fitted with a pressure valve that opens when internal pressures exceed the setting in the valve. Over a prolonged time period, the internal parts of the valve can become corroded due to chemicals in the water. When the corrosion has damaged the valve, water escapes through the decayed part, and we have a leak in the top of the heater (see Figure 7–6).

There is also a drain valve in the lower part of the tank. This is a common type of tap valve with a hose connection thread at its end. When a heater needs to be flushed or drained, a hose is connected to the valve and it is turned on. This valve can also become corroded by chemical action and begin to drip.

Another problem in heaters is that the tank itself can become corroded or clogged with corrosion and cease to allow water to enter properly or exit properly, or it can begin to leak.

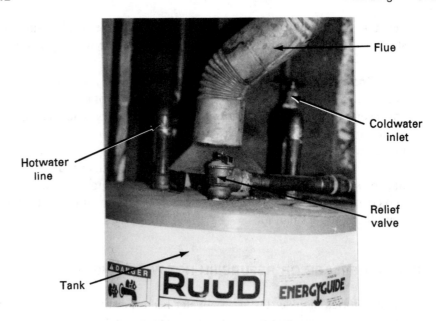

Figure 7–6   Forty-gallon gas water heater.

Finally, the connection between cold water or tank outlet and hot water line can leak.

Alternative solutions to the problem.   What are some alternatives? Obviously, the tank can be removed and replaced. We would expect to do this upon the advice of an expert who has inspected the water heater. Some decisions that would lead to making this decision are clogged or corroded internal areas in the tank. Another would be the age of the tank. Another would be the relative cost of making repairs to a used tank versus the price of a new one. In these times with discounts available because of widespread marketing, customers can often replace rather than repair. In a gas-fired heater, the gas unit can deteriorate over time due to the high heat created by the flames. The heating chamber walls thin with age and can rupture, causing leaks. The gas unit or its control can also fail with age. Any of these problems can be an indication that is usually coupled with aging and provides the inspector with clear indicators that the best solution is to replace the heater. But when there are leaks external to the heater, the owner can opt for repairs and usually reduce overall costs.

Whereas we can choose to let a faucet drip for weeks or months, a leaking water heater or its piping comes very close to catastrophic and usually requires immediate repair. When the heater ceases to produce hot water, we also consider this catastrophic and require an immediate cure.

Some owners can remove and replace the heater, change valves, and generally complete the work efficiently. Naturally, the owner must have the time to procure parts and a new heater. He or she may be able to handle the electrical connections properly and can even make the new gas connections. But the heater weighs quite a bit and the job can be done more easily with two people. Many times the plumber or gas company personnel do the work. A call to the plumber and an explanation of the problem brings the plumber to the house, where he or she performs the entire job, including installation of the new unit. A call to the gas company does the same thing; however, they may require the owner to come to the office to pick out the heater and sign the contract for purchase and installation.

Statement of work and the planning effort.   For the project, we shall assume that a plumber will perform the work and that the work involves decision planning, testing, and ultimately, replacing the heater. Our first statement of work would be *to make an inspection of the heater and determine its state of condition.* Having performed this, we would *recommend removing and replacing the heater, the pressure relief valve, and drain valve and ensure that the flue (used with gas heaters) is sound.* If we encountered a very old tank of 20- or 25-gallon capacity, *we would strongly suggest a minimum tank size of 30 gallons.*

The planning effort parallels the discussion above. The plumber would arrive at the home, make an inspection of the heater, make a recommendation, and provide an on-site estimate. After receiving the go-ahead, the plumber would pick up a new water heater and other parts and supplies, take out the old unit, and install the new one. The plumber would stipulate that payment be made upon completion of the job.

Contract.   To expedite the serious problem the customer is having, the contractor would take a list of costs for equipment and labor to the house and prepare an estimate after the inspection. Using a company estimate/bid form, we prepare it in handwriting using data from the office. The estimate could be similar to the following:

Remove the old heater and replace with a 30-gallon gas water heater.

Install a new relief valve.

Install a new drain valve.

Reconnect the gas line.

Reconnect the flue and check for quality.

Test the system after the tank is filled.

Total estimate $XXX.XX.

Material Assessment

Direct Materials	Use/Purpose
30-gallon water heater	To replace old worn-out unit
Pressure relief valve	Safety valve to prevent excessive buildup in the tank
Drain valve	With hose connection at the outlet

Indirect Materials	Use/Purpose
Plumber's pipe cement	To seal connections
Plumber's pipe tape	To seal connections; polyurethane
Solder	To unsolder and resolder water pipes, if required

Support Materials	Use/Purpose
Plumber's tools	For construction
Garden hose	To drain the tank
Butane torch	To solder connections, if required
Stepladder	To reach the flue above the tank

Outside Contractor Support	Use/Purpose
None	

Activities Planning Chart

Activity	Time Line (Days)						
	1	2	3	4	5	6	7
1. Contract preparation	|_×_|	|___|	|___|	|___|	|___|	|___|	|___|
2. Materials and scheduling	|_×_|	|___|	|___|	|___|	|___|	|___|	|___|
3. Inspecting the old heater	|_×_|	|___|	|___|	|___|	|___|	|___|	|___|
4. Removing and replacing the heater	|_×_|	|___|	|___|	|___|	|___|	|___|	|___|
5. Testing the new heater	|_×_|	|___|	|___|	|___|	|___|	|___|	|___|

Reconstruction

Contract preparation.   Due to the need to expedite this emergency job, the company had the plumber evaluate the job, make on-site decisions about the repairs, and provide the customer with a bid/contract. The estimator provided the probable cost figures for materials and labor, which included an allowance for indirect and support costs. The form used was one that could easily be handwritten.

After the plumber completed the work of installing a new water heater, he or she brought the check and a second copy of the bid back to the office. With the exact figures, the office help divided the amounts according to the various accounts to log the job as complete.

Materials and scheduling.   As we have already noted, the plumber had to drive to the plumbing supply company to pick up a new water heater and transport it to the job site. He or she picked up the other parts as well. Other materials listed in the materials assessment were already in the truck, since they are normally required for all jobs.

When the company received the call for emergency help, they made a trouble work order and as soon as a plumber could be diverted to the job, one was sent. Since the work, including the transportation of the new heater, would take almost a full day, the plumber was scheduled to complete the work prior to leaving the job, even if he or she had to work overtime.

Inspecting the old heater.   During the opening of the chapter and in this project, we indicated that there would be visible signs leading to the final conclusion of what action to take. The inspection included:

1. Examination of a leaky pressure valve. This valve corrodes and the spring holding it closed begins to fail, resulting in a leak.
2. Examination of drain valve and inlet valve. If there was a leak, it could be around the valve or in the valve. The inlet is a gate valve and the outlet is a tap valve (faucet). Each can be replaced.
3. The heater is dripping water at the bottom from inside the tank. Somewhere in the tank there is a leak. It can saturate the insulation and finally drip, or the hole can be in the bottom of the tank.
4. The heater coil (electric type) does not operate when power is applied. It could be burned open. Voltage checks are made in the circuit and at the controls. It could be a bad thermocoupler. (A thermocoupler is an electronic device made from two dissimilar metals that react to heat at different temperatures. When sufficient heat is applied they bend away from each other and open the circuit.) Over time, these can become defective. The problem could also be in the distribution box, where a circuit breaker has changed characteristics; however, this is seldom the case.
5. The gas unit fails to light and/or the pilot light does not stay lit. Water dripping onto the pilot light extinguishes the light. Dampness also extinguishes the pilot light. If the pilot is lit and the burners fail to ignite, the sending unit could be defective. Some units have millivolt circuits and sensors that interrupt the operation of the control unit. This circuit needs to be checked.

The results of the examination are explained to the owner. He or she must agree verbally to the definition of work; then a bid price can be prepared to provide a total cost of repair.

Removing and replacing the heater.   The plumber would follow a series of actions or steps to remove and replace the heater. They would follow this approximate order:

1. Cut off water to the heater at the inlet by shutting off the gate valve.
2. Connect a garden hose to the drain valve and drain the water from the tank.
3. Raise the cover over the flue and remove the flue.
4. Cut off the gas to the unit.
5. Disconnect the inlet coupling from the top of the heater.
6. Disconnect the gas line and move it carefully out of the way.
7. Disconnect the water line at the base of the tank, where it goes to the distribution pipes.
8. Examine the unit for any obstacles that would impair taking the tank out, and remove them.
9. Lift out the unit and with a two-wheel dolly, and move the old tank outside.
10. While the unit is out, examine the plumbing and gas lines for any other problems that may be beginning. These could include weakened solder joints, corrosion on copper or galvanized pipes, and so on.

Installing the new heater begins with installing the pressure relief valve while the unit is resting on the floor. We can also install a new gas control unit if it is not already in place. Then we can set the unit in place and connect the pipes. Sometimes we need to make a slight alteration to the pipe's position by elevating the tank with shims under the feet.

When all connections are made, we fill the tank before attempting to add power (electric) or gas. The tank is full of air, so we open a hot water tap in the house or laundry to permit the air to escape. When all air is out, we have a full tank. Next, we realign the flue pipe over the heater to capture properly the fumes and heat generated by the burner flames.

Testing the new heater.   Now we light the pilot. This may take a few moments since we must purge the gas line until the pilot remains lit. Then we wait for the gas to ignite on the main burner and remain on.

In the case of an electric heater, we reset the circuit breaker and turn on the control. It will take a short while for the heating element to warm up.

If we removed anything, such as doors, to make room to work, we replace these and clean up. We prepare the final bill for payment. By the time these activities are done, we can test the water at a close-by tap and check for lukewarm water. Our final job is to set the temperature to the customer's liking, or about 120 degrees.

Concluding comments.   The project of removing defective heater parts, plumbing connected to the heater, or the heater itself requires a good set of tools, a significant amount of physical strength and agility, and an understanding of the principles of heater operation. Some owners can perform the work, others cannot. The plumber who responds to the emergency can complete the entire job in less than a day, but the time is extended if he or she must pick up a new heater.

Whoever does the work, extra care must be used to follow a safe, standard method when removing and replacing it. Good-quality work is much more important than speed.

PROJECT 4. REMOVE AND REPLACE APPLIANCES THAT USE PLUMBING

Subcategories include: removing and replacing garbage disposals, dishwashers, and ice makers; principle of operation of each appliance; common problems that cause improper operation; and techniques used in restoration.

Preliminary Discussion with the Owner

Problems facing the owner.   Due in part to the long period of prosperity that many homeowners have experienced and the significant advancements made in the production of appliances that use plumbing, most homes have one or more of the following: a garbage disposal unit connected to one drain in the sink, a dishwasher, and an ice maker inside the freezer unit of the refrigerator. These are all electromechanical devices that use electricity, mechanical parts, and plumbing. Our chapter is on plumbing, so we focus our attention there. However, we must also concern ourselves with these other aspects since they may be the cause of non-operability.

Generally, these appliances operate without error for years, but sometime a failure from within an appliance or from an external force damages it. The results vary and we need to address each appliance separately.

Garbage Disposal.   In a garbage disposal (Figure 7–7), small blades spin when electrical power is applied. These cut and pulverize waste food material, then running water washes the residue through the sewer system. When spoons or metallic objects slip into the disposal and the unit is activated, the object damages the blades and from that point on, the noise level of the operating disposal increases dramatically. There is no repair for this.

If the unit fails to operate, the unit can be jammed or blocked, or has electrical problems. A jammed condition can often be cleared without removal of the unit. A blocked unit can be unclogged by clearing the waste lines under the sink. An elec-

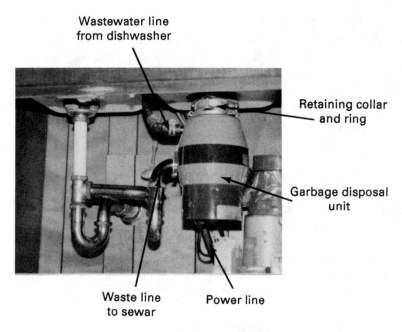

Figure 7–7   Garbage disposal unit.

trical problem can be cleared by resetting the overload button if the unit has one. In each of these situations, the problem may be more serious and require removal and replace action.

The seal at the connection to the sink can leak if damaged. The connecting hose can leak at the connection to the disposal unit or at the sewer pipe connection. These can usually be repaired without replacing the unit.

Dishwasher.   The dishwasher has a timer-control unit which is built to be replaced when defective rather than being repaired. When one or more of the cycles fails to operate, the control part of the timer unit is usually the cause. When it fails to change from the set time, the problem is with the timer part (these situations presume that power is applied). The unit can be replaced easily.

The dishwasher requires high heat to wash dishes. It is equipped with a heating coil that is located under the lower dish tray. When called for, it heats the water or provides dry heat during the drying cycle. If this element does not heat, the cause can be a damaged mechanical terminal or a damaged control unit. It, too, can be replaced easily.

With regard to safety, the unit is equipped with a safety switch located in the door assembly. This switch protects the unit from being turned on when the door is in the open (unlocked) state. Locking the door with the lever closes the contacts of the switch and permits electricity to operate the timer control. The switch can be damaged or burned to the point where it is inoperable. It can be replaced without great difficulty.

The rest of the dishwasher uses plumbing principles. There is an inlet pipe connected to a line that is connected to the hot-water line under the sink. There is a drain line (hose) that directs the wastewater to the sewer lines under the sink. There is a water-level control device located in many units in the bottom front. It looks like a plastic bottle turned upside down. When the dishwasher is filling up, the float rises. At some point the float is high enough and activates a switch that closes the water inlet relay, stopping the water. This happens before the rinse cycle, before the wash cycle, and before the final rinse cycle. If the float is damaged or becomes stuck, the water will flow out of the unit and all over the floor. It is simple to check the float for damage: Just lift it out and examine it. It is also possible to check the shutoff relay by bypassing the interlock switch, allowing the water to enter, and manually lifting off the plastic control. If the water stops, the circuit is okay.

There is an electrically operated pump in the unit. During the wash cycle it pumps water throughout the dishwasher splashing the dishes, rinsing the dishes, and draining the dishwasher. It can go bad because of a worn commutator, brushes, or bearings. It can be frozen in place from a high surge of electricity (a lightning strike). Or the impeller blade can be jammed with an object such as a piece of glass from a dish or glass, a utensil, or a piece of plastic that melted and wedged in the impeller. Replacing the pump is a time-consuming job because it requires removing the dishwasher from under the counter and dismantling quite a bit of it.

Ice Maker.   There are several different types of engineered ice makers in use. Each requires a small (usually $\frac{1}{4}$ in.) pipe to connect it to the cold-water line under the sink. A relay is activated to open and close the water valve, which lets water fill the ice tray. Most home units have a mechanical unit that rotates and dumps the frozen cubes from the tray. Many parts are made from plastic and thus never rust.

When the unit fails to discharge ice cubes, the problem is with the unit and may be electrical or mechanical. We can test the electrical circuit with a voltmeter. We can check the mechanical gears and drive assembly for damage or for misalignment and probably correct the problem. We can check the relay by shorting across the terminals if we can get to it easily. If it closes and opens, it is good. If not, it is not difficult to replace. If the control unit in the ice maker is inoperable, we may be able to obtain a new one or we may be required to replace the entire ice maker.

Alternative solutions to the problem.   Because of the wide variety of problems with appliances that use plumbing, sometimes the owner can repair a problem, sometimes it is better to get help, and sometimes it is better to buy a new appliance.

Let's explore the last idea first. Each appliance has a predictable life expectancy, most ranging from 8 to 10 years. After this time problems occur more often than in earlier years. We must determine the best solution (replace or repair) in terms of costs. Let's use a simple problem to illustrate the point.

Problem Solution.   A dishwasher is 10 years old. The control timer has problems. The dishwasher cost $300 when new. The replacement control timer costs $75 and a service call of $50 is necessary for installation. A new dishwasher costs $375. The expected life of the unit was 10 years.

Average cost per year = $30
Residual value remaining based on life expectancy = $0.
Personal life expectancy of unit = 15 years.
Residual personal value = $100.
Repair costs = $125.

Solution A: Make repairs and assume a 15-year life cycle.

Total personal residual value = $250.
Average cost per year for 5 years = $50.
Total costs for 15 years = $425 or $28 per year.
Expected cost for replacement unit in 5 years = $425.

Conclusion: average yearly cost decreased over 15 years. Inflation costs drove the price of new the unit up and dollars were worth less when buying the new unit.

Solution B: Replace the unit.

Accept the 10-year life span with $0 value left.
Purchase a new unit installed for $375 (present dollars).

Conclusion: The unit lived for its full life expectancy and the new one was bought with cheaper dollars.

Anyone can make such analogies and can include parameters of the type used in the example. It can be carried even further, where we could play with investing the price difference in replacement costs, and this would indicate an even stronger reason to select one answer over the other.

Sometimes it is better to get help. Almost every appliance center can provide service for repairing an appliance if the decision is to make repairs. Many of these companies also sell new appliances and provide for their installation.

Statement of work and the planning effort.   We will assume that the owner decides that the old unit is not economical to repair and that the best solution is to purchase a new one and have it installed. As contractors we are contacted to make the installation. Our requirement is simple: *Remove the old appliance and install a new one. Test it for proper operation, and at the owner's discretion, take the old unit away.*

Planning for this work requires the preparation of documentation, scheduling the work, and installing the new appliance. If we are working with a local retail appliance outlet, they usually charge a flat rate for installation of appliances. When out-of-the-ordinary situations happen that require additional plumbing repairs, we establish the costs with the owner while on-site. We perform the work and adjust the contract price accordingly.

Contract.   In situations like this we may have a standing fixed-price contract with the owner/manager of the appliance outlet. It would be renewed periodically and could have various clauses pertaining to zones of delivery or simple mileage, for example. Our contract with the owner would be for removal and installation of the appliance, and any added costs would be an adjustment to the contract. The outlet manager would, in turn, remit the charges to our office, where we would log the entry and issue a check. In essence, we act as agent for the owner whether we are a plumbing contractor or a general contractor.

Material Assessment

Direct Materials	Use/Purpose
Replacement appliance	Garbage disposal, dishwasher, or ice maker

Indirect Materials	Use/Purpose
Connectors	Replacement flare nuts, pressure nuts, etc.
Solder	To resolder water lines as required
Plumber's tape	To prevent water leaks

Support Materials	Use/Purpose
Plumber's tools	For construction
Voltmeter	To confirm that power is off

Outside Contractor Support	Use/Purpose
Appliance outlet	To provide the appliance

Activities Planning Chart

Activity	Time Line (Days)						
	1	2	3	4	5	6	7
1. Contract preparation	I _×_ I _×_ I ___ I ___ I ___ I ___ I ___ I
2. Materials and scheduling	I _×_ I ___ I ___ I ___ I ___ I ___ I ___ I
3. Removing and replacing the appliance	I ___ I _×_ I ___ I ___ I ___ I ___ I ___ I

Reconstruction

Contract preparation. Our office would receive a call from the appliance center and advise us that we have an installation. They would provide us with contractual information that we would enter into our accounts. Thus a new job is logged in. We would have the name and address of the customer, information about the appliance to remove and replace, and the date the appliance is to be delivered or date we are to pick up the appliance.

After the job is finished, we enter the receipt of funds from the appliance center and allocate it to the various accounts, and if required, pay the plumber his or her fixed rate plus any added work performed.

Materials and scheduling. The plumber usually only needs his or her standard tools and supplies when performing this work. Sometimes, water lines and connections as well as drain system parts are very old. We would replace these and would probably have these materials in the truck.

Our office arranges the date of work and advises the plumber, with a work order, when and where the work will be done. This order could include information needed to pick up the new appliance at the appliance center. The owner would need to be at home on the day scheduled.

Removing and replacing the appliance. For these appliances removal and replacement are similar, but some require slightly different tasks. Therefore, we shall make short lists of tasks peculiar to each appliance.

Garbage Disposal. The tasks are as follows:

1. Remove the power at the circuit breaker or fuse panel. Check that it is off.
2. Examine the unit under the sink for connectivity to the sink, waste lines, and dishwasher.
3. Remove the waste line between the unit and the trap and between the unit and the dishwasher.
4. Disconnect the power line.

5. Place a block of wood under the unit and loosen the holding ring under the sink.
6. When the ring is loosened, lower the unit and remove it from under the sink.
7. If the retaining ring and collar in the sink are in good order, they may not need to be removed. If worn or a different size from the new unit, remove the assembly by backing out the three screws and popping the collar loose.

To install the new one, complete the following tasks.

1. Check the sink rim and clean away any old putty or gasket materials. Apply a new seal and install the new locking ring and sink ring/collar.
2. Position the new unit under the sink and prop it up under the hole in the sink. When the outlets in the unit are aligned with the waste lines, raise the unit and lock it in position with the locking ring.
3. Reconnect the plumbing and electrical connectors.
4. Test the unit by restoring the power and running the water and disposal.

Dishwasher.   The following tasks are involved in removing the unit:

1. Remove the power at the circuit breaker panel or fuse box. Check to make sure that the power is off at the machine.
2. Open the front door and remove the two screws connecting the dishwasher to the countertop.
3. Remove the lower front panel and lower the adjustable legs (bolts).
4. Slide the unit forward until access is available at the back of the unit. There is a copper water line and a hose drain line. There is also an electrical line.
5. Trace the electrical line to the connector nuts and remove these. If there is a ground wire (unshielded), separate it from the dishwasher.
6. Shut off the hot water tap (gate valve) under the sink. Then disconnect the water line at the dishwasher.
7. Disconnect the hose by loosening the hose clamp.
8. Remove the dishwasher. Use caution; there is still water in the bottom of the unit.

To install the new unit, remove any shipping brackets and adjust the leveling feet to permit the unit to fit under the countertop. Then use the same steps in reverse that we used to remove the unit. Turn on the water and check for leaks before sliding the unit all the way in position. Reapply the electricity and check to see that the unit powers up. Slide the unit into final position and level it with the adjuster feet. Install the screws into the countertop and replace the lower panel. Test the unit by running it through a complete washing and drying cycle.

Ice Maker.   Since there are two basic problems that can occur and each requires a different set of tasks, we must make separate lists. The steps in removing the ice maker are listed first and then replacement of the shutoff relay. To remove and replace the ice maker:

1. Unplug the refrigerator from the wall.
2. Remove the ice tray and frozen foods from the freezer compartment.
3. Determine how the unit is fastened onto the wall of the freezer and remove the screws. If the owner's manual is available, some directions may be provided to guide the work.
4. Lift out the unit and set it aside.

To install the new unit, apply the steps in reverse. Plug in the power cord and test the unit. It should fill with water. Since it will take several hours to make the first batch of ice cubes, the owner would not expect the plumber to wait.

To remove and replace the water-control relay:

1. Unplug the refrigerator from the wall and roll it forward. All modern units have casters.
2. Turn off the cold water gate valve under the sink and open the faucet.
3. Locate the copper line feeding into the back of the unit and find the connecting nut.
4. Remove the nut and move the line away, slightly.
5. Locate the relay and remove the wires connected to it. Since electrical wires are connected, we must observe the exact color connected to each terminal on the relay. The best way is to make a drawing and label the colors of the wires. (*Note:* The diagram of the refrigerator may show where the relay is located.)
6. Disconnect the relay assembly from its mounting by removing the screws.

To install the new relay, use the same steps in reverse. Before rolling the refrigerator back against the wall, make sure that the new relay works. The water should be filling the ice tray and shutting off when it is full.

Concluding comments. An owner with a simple set of tools and some agility can remove and replace these appliances. The tests provided in the project are simple to perform. The appliances can be purchased in a wide variety of appliance centers, so one can shop for best price and quality.

Always make sure that the power has been shut off before starting any removal tasks. Make sure that the water is turned off before disconnecting pipes, and make sure that all connections are dry after reconnecting the pipes.

If the plumber installs the new unit, the time can vary from 1 hour to most of the day. The time increases when problems happen during removal tasks. But if the price for installation is fixed, how long he or she takes does not matter.

CHAPTER SUMMARY

In this chapter we have examined a wide variety of problems that have plumbing requirements. It is often best to have the plumber make such repairs. Sometimes, the owner can make them since most parts are simply connected and simple to understand.

In almost every problem there is a very real possibility of water damage to floors, baseboards, cabinets, and walls. So it is very important to shut off water to the damaged unit immediately. We must also be concerned with possible damage to such things as vitreous china items, since, like ceramic, they crack when force is applied. We must also be sure that all pipes reconnected are dry. Applying too much force can create as many leaks as not assuring enough tightness in the coupling or nut.

We also learned that safety is a major concern. By itself, electricity is dangerous and can cause serious burns or death, but when in the vicinity of water, it is more dangerous than ever. Water acts like a bare wire and conducts electricity. Caution is essential. Always be safe and shut off the power; then double check that the power is indeed off.

Safety also means that cuts, bruises, and other injuries can happen easily due to the close quarters that generally exist while making repairs and restorations. Lying cramped in the sink cabinet, reaching up to make pipe and drain connections, climbing behind the refrigerator to make repairs, and improper lifting of a heavy commode are prime examples of the circumstances that cause nonexperienced people to get hurt.

8

STAIRCASES

OBJECTIVES

To understand the construction of stairs and staircases

To recognize the various techniques used in staircase construction

To remove and replace defective stair treads and risers

To replace a stringer

To restore customized trim and molding to a staircase after making repairs to the assembly

To add carpeting to stair treads and risers

To refinish wooden stairs with stain and varnish

To restore a newel post and balustrade to their original condition

To resecure a handrail or banister

OPENING COMMENTS

Conditions or circumstances that necessitate corrective action. There are a wide variety of stairs in homes across the country. All two-story homes have at least one. Homes with basements have a set of stairs. Some of the stairs are a set of treads set on stringers. Others are elaborate, with numerous design features and much beauty. Some have landings and others do not. Some are curved and some are circular. Some are made from steel but most are made from wood. In this chapter we concern ourselves with the wooden staircase. Further, we focus our coverage on the set of stairs leading from the ground or first floor to the second floor. By doing this we incorporate all of the principles used in building and restoring less complex types.

Let's begin to define the conditions and circumstances that cause owners to take corrective action. Things that can be annoying but not catastrophic include squeaky stair treads, loose handrails or parts of the banister assembly, loose or worn carpet covering, badly worn finish, stained wood, worn tread edges, split treads, loosened riser boards, loose newel posts, and loose molding on the stairs or adjacent walls. The more serious problems that cannot be overlooked include physical damage to the banister assembly, where almost all safety is lost, a damaged or split stringer, a loosened stringer, rotted treads and risers, seriously loose handrails, torn carpet on treads, rot, and water-damaged finish.

Any single item or a combination of items from the list can be enough to require attention to the stairs to ensure the greatest safety possible. Where a home was damaged by violent storms or fire, for example, we might be faced with rebuilding the stairs or buying a new staircase.

Contractor's responsibility.   Stair building is almost an artform. To build one requires precise measurements, full use of design concepts, very experienced use of electrical and hand tools, and many years of construction experience. To restore a heavily damaged, well-designed, splendidly finished staircase definitely limits the work to those who can perform such work. All too often, the contractor resorts to replacing the stairs with new ones primarily because he or she has no one with the needed skills and knowledge to restore a severely damaged staircase.

As the contractor who makes the examination of the damaged stairs, we must first be able to recognize the design principles employed. Then while assessing the damage, we can begin to describe the fundamental problems the owner has with the stairs. On site, we can point to the various pieces that sustained damage and generally or specifically describe the actions required to restore the stairs. In Figure 8–1 we see drawings of the stair with all parts named. When the contractor says that the treads are beyond repair and must be replaced, we see that most of the time there is a bullnose on the outer or leading edge. When the contractor points out that the stringer is cracked and needs to be replaced, we see in the figure that there are usually two and sometimes three stringers. When the banister assembly is loose or some of the spindles are missing, we see that there are usually two spindles per step. These are toenailed to the tread and under the rail. The figure also shows that there are many pieces that have bevel cuts.

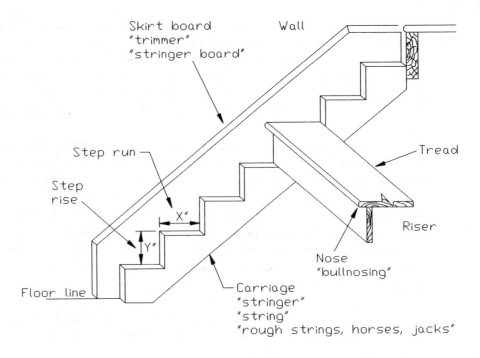

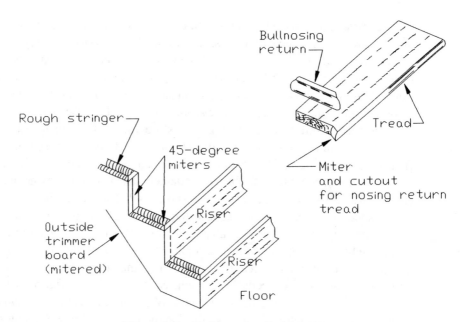

Figure 8–1 Staircase detailed drawings.

When discussing costs associated with the restoration, we make it clear that the work is classified as finish and only experienced carpenters can perform the quality of work required. These people are in demand and they frequently command higher wages. As a rule, they also work efficiently, which results in a saving in time. In addition to labor costs there are material costs. Except for the stringers, all other wood products are first-quality clear stock. This quality of wood always costs more than the construction grades. The finish applied to the stairs is usually equal to the types used on hardwood floors and is relatively expensive. All these factors must be made known to the owner in some form, whether it is an oral discussion or a written estimate.

Homeowner's expectations.   Many owners have no idea what to expect when a staircase requires restoration or replacement. Some will trust the contractor to make the proper decisions that will automatically minimize the costs incurred. Others will seek the lowest price with no regard to the services and materials that the contractor will use. Hopefully, the owner will require a detailed contract offer or bid.

The owner expects immediate restoration when catastrophic problems make the stairs unusable. But he or she may procrastinate a long time before making restoration, being willing to wait for the best workmanship.

Scope of projects.   In this chapter, one problem we are going to solve is a badly damaged staircase that requires extensive finish work. Another is refinishing the staircase with varnish or with stain and varnish. A third project is to remove and replace the carpet on the stairs.

The first project is very extensive and we will carefully discuss each aspect of the restoration. By adopting this approach, the owner and the contractor can arrive at a common understanding if only a part of the staircase requires restoration.

PROJECT 1. RESTORE A STAIRCASE BY CHANGING STRINGER, TREADS, AND RISERS, AND INSTALLING MOLDINGS AND TRIM

Subcategories include: design of staircases; components in the assembly; removing techniques for tread, riser, and stringer banister; spindles, moldings, and trim; cutting and installing a new stringer; making and installing a new riser and tread, anchoring techniques for stringers, banisters, spindles, and newel post; reinstalling moldings and trim; principles of handrail installation; various techniques of fastening the handrail to wall; types of materials used; removing and replacing the 1-in. finish board against the stringer and alongside the wall; joining baseboards properly; joining shoe moldings properly; adding cove or quarter-round to finish a joint and replacing the bullnose at the top step; and safety considerations.

Preliminary Discussion with the Owner

Problems facing the owner.   This catastrophic situation requires an extensive amount of effort by carpenters and others who will restore the staircase. The owner will not have ready access to the upstairs rooms for a period of time ranging from 1 to 3 days, except by ladder. If all the bedrooms are upstairs, the family may need to seek other lodgings, or would need to use a ladder. Any carpeting would be removed and either replaced or reinstalled. Baseboards and shoe moldings probably would be removed to gain access to the stairs. Built-in closets under the stairs will be affected when the staircase is removed or when a new stringer is spliced in place.

After all wood parts are restored, the painter or carpet people must finish the stairs. The painter will apply the finish and the carpet people would install carpet on treads and risers. (In this project, only the carpenter's tasks are described and explained.)

Alternative solutions to the problem.   Several alternatives might be used in this project. First, a new staircase can be purchased and installed. This could mean somewhat less time on the job, but how much is difficult to determine. The removal tasks are many and time consuming. The restoration of the staircase is labor intensive, but a new staircase is expensive and must be fit into the opening.

Next, the staircase can be dismantled in place if the pieces are not glued together. However, some parts of the better-built units are glued to reduce squeaking. Therefore, this would be a trial-and-error approach. If successful, the restoration time can be reduced considerably.

The owner can attempt to perform the work alone or with a friend. We know that the job is very detailed and requires high-quality work. If the owner or friend can perform the work, the first consideration for self-help is met. Next, the owner must determine if the economies of scale are in favor of this solution. Does giving up 3 or more days of wages costs less than hiring the work done? If not, the contractor would do the job.

Statement of work and the planning effort.   Due to the extent of damage in our project, we begin with the statement of work: *Restore the staircase to its original condition.* Now we add significant details: *Retain its original character and style, remove and replace all damaged wood, and where wood shows, use clear oak on the stair treads and risers and elsewhere that matches the type used previously (e.g., red, white, or black oak).* Some trim, baseboard and shoe molding will be replaced; *use miter techniques where required to make all joints accurate with-*

out use of putty. We must also address the banister or balustrade assembly. *Original parts of the old banister assembly may be used if there are sufficient quantities; if not, all new matching pieces will be used.* In addition, *all wall or other materials attached to the staircase will be reinstalled and finished to match the original style, texture, and color.*

For this planning effort, we, as contractors, would require careful consideration of all aspects during the examination. We would probably send the estimator to the job site to make the inspection, then determine the types of materials and work to be done. We would plan to provide the owner with a contract/bid price very quickly since the urgency of the job is so evident.

At the office we would begin immediately to determine who would best perform the work and recognize that an apprentice or laborer could make work go more quickly. The effect of this would be a small reduction in overall costs.

Contract.   This contract could be a fixed-price type or a time-and-materials type. If the carpenter who performs the work were well skilled for the job and we were sure of all aspects of the work, which included custom-made materials and finishes, we would present a contract/bid in fixed-price format. If, on the other hand, we have reservations about certain aspects of the job, whatever they might be, we would be more cautious and present a contract/bid in time-and-materials format. A fixed-formatted contract could appear as follows.

We agree to restore the main staircase leading from the first floor to the second floor to a style, quality, and character equal to the original. Certain qualifications must be included:

  a. Walls and floors affected by the restoration would need to be restored and are included in the cost.
  b. The finish would be the same color and durability as the old, but modern materials would be used.
  c. The materials making up the staircase with attachments would be made from the same materials as the original. This implies cabinetmaking requirements or custom-made parts for banister, spindle, newel post, and various moldings.
  d. The workmanship will be without error and all joints will be made without use of fillers. However, fillers may be used by the painters in the finish process.

We agree further to complete the job within 10 days after securing the custom-made materials. Until that time a temporary staircase arrangement will be installed to provide access to the upstairs rooms.

With acceptance of this contract, the owner agrees to provide a deposit of one-third the total cost. The balance is due upon completion of the job or in the case of the insurance settlement, consigned to this company.

The total price for materials and labor is $XXX.XX.

Material Assessment

Direct Materials	Use/Purpose
Stringers	Foundation for the staircase
Treads	Treads
Risers	Vertical members of the stairs
Assorted trim	Applied to the stairs
Assorted molding	Shoe and cove are two types
Newel post	Lower end of the banister
Banister rail	Part of the balustrade
Spindles	Two per step
Stain	To color the stairs
Paste-wood filler	Used before stain is applied
Floor finish	Clear polyurethane liquid finish
Nails, screws, and bolts	Fasteners
Glue and wedges	Used in constructing the stairs

Indirect Materials	Use/Purpose
Wedges	To align the stairs to upstairs floor
Lumber	To repair walls under the stairs
Drywall, joint compound, and tape	To cover walls
Paint	To repaint walls
Sandpaper	Sheet and disk for smoothing wood and drywall
Temporary stairs	Temporary access to upstairs

Support Materials	Use/Purpose
Ladders	Access to upstairs
Workhorses and bench	Work surface for constructing the stairs
Carpentry tools	For construction
Painting tools	For painting
Router, drill, saws, and sanders	Power tools necessary for the job
Miter box	To cut miters in trim and moldings
Drop cloths	To protect furniture and carpets

Outside Contractor Support	Use/Purpose
Cabinetmaker	To custom-make parts for the stairs
Painter	To finish the stairs

Activities Planning Chart

Activity	Time Line (Days)							
	1	2	3	4	5	6	7	8
1. Contract preparation	_×_							
2. Materials and scheduling	_×_							
3. Removing the damaged staircase		_×_						
4. Constructing the new staircase			_×_	_×_				
5. Installing the new staircase					_×_	_×_		
6. Restoring the walls							_×_	_×_
7. Finishing the new stairs	Days 9 and 10 covered in project 2							

Reconstruction

Special Note.   After the following restoration detail analysis, there are several quick-fix solutions to staircases with minor problems.

Contract preparation.   The office personnel will need to build a contract from the worksheet provided by the estimator. Having come from the job site, the estimator has the necessary information about the damaged staircase, its style, its construction characteristics, and types of materials and finish. He or she then uses the company database or hardcopy estimating manual to organize the worksheet to include the bill of materials and labor costs for the job. After this, allowances for overhead and profit are applied. This sounds very simple, but in fact, the work many be very intense and require considerable effort in locating the exact materials needed and a qualified carpenter among the company employees. The estimator must also obtain bids from each subcontractor.

The office person completes the contract/bid in the standard company form. This single document also includes the subcontractors' best estimates. With this document in hand, the contractor or estimator meets with the owner to obtain approval of the contract and determine the date that work should begin.

Materials and scheduling.   As we saw from the materials assessment, there can be a wide variety of specialized materials needed to restore the staircase. Even if the decision was to replace the entire staircase with a new one, there would still be a large number of pieces in the job.

Where custom-made parts are needed from the cabinetmaker, we would need to have the cabinetmaker obtain samples from which to make copies. Then we would need to program our carpenter's efforts based on the availability of all materials. In addition, we must also schedule the painter.

As the activity chart shows, each craftsperson requires a specific number of days to complete his or her work. Our activity chart is not an actual time-line chart since in real time there can be days of separation for various phases of the work.

Removing the damaged staircase.   Removing the staircase is like building it in reverse. We start by removing the last pieces installed and work backward until the stringers can be removed. Essentially, we remove the carpeting, if any, then the banister or balustrade assembly. In case of the carpet, we may save it or not, but we should save as much of the banister assembly as possible. Next we remove the molding, which is usually quarter-round and cove. After this we remove the top tread. Following this, we remove the wood trim. If the staircase is a glued unit, we remove it next. If the staircase is a built-up type, we remove the treads and risers from the stringers. Finally, we remove the damaged stringers.

Constructing and installing the new staircase.   Now we are sure of the parts that have to be remanufactured and all of the work required to rebuild the staircase. Let's discuss the built-up type first, then the unit type.

Built-Up Staircase.   We have removed the damaged stringer. From it we lay out and cut a new one to match. Usually, we use a 2×12 stress-rated fir or yellow pine for the lumber. Once it is cut, we install it in place of the old one. If the one against the wall was replaced, we might have to replace the trim board first, since it goes behind the stringer. Then we install the treads and risers. Where the old ones had grooves and rabbets, we must make these cuts in the new ones. The risers may be mitered with a 45-degree angle to complete the joint of the trim board applied to the outside of the stringer. To ensure a high-quality job, we would screw and plug each tread onto each stringer. This eliminates the squeak. If the bullnose returns were not installed on each tread, we can do this now.

Unit Staircase.   We would either buy a new unit staircase or rebuild the old one on site. If building it on site, we would need to remove the side that was damaged, or lay out and cut two new sides, as the case may be. This unit is almost always glued, and the treads and risers are forced into placed with wood wedges. As we can see in Figure 8–2, there is a great deal of routing to do to make the dadoes for each tread and riser. The 90-degree angle is always maintained as shown. But each dado is flared to make room for the wedge. When assembly begins, the treads and risers are glued into place, and a wedge with some glue on it is driven into the dado, forcing the piece against the other shoulder of the dado. The underside of the tread often has a groove $\frac{1}{4}$ in. deep by $\frac{3}{4}$ in. wide to house the riser's top edge. The front side of the riser can have a rabbet $\frac{1}{4}$ in. deep by $1\frac{1}{4}$ in. wide to fit against the back of the tread. The riser can be nailed into the back of the tread. We

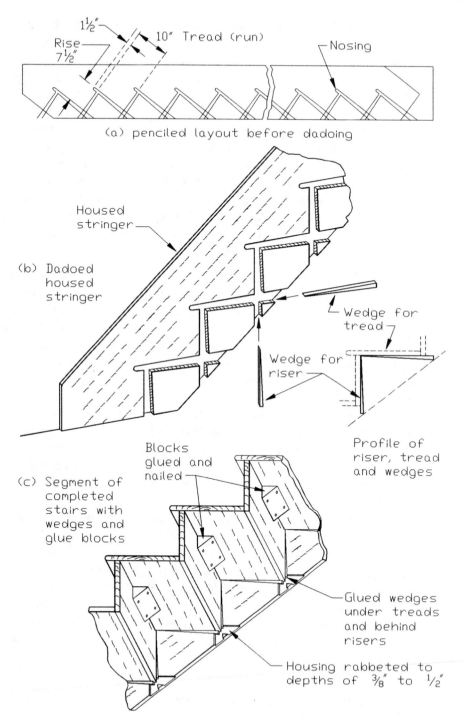

$1\frac{1}{2}''$

10″ Tread (run)

Rise $7\frac{1}{2}''$

Nosing

(a) penciled layout before dadoing

Housed stringer

(b) Dadoed housed stringer

Wedge for tread

Wedge for riser

Profile of riser, tread and wedges

Blocks glued and nailed

(c) Segment of completed stairs with wedges and glue blocks

Glued wedges under treads and behind risers

Housing rabbeted to depths of $\frac{3}{8}''$ to $\frac{1}{2}''$

Figure 8–2   Unit-type detail work.

also cut angle blocks about 3 to 4 in. long and glue these in back of the joint of the riser and tread to add a measure of rigidity. In this arrangement there is seldom a middle stringer. The outside pieces are the only stringers.

All of this work is performed on the ground or on a workbench. Only after the unit is fully complete is it brought into the house and installed. In this case the installation requires positioning the unit against the wall and adjusting its position. When located accurately, we nail it to the second-story headers and first floor. We also anchor it to wall studs. At this point we can complete the work of adding the banister assembly and moldings as well as the piece of tread.

Comment. Although either type can be used anywhere, the built-up type is used more often where one side of the staircase is open and the other side is against the wall or where both sides are open. In contrast, the unit type is used more frequently between walls. Its design minimizes the need for customized fitting and simplifies installation and finishing.

Installing the Banister Assembly and Other Trim.   Our next job is to reinstall the newel post and banister assembly. First the newel post is set in place and anchored firmly. Then the handrail is positioned and cut to fit. Most of the newer handrails have two pieces: the shaped top piece, which we use to hold on to, and the slim narrow piece, which we use to nail to the tops of the spindles. Since we are replacing the spindles either with all old ones, some new and old, or all new ones, we must use one of the old ones for sizing purposes. Actually, there are two different lengths since there are two spindles per step: a shorter length near the bullnose of the tread and a longer one farther back. We toenail these to the treads and nail through the narrow piece on the top. When all are in place firmly and accurately, we screw the handrail to the narrow board and newel post or posts.

Where the staircase is between two walls, the banister or handrail is fastened or anchored to the studs in the wall. Special stand-off metal brackets are made for the job. This handrail is set at 34 in. above the stairs.

The trim and molding are always custom fit to the staircase by the carpenter. Because of the wide variety of treatments of blending the staircase in with the baseboard and floor or closet/storage space under the stairs, we can say that an extensive knowledge of wood, mitering, and joining pieces at various custom angles is required. Several techniques are shown in Figure 8–3. By using these representations, an inexperienced carpenter can make appropriate adaptations. The owner reading and studying this figure can gain an understanding of the work involved. With this knowledge, he or she can better understand the ramifications with regard to work, time, quality, and cost.

Restoring the walls.   All too often the walls adjacent and under the staircase are damaged when the staircase receives severe damage. This problem is further aggravated when the carpenters remove the damaged unit. Drywall, for

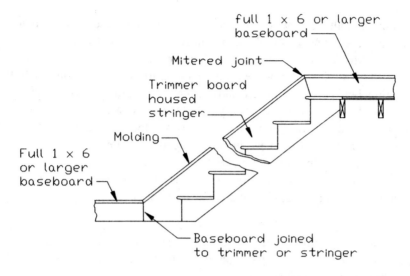

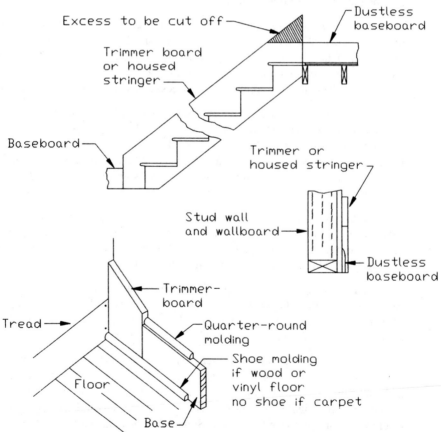

Figure 8–3 Customized fitting of moldings.

example, is almost always installed before the staircase is set in place. So if it is damaged, we expect to replace the entire sheet or sheets while the staircase is removed. All the activities studied in Chapter 1 come into play in this part of the job.

Many of the older homes and the more affluent ones today include extensive paneling between the staircase and ceiling. The paneling may be made from a wide variety of wood and molding. Plywood or wainscot may also be used. The same treatments can be used under the stairs to the floor. Sometimes built-in bookcases are site constructed. If these were damaged with the stairs, the carpenter would need cabinetmaking skills to make the restoration.

In these situations the contract we described earlier in this project would be totally inadequate. Many more details would be required.

Simple problems and corrective actions.   We stated in the beginning of this section that some simple problems can be fixed without removing and replacing the staircase. Here are a few:

1. *Loosened bullnose.*   Remove the bullnose, clean off any dirt and old glue. Predrill holes about 8 in. apart with a $\frac{3}{8}$-in. recessed drill bit. Then align the bullnose and continue the pilot hole a short way into the stair tread. Apply a thin coat of carpenter's glue to the back side of the bullnose and screw it in place. Fill the recess with wood plugs purchased from the hardware store. Trim the excess and sand smooth. Refinish the step.

2. *Squeaky stair treads.*   Locate the stringers and try to determine how the risers fit onto the treads. If there are stringers under the treads, drill two screw holes with recesses; install two screws and plug the recess. Trim off excess plug, sand, and refinish the tread. In the case of a stair whose stringers are dadoed, locate the wedges under the stairs. Either drive the wedges in tighter and nail the wedge in its new position, or add glue blocks between the riser and tread.

3. *Loose newel post.*   Inspect the post for anchoring technique used. Determine where an added lag screw can be installed. First tighten the original lag screws; sometimes the trim must be removed to gain access to the screws. Next find a solid reference such as a stringer and add a new lag screw to stiffen the post.

4. *Loosened spindle.*   Unless the spindle is split badly, the spindle can be removed carefully, glued to add new strength, and replaced. It is far better to use several 4d finish nails than one 8d finish nail. All nails must be set and the nail hole filled with wood dough. Sand and refinish the spindle.

5. *Loosened handrail or banister.*   Where brackets hold the rail in place, first determine how the rail is fastened. Generally, we remove the rail, reset or anchor the brackets, and after filling the old holes with glue and wood plugs, we reinstall the rail. In the case of a banister with spindles, we might have to reset all nails toenailed into the banister or rescrew the banister to the filler piece. Sometimes the nails holding the banister to the post work loose. First, try pulling the joint together by setting the nails a little bit more. When this fails to cure the problem, cut the old nails off with a hacksaw. Add glue to the joint and draw the post and handrail together with a bar clamp. While the glue is drying, drill a pilot hole and install a screw from the handrail into the post.

6. *Split tread or riser board.*   If the piece that is split can be removed, do so and either glue it together and replace it, or make a new one and install it. If the tread or riser cannot be removed, although there should be no situation where this exists, try to force glue into the split and apply a bar clamp. This means that a separate block of wood may need to be screwed to the tread or riser and act as an end for the bar clamp to tighten against. After the glue dries, sand the tread or riser and refinish.

Concluding comments.   Restoring the severely damaged staircase is not an easy or simple undertaking, even though one might think so from reading this project. A great deal of skill and experience as well as understanding is required to make the restoration. A great deal of expense is associated with this undertaking. Many carpenters are not qualified for the work. A contractor would assign one of the best carpenters to perform the work. The estimator would probably be schooled in the mechanics of the work and may even have performed some. He or she would make a careful detailed examination to make sure that an accurate restoration would be made.

Most homeowners could perform the six small problems identified and described ahead of this conclusion. The tasks are fairly simple and do not require a great deal of specialized tools.

PROJECT 2. RESTORE THE FINISH TO A WOOD STAIRCASE

Subcategories include: sanding machines to use; sandpaper to use; other tools to use to remove old finish; application of stain, sealers, and top coats; and application of principles to balustrades and newel posts.

Preliminary Discussion with the Owner

Problems facing the owner.   Regardless of the type of construction used to build and install the staircase, there is a time when the finish on the staircase has deteriorated and needs replacement. In this project we discuss many of the problems facing the owner whose staircase is in need of restoration.

When we, the contractors, are called by the owner to examine and determine what can be done to the staircase, we need to describe what we find and translate the findings into restoration techniques and costs. Some of the usual situations we encounter are related to abrasion, indentations, weathering, and natural aging.

Although most varnish and polyurethane finishes are hard and abrasion resistant, they do wear thin and wear out. Sand particles that are carried into the house on the soles of shoes have sharp edges, and since we always slide forward ever so slightly when climbing or descending a staircase, we grind the sand and grit into the varnish finish. Since we walk in the center of the length of each tread, the most severe abrasion occurs there. After the varnish is worn away, continued use causes the sand and grit to wear away the softer cells in the tread. Eventually, the harder cells wear away, too. In severe cases the result is a definite, measurable depression in the tread.

Abrasion also occurs on the lower part of the riser. People climbing the staircase with hard leather soles or boots will kick the riser, thus causing a small abrasion. Over time (years) the varnish wears thin and finally wears away. When black marks are made on the riser, cleansers are applied to remove them. These products invariably contain abrasives in the form of pumice. The rubbing action of the person cleaning the riser causes the varnish to wear off. The results are the same. Carried on long enough, the wood of the riser is also worn away.

Indentations also create an unsightly appearance in the staircase. The most common locations for indentations are on the handrail or banister, on the cap of the newel post, on the stem of the newel post, and on the bullnose of the treads. Sometimes there are indentations in the trim of the staircase which might have been made by carrying furniture up or down the stairs. These are difficult to deal with and sometimes are minimized by sanding or filling. In the most severe cases, pieces of the stairs are removed and replaced.

Weathering and natural aging of the varnish or polyurethane are two very common similar causes for refinishing the staircase. Although there is little possibility that rain or snow will touch the staircase, the interior climate of the home can have an effect on the finish over time. When the finishes are first applied, the chemicals in them are soft, and these harden with curing. After the curing period, the product is very stable. However, with each season the house has a different set of temperature and humidity conditions that affect the finish. The sun shining on the staircase, the dry heat in winter, the humid air in spring, summer, and fall, and the cold of winter all contribute to changing the properties of the finish either directly or in conjunction with the wood to which it is applied. The chemicals in the varnish especially, but all floor finishes as well, are subject to darkening with age. The change is very subtle but does occur. There is no stopping this action.

Also aiding the darkening process is repeated polishing. Each coat of polish on the spindles, trim, and handrail, for example, leaves a slight residue that darkens the finish ever so slightly. Granted that the polish removes fingerprint grease, food stains, and the like, and leaves a fine satin sheen, we are still adding to the darkening process. Some polishes have stain as part of their makeup. The stain darkens the dents and other mars caused by normal or abusive use, and these stains add to the overall darkening.

Some staircases are painted rather than stained and varnished. Paint ages, too, over time. It can pick up household products such as grease from the heating system, nicotine from smoke, and other airborne agents that are deposited on the staircase and cause darkening.

Alternative solutions to the problem.   There are several alternatives to the problem worth discussing, which include, at one extreme, complete restoration, and at the other, minimum treatment. Complete restoration involves stripping the old finish with chemicals or mechanically using sanding machines. This is followed by the application of new finishing materials. Minimal effort is to remove the finish partially without disturbing the wood beneath, then apply new finish.

The owner can hire a contractor to perform the work required in refinishing the staircase. The best contractor for this type of work is the floor finisher. The workers employed are trained to solve the problems listed in the opening paragraphs. They can quickly and expertly remove the old finish and apply new finish. Further, they can often do minor restoration work that can blend the new finish with the old.

Where a problem with the treads and riser boards involves damaged wood, the alternatives are very limited. The first solution is to attempt to sand the entire surface to remove the wood surrounding the damaged area to create a new flat surface. When the tread or riser can be removed, the job goes easier, but this is seldom an easy task, since the pieces are generally glued in place. The work requires using a belt and disk sander, first with coarse sandpaper, then graduating to smooth. The corners are scraped.

The second solution is to remove and replace the damaged tread and riser board. Getting the boards out can be the simpler task, since they can be cut through the center. Getting them back in may be difficult or simple depending on the type of stair construction employed. In any removal project, the spindles would be removed and replaced.

The solutions examined above apply also to the balustrade assembly, which includes the newel post, banister or handrail, and spindles.

Statement of work and the planning effort.   For this project we will plan to refurbish the entire staircase together with its trim and moldings. Our initial statement of work begins with *refurbishing the staircase between the main floor and second floor.* Now we add detail statements that include: *All wood on the staircase, trim, and moldings attached to the staircase will be stripped of old finish,* *lightened, and refinished.* One stair tread is heavily damaged, so we will *remove and replace the tread,* since its worn surface is so deep. The quality of work needs to be stated as: *All work will be of first-class quality; all finish materials will be of high-quality and capable of long wear resistance.*

The planning effort for this job begins with a decision by the owner to have a contractor perform the work. The contractor's planning begins with sending the estimator or an expert to the job site to make the initial assessments. The estimator collects facts about the extent of damage to wood pieces, extent of deterioration of the finish, overall condition of the staircase, types of woods used for staircase, trim, and moldings, and the dimensions of the staircase. With these facts, he or she can plan the work to be done and estimate the costs.

The contractor would plan to meet with the owner to discuss the costs, time requirements for performing the work, and obtain consent to proceed. Since the work will take several days, the owner's family can expect to be inconvenienced. First someone must be home while the workers are present. Next, safety must be considered when the tread is removed and a new tread is being prepared. Because of the dust generated by sanding, care must be taken to cover furniture and pictures on walls and the like. Then for a period of one day, no one will be able to use the staircase because the new finish must set and begin curing. Finally, the contractor must use a cleaning service to vacuum and dust the house to free it from sawdust that escaped the collection bags on the sanders.

Contract.   For this job we can use a fixed-price contract. There are no hidden factors that could cause added work or costs. This decision is best for the owner and also sets the terms for the contractor. The body of the contract needs to stipulate all of the statements of work as well as some of the planning items.

For the price stipulated below, we agree to refurbish the staircase. The damaged tread will be removed and a new one installed. All old finish will be removed, lightened, sealers applied, and a clear wear-resistant finish applied.

Protective cloths will be used to cover furniture and personal objects that cannot be moved into other rooms. Upon finishing the job, a cleaning service will vacuum and dust the house.

The owner agrees to have a family member or other person of his or her choice on the premises while workers are present. The owner also agrees to participate in safety practices by using caution when workers are repairing the steps and doing other work. He or she also agrees to refrain from using the staircase for 12 hours after the top coat is applied to the staircase.

Total materials and labor: $XXX.XX

Payment in full is expected when the final inspection is made.

Material Assessment

Direct Materials	Use/Purpose
Tread	Oak or pine as required
Riser	Oak or pine as required
Sealer	To seal raw wood cells
Floor finish	Polyurethane/varnish
Glue, screws, nails	To install new wood pieces
Wood dough or filler paste	To fill holes and the like
Cleaning agents	Mineral spirits, etc.

Indirect Materials	Use/Purpose
Sandpaper	Sheet sandpaper (60, 80, 100 grit)
Sanding belts	Cloth belts (60, 80, 100 grit)
Disk sander pads	Circular disks (60, 80, 100 grit)
Liquid paint/varnish remover	To chemically remove old finish
Scraper blades	Expendable blades for hand scrapers
Masking tape	To attach protective covering to adjacent walls
Plastic sheets	To protect walls and rugs
Steel wool	To polish the top dressing

Support Materials	Use/Purpose
Floor finisher's tools	For construction
Carpentry tools	For construction
Power saw, belt sander, disk sander, palm sander	To simplify the work
Paint brushes	To apply stripping agent and new finish
Drop cloths	To cover the furniture and personal articles

Outside Contractor Support	Use/Purpose
None	

Activities Planning Chart

Activity	Time Line (Days)						
	1	2	3	4	5	6	7
1. Contract preparation	_×_						
2. Materials and scheduling	_×_						
3. Repairing the staircase		_×_					
4. Removing the old staircase finish		_×_	_×_				
5. Applying the sealant and finish			_×_	_×_			

Reconstruction

Contract preparation.   Compared with the contract preparation of the first project in this chapter, this one is much simpler. The estimator makes out the job analysis worksheet, which includes pricing the labor and materials, adding allowances for overhead and profit, and logs the job into the database. The other office personnel prepare the contract in standard form and add the pricing from the worksheet. After a review by the office manager or contractor, the contract is presented.

Materials and scheduling.   The materials list for this job is quite extensive considering that the major items are the wood replacement pieces and finish materials. However, we can readily understand the need for all the other items. All the items are available locally, so there should be no delay in completing work after the contract is signed.

The office manager or contractor would set the dates for work with the owner. This effort is an agreement that satisfies the owner and one that permits the contractor to have a qualified worker or workers available. We see that the project is scheduled for 3 days at the owner's home.

Repairing the staircase.   To remove and replace the damaged tread and riser, we must first remove the spindles attached to the thread. The problem with this job is that each spindle is subject to splitting where the toenails are driven through the lower part of the spindle. One very possible way to avoid the splitting problem is to lift the spindle slightly with a wood chisel and then cut the nails with a hacksaw. We can then pull the spindle free from the piece under the handrail.

Next we must remove all moldings attached under the bullnose and at the rear of the tread, if any. Most of the time these pieces can be taken off without splitting; however, it is best if we have new stock for replacement.

The details in Figure 8–4 show that we remove the damaged tread and riser in one of two ways. If there are wedges under the staircase, we drive or chisel these out, crack the tread and riser free and slid them out. If the tread and riser are screwed to the stringers, we remove the plugs with a wood chisel, remove the screws, and pop out the tread and riser. If neither of these two processes works well, we can always cut through the tread and riser with a power jigsaw and finish the cut with a handsaw. Then we pry out the four pieces.

Before we can install the new pieces, we must cut them to fit. In this case each one is custom-made from clear stock of matching wood: red or white oak, for instance. We must add a bullnose to the tread with glue and using screws placed as in the old one. If the riser has a miter on one edge, we would need to make it fit onto the stringer trim board. Then we can sand them smooth and install them using the

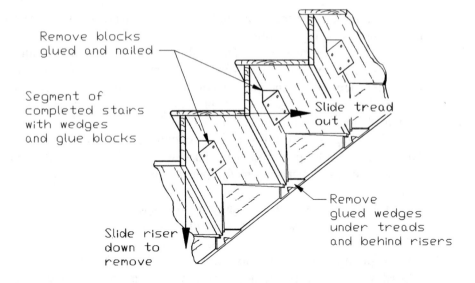

Remove blocks
glued and nailed

Segment of
completed stairs
with wedges
and glue blocks

Slide tread
out

Remove
glued wedges
under treads
and behind risers

Slide riser
down to
remove

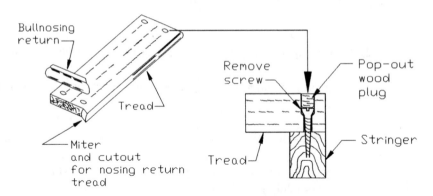

Bullnosing
return

Remove
screw

Pop-out
wood
plug

Tread

Miter
and cutout
for nosing return
tread

Tread

Stringer

Figure 8–4   Removing and replacing the damaged tread and riser.

same techniques as used in the original design. If there was quarter-round molding
on the tread under the bullnose, we would either replace the old molding or cut new
molding and fit it properly. To finish the carpentry work, we set the nails and fill
the holes with wood putty or wood dough.

   Removing the old staircase finish.   The removal of old finish materials is
difficult, time consuming, and involves the use of chemicals that can be toxic.
Proper ventilation and plenty of it is essential for safe breathing. Since the chemicals are strong enough to burn into the finish, we need to wear gloves to protect our

skin. We must also cover all floor and wall surfaces to prevent staining or otherwise damaging their finish or fabric.

There are two schools of thought about removing the finish with chemicals. One, start at the top and work downward. This method allows materials removed to fall on the steps below and be scraped away. Using the second, starting from the bottom, the cleaned wood must be kept clean and the worker must kneel or walk on chemically treated surfaces that have not dried.

If sanding is used in lieu of or in conjunction with chemicals, we first use 60-grit paper in the power sanders. Then we use the 80-grit paper, and finally, the 100-smooth-grit paper. In many spots we use hand scrapers and sandpaper by hand.

The removal part of the total job is complete when all the finish has been removed and the staircase wood is free of finish.

Applying the sealant and finish.   The finishing operation can be done in several ways to provide a high-quality, long-lasting durable surface. Some owners prefer high gloss, others prefer a satin finish. Each requires different materials and applications. Common tasks include:

1. Fine sanding.
2. Application of sealer. This may be a clear sealer or one that contains a small amount of stain.
3. A light sanding after the sealer dries to remove the burrs and wood grain that has risen.

For a high-gloss finish:

1. Apply the first of two coats of high-gloss polyurethane. After the coat dries, the entire surface is lightly sanded.
2. Apply the final coat.
3. After a curing period as specified by the manufacturer of the finish, a good polishing is applied.

For a satin finish:

1. Apply a satin-finish polyurethane. After this coat dries, sand lightly with 100-grit paper.
2. Apply the second coat of polyurethane.
3. Hand rub with steel wool to an overall sheen.
4. Polish with furniture polish. (*Caution:* Polish should be used very sparingly on tread surfaces. All other surfaces can take more polish.)

In most cases the manufacturer supplies the instructions with the materials to finish the wood. This information also details the approximate square feet of coverage per gallon. The individual coats must be applied thinly (about 1 to 1.5 mils thick) to cover best and prevent runs. Cleanup of the brushes and spills should be done with the appropriate agent. Most polyurethane and all varnishes require mineral spirits for cleanup.

If the staircase is to be darkened, stain must be applied. There are two ways to do this. A wiping stain of the appropriate color can be applied with a brush or rag, permitted to soak in for a few minutes, and then wiped off. When this is the technique used, a drying time of about a day is required before the clear coats can be applied. Sometimes, though, stain is mixed with the clear coat at the factory. This produces a fixed color. It is also uniform, and many find that the grain is slightly obscured. For this reason, separate application of wiping stain and top finish are frequently preferred.

Concluding comments.   The homeowner who has some skill with carpentry tools can make the repairs indicated in this project if time and patience are used. The stripping and finishing tasks are well within the capabilities of most owners. However, the time it takes to perform the various stages of the job may be more costly than having a contractor perform the work.

The work is all finish type, so mistakes are not permitted. Caution must be used to remove the spindles to preserve them for reuse, for example. Sanding operations with power types can create gouges and sanding marks that are almost impossible to remove if the machines are used improperly. This could further damage the staircase and add to the overall cost.

PROJECT 3. RECARPET TREADS AND RISERS

Subcategories include: types of carpets used—advantages and disadvantages; installation techniques; components used in the installation; and quality standards to meet.

Preliminary Discussion with the Owner

Problems facing the owner.   Over time carpets wear thin and wear out. They are also abused by food spills, tracked-in dirt and grease, and the like. We also know that the sun striking the carpet alters its color. Sometimes the anchoring techniques used to hold the carpet in place give way and the area becomes loose and unsafe. In other installations, a bar is fastened across the back of the tread to keep the rug tight.

The owner can quite easily remove the carpet from the staircase. When safety is involved, this immediate solution is best. After the carpet has been removed, the carpet tacks and tack strips can be removed. The owner can also pull free carpets glued or cemented in place, but much more effort is required.

Another problem facing the owner is matching the replacement carpet with the type and color of carpet now at the base of the staircase or on the staircase. Carpets are manufactured in dye lots. Even though the dyes are controlled, there is almost always a slight variation between lots. Couple this with the time difference in years and the differences in manufacturing processes and materials used, and it is clear that a match is almost impossible.

The choices of carpeting are many; the styles, textures, colors, materials used, dimensions, twists, backing, and subbacking are many as well. Let's identify just some of the more popular kinds.

Most carpet consists of pile yarns and backing yarns. The pile yarns are principally tufted, woven, and knitted and are the wearing surface. The pile yarns also identify the carpet and include wool, nylon, acrylics, polyester, and polypropylene. The backing yarns hold the pile in place and include jute, cotton, and polypropylene or acrylic. The jute and cotton cannot be used in or around damp areas, whereas the polypropylene and acrylic types can stand dampness.

For our purposes, several comparative factors may be important in identifying carpet quality. Pile density, which is a combination of pile thickness and weight, is an important characteristic. It forms the weight of the carpet. Other factors of importance are the number of tufts per square inch: the closer the tufts, the more dense the carpet. In summary, the yarn size or weight, the number of piles to strands twisted together, and the number of tuffs per square inch are measures of quality.

1. Wool carpet provides good resistance to abrasion, hence would be a good selection for staircase use.
2. Nylon, the most used carpet, has excellent resistance to abrasion and high fiber strength (resistance to tear).
3. Acrylic carpets have the durability of wool and its appearance as well. They have good abrasion resistance.
4. Polypropylene (olefin) carpet has a very low moisture absorbency rate, which makes it suitable for damp areas. It also has good abrasion resistance.

Other factors to consider in making the selection for carpet replacement include resistance to alkali and acids, insects and fungus, and burns and melting points; appearance retention; recovery from compression; crush resistance; and ease of maintenance. Since each of these is an important factor in carpet selection, the wise owner or contractor will look for the quality items first before judging the price.

Alternative solutions to the problem.   The first alternative to the problem is to eliminate the carpet from the stairs. The treads can be sanded and varnished. Holes from tack strips and other anchoring devices would be filled and sanded prior to varnishing.

The next alternative is for the owner to perform removal and replacement himself or herself. If the carpet is a strip that does not reach the full width of the tread, the project is less difficult. If the carpet can be cemented in place, the job is not difficult. But if the carpet must be lapped over the bullnose and ends of the treads and cut around the spindles, the job becomes increasingly difficult. As the installation techniques grows in complexity, the time for installation increases and the tasks and materials differ.

The final alternative is to have the work done by a carpet contractor. The contractor, who may be a carpet outlet merchant, would have a salesperson make the inspection and provide advice about the exact replacement style.

Statement of work and the planning effort.   For this project we will have the carpet installed to cover the entire tread and riser. Our primary statement of work is to declare that *the carpet will be of the style and quality selected by the owner.* Further, *the carpet must be laid to cover the entire staircase's treads and risers and be installed over the bullnose on the ends of the treads that are exposed to view.* To extend the life of the carpet, *we need to install a $\frac{1}{4}$ in. pad under the carpet on the tread surface. Glue or carpet tacks will be used to fasten the carpet over the bullnosed ends of the treads.*

The planning effort requires that the owner selecting the carpet, negotiating the price of the contact and agreeing to a date for installation. The contractor must provide a salesperson to represent the company, work with the owner to make the carpet selections, and price the job. Then he or she must obtain the carpet and padding, schedule the workers for installation, inspect the completed job, and secure payment. The workers must bring the tools and carpet to the job, remove the old carpet, and install the new carpet.

Contract.   For this work a standard fixed-price contract is suitable. The carpet store or outlet usually has invoice/contract forms already prepared with space for all the requirements for a legal contract. The company name and address are included. The guarantee is usually a limited variety and printed on the form. The salesperson completes the remainder of the form using either handwritten or type-written details. In many companies today, the data are entered into a computer and the contract form is printed out in multiple copies.

Material Assessment

Direct Materials	Use/Purpose
Carpet	Replacement for damaged carpet
Pad	$\frac{1}{4}$-in. foam
Carpet tack strips	To secure the carpet to the treads
Carpet tacks	To fasten the carpet ends
Carpet glue	To hold the carpet in place

Indirect Materials	Use/Purpose
Blades	Throwaway blades used to cut carpet

Support Materials	Use/Purpose
Carpet layer's tools	For construction
Carpet stretcher	To tighten the carpet

Outside Contractor Support	Use/Purpose
None	

Activities Planning Chart

Activity	Time Line (Days)						
	1	2	3	4	5	6	7
1. Contract preparation	_×_						
2. Materials and scheduling	_×_						
3. Removing and replacing the carpet		_×_					

Reconstruction

Contract preparation.   The office personnel obtained the specification for the job from the salesperson. They log the job and place the order for the carpet or make arrangements to have stock taken from warehouse inventory. This is the worksheet part of the contract preparation of the contract. The office personnel verify the estimate the salesperson provided to the customer and make adjustments accordingly. They authorize the job and approve the sales contract.

Materials and scheduling.   The length of the job could be 2 days, as indicated in the chart above. However, there is usually a gap in days, for several reasons. Selecting the carpet is not a simple task for the owner. Even when the salesperson is expert, the task can take several days. Swatches are selected, brought to the home, and placed against the surrounding carpet for match. Once a selection is made, the order is placed. The time for acquiring the required amount can range from an hour to several weeks.

The scheduling of the installation cannot be made until a delivery date for the carpet is firmly established. Once this date is firm, the job is logged in for completion. As soon as skilled workers are available, a date is provided to the owner. He or she may agree to the date, or in case of conflict, suggest an alternative date. In the end, a date for installation is agreed to.

Removing and replacing the carpet. The carpet installers first remove the old carpet by cutting it at various places to simplify removal. If the old carpet was tacked in place, the tacks would be removed. If it was glued in place, the work takes longer since the carpet must be scraped free. If tack strips were used, the carpet is pulled away from these. In any event, an hour to several hours are employed in the removal process.

The installation process is more time consuming. The tasks include:

1. Measuring the carpet and cutting the piece or pieces to approximate size
2. Preparing the treads with tack strips (or gluing if that were selected)
3. Cutting pad to fit
4. Installing the carpet from bottom to top
5. Finishing off the stair tread ends and around the spindles
6. Cleanup

Concluding comments. Installing carpeting on a staircase is not a simple job. There are many problems to deal with: removing the old carpet, preparing the treads and risers for the new carpet, selecting the method of installation, and making the finished project professional looking.

Owners can do the work if they have some skill in carpet installation. The work is tedious; many cuts are required to fit the carpet around spindles and over the end bullnose. However, in staircases without exposed ends of treads and rises, the job is quite simple.

Contractor personnel are usually very helpful in obtaining the exact replacement carpet and performing a high-quality installation. They are usually efficient and rarely make a mess.

CHAPTER SUMMARY

The need to restore the staircase in a home is primary when it has been damaged by storm, fire, rot, or infestation. Lesser problems can be postponed if necessary without affecting safety or appearance.

When restoration work is required on a staircase, skilled workers must perform the work. There is no alternative, since safety is crucial. Even the task of removing squeaks from a staircase requires considerable understanding of stair construction.

From the descriptions provided in this chapter, we can visualize the complexity of a staircase. The stringers must provide support for the treads and risers and the traffic it bears, for example. Fortunately, in a restoration effort, we do not have to design the staircase, but merely copy the design. This simplifies the work considerably.

Finishing a staircase requires the use of good-quality materials and considerable attention to detail. Preparation for the finish must be complete and performed with considerable attention to detail. Transparent finishes do not hide anything. They do not fill in anything either. Therefore, fillers, sanding to remove old blemishes and stains, and the like are critical preliminary steps to applying the clear finish. Then the final task of rubbing the surfaces with steel wool or pumice to a polished, smooth surface competed the job.

Where the staircase is carpeted, the restoration is usually a replacement. New materials are bought and installed. The job may be simple or complex, depending on the design of the staircase and method of installation selected. Sometimes the owner can do the work; sometimes it is best to have the work done.

Although the restoration of a staircase appears to be simple, there are many specialty tasks involved. These require years of practice to obtain the necessary degree of skill. Since none of these are easy to learn, the owner should use sound judgment in approaching restoration work.

9

WOOD CABINETS
AND COUNTERS

OBJECTIVES

To understand the principles of wood cabinet construction

To understand how countertops are built and installed

To restore the finish to wood cabinets

To renovate cabinet interiors

To add shelving while restoring cabinets

To rehang poorly fitted doors

To replace the catches that keep doors closed

To replace worn-out runners and guides

To replace or cover over the damaged side of a cabinet bottom

To replace hardware: hinges and handles or pulls

To repair ceramic countertops

To remove and replace a countertop with a new one

To clean and regrout ceramic tile counters and back-splashes

To refurbish a back-splash

OPENING COMMENTS

Conditions or circumstances that necessitate corrective action. Wood cabinets are located primarily in kitchens, bathrooms, libraries, and dens. Cabinets will sometimes be built in as a permanent structure in a house. In this chapter we focus on the problems that owners have with wood cabinets and solutions that will restore the cabinets.

If we count the objectives, we quickly identify 15 conditions that can develop in a home. Some of the simpler problems, such as a loose hinge, may appear to be major but can usually be solved with a simple, effective solution. Problems that involve a damaged finish require much more labor and material to restore.

Due to the gradual deterioration of cabinets, owners seldom take notice of any change and tend to ignore it. However, there is a point where we can no longer ignore the condition, and we must take action. Some of these conditions include doors that refuse to stay closed or to close at all, broken hinges, loose or missing handles, broken tracks of drawers and roll-out shelves, damaged finish inside and outside a cabinet, damaged countertops and back-splashes, missing ceramic tiles from counters and back-splashes, and the like.

Contractor's responsibility. When we, as contractors, are called by an owner to help solve a problem, we usually find a condition that has not only been damaged over time or by a physical impact, but we also have to deal with the owner's attempts to solve the problem. In extreme cases we may find that nails were used rather than screws, or that unsuccessful attempts have been made to remove finishes or to apply new finishes. Many owners have had experiences trying to get assistance with repairs and have not succeeded, or believe that no contractor will take on a small job.

In part the owner is correct. A small job is cost prohibitive from the owner's viewpoint. However, if the job is allowed to deteriorate further, the costs of restoration increase regardless of the length of the job. As contractors, we have an obligation to support the owner in his or her need for skilled work, and we must be able to respond to small jobs and charge a fair and reasonable price for the work.

When we assess a restoration project we need to provide the owner with clear explanations of the various solutions. For example, damaged finishes on a cabinet surface can be refinished in more than one way. We might opt for partial stripping and refinishing, or for complete stripping and refinishing. We might also suggest, after close examination, that the owner select a painted finish rather than a clear coat finish because the original finish was a laminated-painted pattern over a sub-surface wood that lacks good-quality graining. If the outer surface of the cabinet is severely scarred or even slightly scorched, we might even need to suggest laminating a thin plastic material that has a wood grain pattern. Finally, we might need to recommend removing and replacing the damaged cabinet as being the most cost-effective method of restoration.

When we must advise the owner about restoration of countertops, our responsibility requires that we provide enough detail to satisfy the owner. If the countertop is laminated with plastic, a new one could be installed over it. But when the countertop is covered with ceramic or other specialized materials, our recommendation will vary from making repairs to total replacement.

Homeowner's expectations.   On a simple repair job, the owner expects a quick fix with little explanation at a very modest cost. However, this seldom happens, since the owner will usually attempt to make all simple repairs. Therefore, we can expect the owner to show us a problem that requires a skilled solution, and he or she is somewhat prepared to expect a hefty bill for services. All cabinet restoration work is classified as finish type. This means that skilled, knowledgeable workers must be used to do the restoration. These people include highly skilled carpenters, cabinetmakers, tile setters, countertop specialists, and painters. The hourly rates for these workers varies from locale to locale but are somewhat higher than those of general carpenters and other construction workers. The owner needs to equate the quality of work required with the cost of restoration: the better the quality, the more costly the project.

Scope of projects.   We can reduce problems with cabinets and built-ins to six major areas: cabinet doors, interiors of cabinets, ceramic and other types of countertops, refinishing the exterior of the cabinets, and restoration of physical damage to panels and shelves of cabinets.

PROJECT 1. REFIT AND HANG CABINET DOORS AND THEIR HARDWARE

Subcategories include: repairing screw holes that have worn out; adjusting the position of a door; removing hardware, cleaning, and replacing; replacing cabinet catches; and replacing damaged or worn-out self-closing hinges.

Preliminary Discussion with the Owner

Problems facing the owner.   Most kitchens and bathrooms have quite a few cabinet doors. Some are on base units, others are on floor-to-ceiling units, and the rest are on wall cabinets. They all have hinges and pulls of some sort, and many have cabinet catches that hold the doors closed. These mechanical parts wear out and frequently work loose. Some hinges freeze up and do not function. Handles and knobs are stripped by overtightening, and cabinet catches cease to function.

When screws work loose, we cannot use a larger or longer screw to hold the hinge in place, but many owners try this as a cure. When a door sags, slamming it shut damages the frame and door but does not cure the problem. Something happened to make the door sag, and we must find the cause.

Hardware is made to add character and style to a cabinet. The hardware's finish may be painted or applied to resemble antique or early American styles and colors, or might be bright brass, for example. Over time the finish dulls, tarnishes, erodes, or peels. The owner may try to clean and restore the hardware, but all too often he or she actually ruins the applied finish and exposes the base metal. When he or she does this, the alternatives are to paint or to replace.

Doors made from pieces are called frame and panel doors even if they have glass in place of raised panels. Over time the glue bond fails and the door either parts or sags. Most of the time the door can be salvaged. However, the work requires skill and understanding.

Alternative solutions to the problem.   The owner can make some repairs, such as replacing a broken hinge or replacing a knob or pull. But when the door must be retrofit and rehung, the work is much more demanding and a skilled person such as a cabinetmaker should do the work. Similarly, when a magnetic catch fails, the owner can replace it, but when a door binds or otherwise hits the frame improperly, no catch can hold it closed. The carpenter or cabinetmaker has the skills to refit the door so that the catch can function correctly.

If the entire kitchen is to be retrofit, the contractor will set up an area to work that expedites removing the doors, cleaning them and the hardware, preparing them for refinish, making repairs to panels and frames, and the like. He or she, if required, would know what sources are available to replace old, worn-out hardware. This could be simpler for the contractor to do than the owner, because the contractor will know where to find the hardware.

Statement of work and the planning effort.   Bathrooms and dens usually have fewer wood cabinet doors than kitchens do. Most kitchens have more than a dozen doors on base, wall, and floor-to-ceiling cabinets. So we shall use as our project restoration of **16** kitchen cabinet doors. Our first statement of work is: *Remove the cabinet doors and after making repairs to them, refit and hang them.* We also need to include the requirement to *replace all damaged hinges, handles, and catches if self-closing hinges are not used.* We need to state several facts about the quality of work: *We will ensure that the doors fit accurately and are in alignment, that all hardware is aligned properly, and that all doors remain shut when closed.*

We need to plan to set up a workstation in a carport or similar area to increase the efficiency of the job. We need to make an appraisal of the conditions of the doors and hardware to determine what replacement parts to bring and what kinds of special tools, such as clamps, we might need. Since we will be cleaning the doors during the retrofit, we require cleaning agents, sandpaper, and other supplies. We can use mass production techniques during the work by removing all doors at one time, all hardware at one time, and the like.

We must select a highly qualified carpenter or cabinetmaker to perform the work. One will need to be selected from our workforce or subcontracted.

The contract must be prepared and an estimate presented to the owner.

Contract.   We have already identified quite a few variables to deal with in this project; however, fortunately, we can reduce the work per door and per pair of doors to a manageable time frame for each. Then we can multiply the number of doors times the average time for retrofit and add time for the special things that must be done, such as regluing doors, or deep cleaning in paneled doors, to arrive at the total worker-hours for the job. In addition, we can determine what, if any, replacement hardware we need and where to obtain it. If the hardware is modern, its replacement is almost assured; however, if it is very old and not re-placeable, we would need to have the owner select an alternative style. Based on these relatively simple conditions, we can usually offer a fixed-price contract. There may need to be one clause that is price driven, where the owner selects new hardware.

The body of the contract would include the following items:

Remove, clean, and rehang all doors.

Ensure accurate fit and alignment.

Ensure that all doors latch correctly if non-spring-loaded hinges are used.

Replace hardware if old hardware is broken or damaged; owner will pick out new hardware.

Total cost for materials and labor except for new hardware: $XXX.XX.

Material Assessment

Direct Materials	Use/Purpose
Cleaning agents	To degrease and remove smoke and other agents from doors
Hardware	Replacement hinges, catches, pulls
Wood plugs/fillers	To drive into holes before reinstalling screws

Indirect Materials	Use/Purpose
Glue	To reglue door parts
Paste wood filler	To fill scratches, and gouges, as well as broken door edges
Sandpaper, steel wool	To clean and smooth door edges and surfaces

Support Materials	Use/Purpose
Carpentry tools	For construction
Bar clamps	To reclamp panel doors
Workbench	Work surface
Pails and rags	Cleaning supplies

Outside Contractor Support	Use/Purpose
Cabinetmaker (optional)	Will perform the work if a qualified carpenter is unavailable

Activities Planning Chart

Activity	Time Line (Days)
	1 2 3 4 5 6 7
1. Contract preparation	I _×_ I ___ I ___ I ___ I ___ I ___ I ___ I
2. Materials and scheduling	I _×_ I ___ I ___ I ___ I ___ I ___ I ___ I
3. Retrofitting the cabinet doors	I ___ I _×_ I _×_ I ___ I ___ I ___ I ___ I

Reconstruction

Contract preparation.   The office personnel will prepare a worksheet for the job. The estimate of time for retrofitting each door is determined by empirical information coupled with the type of cabinet door and the level of restoration required. In the event that the office has no data, the carpenter, cabinetmaker, or contractor must make a calculated judgment that includes travel time, time to pick up materials, time on each door or pair of doors, and the like. With these data, he or she can prepare the contract forms. Along with contract preparation, the job is logged into the ledgers.

Materials and scheduling.   Due to the nature of the job, few specialty materials are needed. Those listed in the materials assessment are readily available. Regarding sandpaper, we would bring 100 grit and 120 grit to the job. We would also bring number 00 or 000 steel wool. Both of these products would speed up the cleaning operation. The use of sandpaper would also be appropriate for the final shaping of the filled-in hole or would be built up of plastic wood or wood dough.

From the activity list, we see that the job is expected to take 2 days at the owner's home to retrofit the 16 doors.

Retrofitting the cabinet doors.   The tasks we must accomplish are these:

1. Examine each door before removing it for fit, problems, and overall condition.
2. Number each door as it is taken off the cabinet. We number the upper doors on top with a wood chisel or awl, beginning on the left and counting clockwise. We number the base cabinet doors on the bottom edge, also in a clockwise direction.
3. Add a special mark to pairs of doors.
4. Strip all hardware from the doors and catches from the cabinets.
5. Soak hardware in a strong detergent, rubbing the pieces occasionally.
6. Clean the door surfaces and edges with detergent and steel wool. Dry.
7. Examine the door and make repairs using wood plugs and filler; sand smooth.
8. Rebuild damaged edges of doors.
9. Examine stiles and other frame parts on the cabinets.
10. Plug screw holes as needed to provide a more solid base for screws.
11. Reinstall old hardware or install new hardware in the same place on each door.
12. For each door as shown in Figure 9–1:
    a. Place the door in position, check for clearance, raise it up until it just touches the top of the frame, lower it slightly, and install a screw in the top hinge.
    b. Check for alignment and install a screw in the bottom hinge.
    c. Check for swing. No part of the door should touch any part of the frame except for the door's lip. On doors hung with mortise hinges or surface mount hinges, maintain proper clearance.

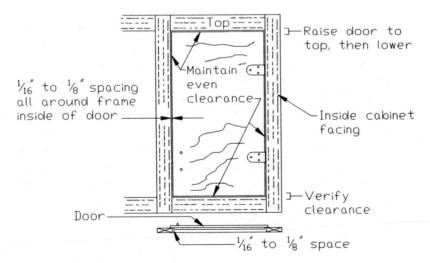

Figure 9–1   Fitting cabinet doors to their openings.

d. Install the remaining two screws and recheck for proper door operation.

e. For pairs of doors, ensure that the gap between doors is even at about $\frac{1}{8}$ in., top to bottom.

13. Install the pull using the old holes.

14. Install a new catch on the door and frame (none required if the hinges are self-closing).

15. Inspection: verify that the following are accurate and proper:

a. Doors are in alignment with stiles.

b. Doors are in alignment across the top from door to door.

c. Parallel doors are gapped at $\frac{1}{8}$ in. between doors and the same edges are in alignment top to bottom.

Concluding comments.   The job of restoring proper operation of cabinet doors is classified as finish work. Granted that door removal is simple and that almost anyone could do it. Most owners can also scrub the doors clean of cooking oils and household smoke, but only people with cabinetmaking experience should perform the work of installing and aligning doors.

PROJECT 2. REFURBISH THE INTERIOR OF CABINETS

Subcategories include: adding new shelves; replacing the drawer and roll-out guides; regluing the drawers; and replacing rotating corner unit hardware.

Preliminary Discussion with the Owner

Problems facing the owner.   It may seem strange to consider refurbishing the interior of cabinets but quite a few things do go wrong. Owners frequently have drawers that work poorly. Sometimes the track works loose or the wheel assembly at the rear of the drawer works loose. When this happens, the drawer falls down when pulled out. Or it travels badly and must be shifted or slammed to get it to shut. All too often the drawer front cracks loose from the rest of the drawer. This happens more often when a wood drawer front is screwed to a plastic drawer unit. Screwing it back on with larger screws is not the correct solution. Drawer sides frequently come apart and the bottom falls out, rendering the drawer useless.

Roll-out shelves are guided on tracks that telescope in and out. These generally operate for years without error. But sometimes the bearings in the wheels freeze or guides break off and the guide fails. Most of the time the drawer or shelf can be reused with a new pair of guides.

When silverware is dried, it is usually tossed lightly into a compartment in a drawer. Over time the tongs of the fork and the end of the knife damage the wood at the rear of the drawer and even slide between the drawer back and the drawer bottom. Major drawer repair is required to replace these parts.

Rotating shelves in corner cabinets are installed before the cabinet top is installed. They operate on the same principle as that of a rotisserie. There is a metal base on which the cabinet is fastened. Frequently, there is a metal assembly on top of the shelves that steadies them. The doors are fastened to the shelves permanently and form a right angle so that when they are in the rest position, one surface is even with the face of cabinets on two different sides. In fact, a corner is formed by the doors. Over time the mechanisms wear out and the unit ceases to function properly. This is a difficult problem to solve and may require removing the countertop.

Shelves are either fixed in place or adjustable. The fixed shelves are usually set into dado joints, as shown in Figure 9–2. These seldom require replacement except when physical damage or fire damage occurs. More often, adjustable shelves give us problems. These shelves are held up with small brackets. Some are metal and others are plastic. There are holes drilled in the sides of the cabinet where the shelf supports are plugged into. Plastic supports shear off and the shelf falls. Metal ones are made from two pieces and the joint works loose over time. The holes also wear out, especially if they were too large to begin with.

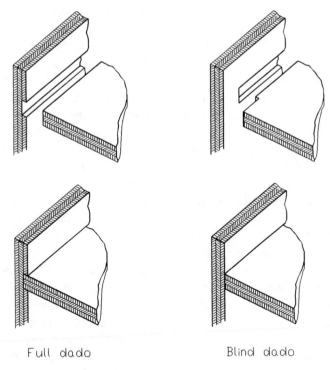

Full dado   Blind dado

Figure 9–2   Dado joint for shelving.

Finally, the insides of cabinets can be stained, accumulate dirt, and generally deteriorate. We can solve this problem in several ways.

Alternative solutions to the problem. First, the owner can make all necessary repairs himself or herself or with the aid of a friend who has the necessary skills. Or the owner can hire a contractor to perform the work.

Owners who decide to make the repairs themselves will require carpentry tools and bar clamps and may also require machines to make new parts for drawers and shelves. Plumbing may also need to be disconnected to remove the countertop to get to interior parts of the base cabinets. These are not things done easily when owners have little skill or knowledge of cabinetmaking.

The owner who opts for a contractor must be assured that the contractor has the skills, or that his or her workers have the skills, to make the repairs. We can do this by requesting references and placing several phone calls. If the contractor has the capability to do the work, he or she should be able to explain the types of repairs that he or she expects to perform. Thus owners can gain a sense of the difficulties that need to be overcome so that they can assess the fairness of the contract.

With regard to the practical parts of the job, let's say that there are eight drawers, four roll-out shelves, and several adjustable shelves that are to be retrofitted. We could have new drawers made and new hardware used to install them, or we can have the old ones repaired. We can have new roll-out shelves made, or we can have the old ones repaired and new hardware installed. Where shelf supports have sheared off, we can simply replace them with new ones, but if the support hole is damaged, we can either lower or raise the shelf by drilling new holes, or we can fill in the hole and after the glue dries, drill a new hole in the same place. If the supports had vertical metal pieces embedded into the inner walls of the cabinet and these became loose or damaged by storms, for example, we would need to replace them. If the new ones were slightly different, we would need to modify the dadoes and then install them.

Statement of work and the planning effort. We know, from the previous paragraph, that we must retrofit eight drawers, four roll-out shelves, and several adjustable shelves. This is our project study and reference. Our statement of work begins: *Perform the cabinetmaking work consistent with restoring the drawers, roll-out shelves, and adjustable shelves to make them functional and operational.* For our project, we need more specifications, such as: *Remove and replace damaged wood products, metal guides and tracks, and supports as required; make repairs to drawers, roll-out shelves, and adjustable shelves where it is economical and cost-effective, ensure that when restored, the unit operates smoothly and accurately.* By "accurately," we mean that the drawer travels smoothly on the guides and the drawer face fits evenly against the cabinet frame, roll-out shelves glide smoothly and rest in the indentation in the track when in the closed position, and adjustable shelves are level and are supported securely.

The planning effort for this project requires us, as contractors, to have a person with proper skills and knowledge determine the quantity and types of restoration to make. With this information, we can accurately establish a plan and derive the costs. After making the bid/contract proposal and discussing it with the owner, we would plan to assign one of our best qualified carpenters or subcontract a cabinetmaker for the work. Acquiring new hardware and materials should not be too difficult, although we might need to substitute more modern hardware for the old outdated type.

Finally, we would require access to the house and would probably request some member of the family be home while the work is ongoing.

Contract.   Two types of contracts can be selected for this project. Where the exact requirements for repair are only rough estimates of materials and time, the best contract is the *time-and-materials* type. But when the exact materials are known since the kinds of guides and tracks are currently available and the drawer or shelf materials are also easily obtained or salvageable, the fixed-price type is more suitable. The body for each type could look as outlined below.

Time-and-Materials Contract

We will retrofit eight drawers, four roll-out shelves, and several adjustable shelves in the same cabinet area. For this effort we will supply all materials at their cost plus a fixed markup of 20 percent. [Note that the customer may ask why overhead has been added. The markup is required for transportation and company overhead costs.] The labor cost for one carpenter or cabinetmaker is set at $32 per hour. [Note that the actual work salary may be only $16 to $20 per hour, but we must add administrative and fixed costs to the contract.] Further, we agree that labor costs will not exceed a limit of 20 worker-hours, but may be less.

We guarantee the workmanship to be of high quality and that the drawers, roll-out shelves, and other work be accurate and secure for one year. We will leave the job site clean.

As a rough estimate, the total for the work could approach $750.00.

Fixed-Price Contract

We will retrofit the eight drawers, four roll-out shelves, and all the adjustable shelves and their brackets in the area for the fixed price shown below. We will restore materials that can be salvaged and replace those beyond saving. All interiors will function accurately and be sound. We provide a guarantee of one year for serviceability provided that no physical damage is caused by the owner or persons in the house damaging the units.

The total fixed price is $XXX.XX.

Material Assessment

Direct Materials	Use/Purpose
Metal drawer guides	To replace old, damaged guides
Wood drawer guides	To replace worn or broken guides
Roll-out shelf guides	Sixty or 100 percent expanding guides
Shelf supports	Plastic or metal supports
Powdered, dough, or plastic wood filler	To fill holes to form a base to redrill
Carpenter's glue	To reglue drawer parts
Drawer parts	Custom-made replacements
Wood shelf pieces	Replacements for damaged roll-out and adjustable shelves

Indirect Materials	Use/Purpose
Sandpaper	To smooth filled areas
4d finish nails	To nail drawer sides to front and back

Support Materials	Use/Purpose
Carpentry tools	Cabinet work
Bar clamps	To clamp pieces while glue dries
Workbench	To make repairs

Outside Contractor Support	Use/Purpose
Cabinetmaker	(Optional) Required if carpenter lacks cabinetmaking skills

Activities Planning Chart

Activity	Time Line (Days)						
	1	2	3	4	5	6	7
1. Contract preparation	_×_						
2. Materials and scheduling	_×_						
3. Restoring the drawers		_×_	_×_				
4. Restoring the roll-out shelves		_×_	_×_				
5. Restoring the adjustable shelves		_×_	_×_				

Reconstruction

Contract preparation. We have already seen that two types of contracts can be used for this project. Our estimator would be the one to gather the exact details in order to develop the worksheet for the job. He or she would determine the type of guides needed, measure and define the type of wood needed to restore broken drawer sides, backs, or bottoms, determine whether or not the roll-out shelves need replacing, and determine the extent of repair to adjustable shelves and supports.

Then he or she would decide if the regularly employed carpenter had the skill and knowledge to do work of the quality required. If, yes, no subcontractor would be required and the contract/bid could be prepared. If, no, then a specification sheet would be made for the cabinetmaker. With it, the cabinetmaker would submit a bid for the job.

The office personnel would load the job into the files or database and set up an appointment with the owner to discuss contract details and pricing.

Materials and scheduling.   If the materials used in the original cabinet interiors were fairly modern, replacement parts could be obtained easily. However, we may need to fabricate (on site) handmade cabinets, or the existing cabinets, including the drawer guides and roll-out shelves, may no longer be widely available. This could add to the materials list.

The activity chart indicates 2 days for the three parts of the job. The reason for the overlap is that we need drying time for the glue. Therefore, we would schedule removing all damaged parts in all three areas on the first day. Following this, we can glue all pieces or fill all damaged or split holes. We should finish the job on the second day unless unforeseen problems occur on the first day.

Restoring the drawers.   Figure 9–3 shows the drawer, its parts, and its guides. In our project we have eight drawers to restore. After carefully marking each for exact replacement, we can remove the old guides and fill the screw holes. We can also reglue the pieces if needed or cut and fit new pieces, then glue the drawer or drawers. The old guides in the drawer opening in the base cabinet should be either reanchored or removed to make room for new ones. Where the drawer must be taken apart to install a new bottom or back piece, for example, we would apply glue to the mating surfaces and after clamping add either slender screws or finish nails. The following day, we would sand various surfaces as needed to ensure a hand-felt smoothness.

Restoring the roll-out shelves.   Figure 9–4 shows an example of the roll-out shelf and its guides. Many roll-out shelves are built with a band on all sides but the front. Since the roll-out guide is side mounted and is about 2 in. high, we find a wood band at least 2 in. wide. This provides an excellent base to screw the guide onto.

These guides are pound-rated. Some can support 35 pounds, others 50 and 75 pounds. If the self-weight exceeds the rating and the shelf is fully extended, the screws will give way and rupture the wood or split it. In that event we would have to remove the band piece or pieces, reestablish a flat, smooth edge on the shelf, and

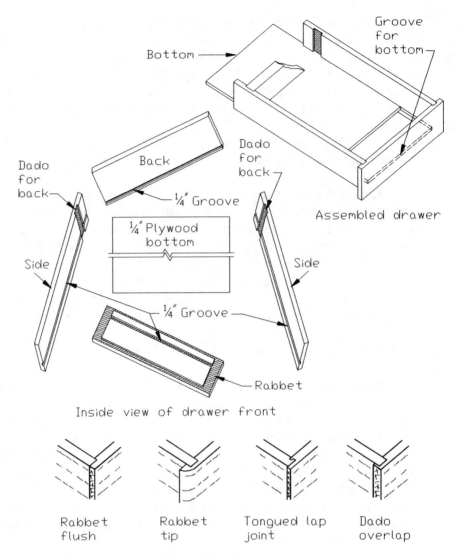

Figure 9–3 Drawer, parts.

make and glue a new piece in place. This repair would need to be done the first day. Installing the new guide does not take very long unless it is done inaccurately the first time.

Restoring the adjustable shelves.   Figure 9–5 shows an adjustable shelf. Shelves with an inset metal track seldom need replacement; however, the support that connects to the track does fall out and needs replacement. The most common varieties are the plug-in types, made from either metal or plastic. Both shear off and allow the shelf to sag or fall. In many cases the pilot hole was drilled for a larger

Figure 9–4   Roll-out shelf and guides.

($\frac{1}{4}$ in.) support and replaced with a smaller ($\frac{3}{16}$ in.) one. This causes wear on the hole, and eventually the hole cannot hold the support securely. When this happens, we usually fill the hole with a putty that hardens like wood. Then we drill a new pilot hole into the shelf. The trick here is to get it exactly right. The exactness of position must be relative to the cabinet floor or top, not front to back. When done inaccurately, the shelf rocks and is unacceptable.

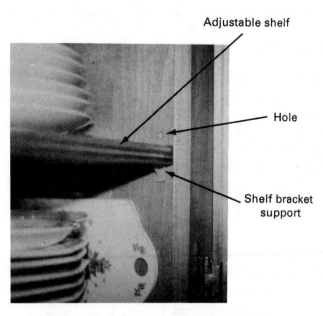

Figure 9–5   Adjustable shelf: interior of cabinets.

If the shelf is damaged, we might have to cut a new one. Almost all shelves have a finished leading edge. We have to match the old one.

Concluding comments.   Restoring the interiors of cabinets is cabinetmaking. It requires skill, knowledge, and quality work. Speed is not a factor, but accuracy is vital. This means that an owner who would attempt the project would need to be a qualified cabinetmaker.

When a contractor is selected for the job, his or her worker must have the cabinetmaking skills or he or she is the wrong person. The owner must always question the contractor about the need for a skilled person and the absolute requirement for accurate, high-quality work. Mistakes are not permitted.

Sometimes it is very difficult for the owner and contractor to agree on price and type of contract. This places a greater burden on the contractor, who must convince the owner through dialogue and persuasion that the work must be done by a very skillful person and that such people demand excellent wages for their skill.

PROJECT 3. REPAIR CERAMIC COUNTERTOPS AND BACK-SPLASHES

Subcategories include: removing cracked or chipped tiles; cleaning out old grout; applying cement and new tiles; grouting; and sealing. (*Note:* The discussions in this project apply equally well to ceramic tiles on floors and walls regardless of size, and to most tiles applied to concrete bases as well.)

Preliminary Discussion with the Owner

Problems facing the owner.   Figure 9–6 is a drawing that illustrates the tiling of a vanity's top and back-splash. Homeowners who have ceramic tile for countertops and back-splashes in kitchens and bathrooms, in specialty places such as bars and cabinet tops in green rooms, and the like, all share the same problems. Several different tiles are usually used to create the finished countertop or cabinet top, including the square tile, edge tiles, border tiles, and decorator tiles. Decorator tiles are embossed with flowers or other patterns before final firing. In terms of problem severity, the problems are:

1. Discolored or stained grout in the tile joints
2. Missing grout in the joints, and finding the correct color grout to use
3. Loosened tile—full tile whose bond to the backing has failed
4. Cracked or broken tile with good bond to backing
5. Chipped tile with good bond

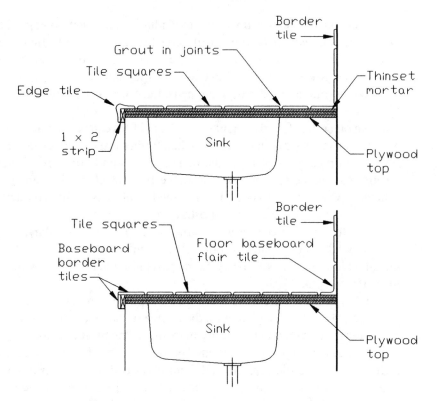

Figure 9–6   Tiling a countertop and back-splash.

6. Cracked or missing tile
7. General failure of bonding cement, resulting in loosened tiles
8. General failure of the backing materials, whether concrete, drywall, or plywood

These eight problems may occur alone or in combination. Staining, for example, happens when fungus grows in unsealed grout. The owner is faced first with eliminating the fungus, then restoring the grout, and finally, coating the grout with a sealer.

Missing grout usually erodes over time with water, but sometimes a physical accident happens to chip a piece from the tiles. This can happen when, for example, a heavy pot is dropped onto the countertop. The owner may not even be aware that the grout is missing. However, from that time on moisture penetrates the joint and seeps into the bond beneath the tile. In the early stages, simply replacing the grout and sealing it stops the deterioration. If left unattended, a general failure of all tiles in the vicinity may occur.

Cracked and chipped tiles that have good bonds are problems for the owner since they must be removed without extending the problem to adjacent tiles. Most of the time the worker (owner or tilesetter) cracks the tile further to make small pieces that are easier to remove. Once the pieces are removed and the substratum is cleaned, a new tile is cemented in place and the joints are grouted and sealed.

When general bond failure happens, the owner can freely lift a group of tiles off the counter or they fall off the back-splash when the grout fails. If there is no problem other than failed cement bond, the old tiles can be recemented in place and new grout can be applied. However, when further inspection reveals damage to the substratum regardless of type, the most serious condition exists. Then extensive repairs must be performed that can range from patching the damaged area with cement or wood filler, to complete removal of all tiles on the countertop or back-splash to access and replace the substratum.

In situations where tiles were cemented in place with portland cement mortar, a failed bond can be treated as follows. A special mortar with a bonding additive is mixed with water to form a paste. Some paste is applied to the new tile and then the tile is reset in place.

Each of the problems in the list and explained in detail above has a cost in time and materials coincident with the degree of damage. The first item is the least costly for the owner, and the eighth in the list is the most expensive for the owner.

Besides the eight problems cited earlier, the need for replacement tiles is very difficult. Ceramic tiles are created from clays and dyes. Even though a batch is quite large in numbers, no two batches are exactly a perfect match. They can be very close in color, but the shade, density of color, brightness of color, and the like vary ever so slightly. When a single tile or a few tiles need to be replaced, the owner or tile contractor will pick a tile whose characteristics closely match those of the original tiles. When the color is markedly off, the only solution may be to remove and replace all the tiles. Even though this could be quite expensive, it may be the wise thing to do.

Alternative solutions to the problem.   Let's use the previous list to examine the alternatives. When a small part of the grout is stained, we can focus in on that narrow area, say a corner, and eliminate the stain. We can also eliminate the stain and the cause of the stain, such as fungus or spores, then regrout and seal as needed. We can also perform the above and eliminate the chance for future growth of fungus by providing natural light and air circulation, which will remove the heat and moisture needed for natural growth.

When tile bonds fail, we can just reinstall the loosened tiles and regrout. Or we can make a full examination of the wall or countertop. Tiles with a poor bond to the substratum have a hollow or dull sound when tapped on with a butter knife, for example. Soundly bonded tiles make a ringing sound. If the failed bond were in the back-splash, for example, it is likely that the same moisture also penetrated the countertop near the wall. Water that gets behind tiles may rot the wood or drywall and cause the tile bond to fail. Sometimes the best solution is to perform a general restoration.

There is no easy alternative solution to chipped or cracked tiles. They have to be removed and replaced. Since we already identified the problem of exact match, we might need to devise a solution where new tiles are scattered throughout the surface area if less than a full replacement is selected. We can replace the entire surface but refrain from redoing adjacent surfaces. This means that we will rely on the light reflections to hide the slight color differences. Finally, we can say "oh well" and chose a tile that is close in color and be satisfied with it.

When the substratum fails in part or fully, we can make local repairs or make a general repair. The first is generally less expensive but leaves us with the problem of matching tiles. The latter solution is more expensive, but it means that we can disregard the problem of an exact match. All the new tiles on the surface will match, even though the adjacent walls or countertop were covered with the earlier tiles.

Statement of work and the planning effort.   For this project we shall assume that the countertop and back-splash have been installed for over 10 years and that during that time the owner has replaced the grout in the wall–countertop joint every year or two. The problem has now reached the place where the plywood countertop substratum has rotted under the tiles and around the faucet assembly. Our first statement of work is *to restore the kitchen countertop and back-splash to its original condition.* Since we know that it has been in place for 10 years, the likelihood of an exact tile replacement is almost impossible, we must *recommend a full replacement of all tiles to ensure a matched tile job.* We must also *replace the substratum on the counter and, where damaged, the drywall on the wall.* To forestall a repetition of the problem, *we will apply a coating over the grout that will seal the porous materials and retard or completely block moisture and water penetration.*

The planning effort requires an examination and evaluation of the damaged counter. After this is done, we would discuss the problem and solutions best suited for the problem. Since we as contractors for this job also operate a tile sales center, we can aid the customer in selecting a replacement. We also have the tools and can easily provide a contract offer. If we were a tile setter by trade, we could provide the same service but would need to obtain the tile samples from our supplier.

We would need a minimum of 2 days for the work since we would have the kitchen sink to remove and reinstall as well.

Contract.   For this job we would probably offer a fixed-price contract. We can readily determine the materials required, obtain current prices, and determine the time required for work. The contract wording would be very simple and would reflect the statements for work.

This contract is for the removal and replacement of the countertop and back-splash of the kitchen. All new tiles will be used. After grouting the wall and countertop, we will seal the grout with a clear coat to prevent the entry of water. Removal and reinstallation of the sink and its rim are included in the contract price.

The tile selected by the owner is lemon yellow and the owner has selected 10 decorator tiles to be installed at random throughout the tiled area.

Someone from the owner's family must be home while we are at work.

Total price: $XXX.XX.

Material Assessment

Direct Materials	Use/Purpose
Tiles	Edge, flat, border
Grout	White or colored as required to fill spaces between tiles
Plywood	Substratum—actually this is the countertop
$\frac{1}{2}$-in. Drywall	To replace the damaged drywall
Nails	Drywall and 6d finish galvanized types
Tile cement	To glue tiles in place

Indirect Materials	Use/Purpose
Tile rod-saw	Special blade used in a hacksaw for cutting tile
New sink rim	(Optional) May need to be used if old one gets damaged removing it
O-rings	(Optional) May need to be used in wastewater system

Support Materials	Use/Purpose
Tile-cutting tool	To mark and crack the tile
Carpenter tools	For construction
Wrenches	For plumbing work
Tile-setting tools	To install the tile and cement

Outside Contractor Support	Use/Purpose
None	

Activities Planning Chart

Activity	Time Line (Days)						
	1	2	3	4	5	6	7
1. Contract preparation	I _×_ I	___ I	___ I	___ I	___ I	___ I	___ I
2. Materials and scheduling	I _×_ I	___ I	___ I	___ I	___ I	___ I	___ I
3. Removing and replacing the tile	I ___ I	_×_ I	_×_ I	___ I	___ I	___ I	___ I
4. Applying the sealant	I ___ I	___ I	_×_ I	___ I	___ I	___ I	___ I

Reconstruction

Contract preparation.   Just because the contract is prepared at the tile outlet store does not change the need for proper preparation. Every aspect of determining the costs for materials, labor, and overhead must be applied. However, the contract form would probably be an invoice style where there is room for a description
and columns for listing pricing, taxes, and the like. Since the owner would be at the
store to pick out the tile, he or she would have the responsibility for selecting the
price range that will be included in the contract.

Materials and scheduling.   In this project we have a very unique situation
that makes it easy to identify the number of tiles needed for the job. We simply
count the number of tile squares, border tiles, and edge tiles. Then we add a few
extra to allow for those that crack or break when we cut them.

All the materials are usually available locally, which simplifies the preparation for the job. It means that when we arrive at the job site, we have everything
necessary to complete the work.

Scheduling is a simple matter of selecting two successive days agreeable to
the owner and to us.

Removing and replacing the tile countertop and back-splash.   Let's
make a list of the sequence of tasks and activities that we must perform in removing
the countertop and back-splash first; then we can make another list identifying the
restoration activities.

Removal Tasks and Activities
1. Disconnect the sink plumbing. (Refer to Chapter 7 for these details.)
2. Remove the sink rim and sink.
3. Remove the covers from all outlets and switches that are on the back-splash tiles.
4. Remove the back-splash tiles by prying them loose with a putty knife or small flat
   bar.

5. Remove the countertop. Where possible, remove the tiles first. If it is a problem, just take off the edge tiles to get to the plywood substratum. The plywood is normally nailed to the top of the base cabinet.

The activities and tasks are really simple to perform. However, caution should always be used, for several reasons. First, there is the need to avoid damage to the base cabinets, plumbing, and sink. Second, the countertop is normally quite heavy, but when the tile is added on top of it, the assembly is really heavy, which means that the person doing the work can sustain back strain if stressed too far. Finally, reaching across the 2-ft area to take off the wall tiles also means stretching and working at odd angles with a bar and hammer. Caution should be used here as well.

Restoration of the Countertop and Back-Splash

1. Install the new plywood countertop using the old one as the pattern for the layout for the sink and other special conditions. Make sure that the countertop is fastened down securely.
2. Install the new drywall behind the countertop and fill the nail holes with joint compound or spackling paste.
3. Install the new tiles on the countertop following the pattern of the old countertop.
4. Install the back-splash tiles.
5. Grout the entire surface.
6. Apply the sealer to the grout.

The tile cement is ready-mixed and is sold in 1-gallon cans, which makes it easy for us as installer. We would use a special trowel with notches cut along one end and one long side. This makes it possible to have just the exact amount of cement on the plywood or drywall. Then we simply press the tiles into the cement and a firm bond is established. This sounds very simple, but the layout and planning tasks must be done first.

We need to apply the edge tiles or mark their location first, since these can only be cut off for length. Then we can install all the whole tiles and cut those that fit against cabinets and outlets as we get to the tiles in question. The border tiles are installed last.

Concluding comments.   Who should do this work? A person who has a very good background in the trades. He or she must have carpentry skills, plumbing skills, and tile-setting skills as a minimum. He or she also must be able to plan the work as we have described it here.

The job is moderately difficult and moderately expensive as well. Prices of tile and other materials listed vary with quality and mark-up. Prices for labor also vary from company to company, so references should be used by the owner. The contractor should supply these readily upon request.

PROJECT 4. REMOVE AND REPLACE DAMAGED COUNTERTOP
AND BACK-SPLASH

Subcategories include: techniques of on-site countertop construction; mechanics of removing and replacing commercial-built tops; and installing back-splashes using sheet plastic products.

Preliminary Discussion with the Owner

Problems facing the owner.   When the contractor is called to the home of the owner about a countertop problem, the condition is usually far advanced. The contractor will find one of three basic construction techniques used in building the countertop and back-splash unit. Figure 9–7 illustrates the parts and details about the construction. Sometimes the countertops are built on-site by carpenters and they also install the plastic top. Although Formica is the name of a company famous for its plastic goods, the name has become generic for plastic countertop materials. These products are usually glued or cemented in place over plywood or particleboard. The edges can easily be made of the same materials, which eliminates the need for metal edging. But in the early days of modern kitchens metal edging held the countertop material in place. In more recent times specialty shops have equipment that can mold the plastic to a formed substratum of plywood or particleboard.

Since the owner has one of the three kinds, some of the problems that he or she faces include worn-out covering, scorched spots, cracked top, damaged or broken edges, or rotted plywood or particleboard. Over time the surface material dulls and erodes, due to abrasives in the cleansing compounds and careless regard for the surface, which gets marred by knives, pots, and other items around the house. The cement sometimes fails, which causes a separation of plastic and substratum. This happens most often at the edge, at the joint of back-splash and top, and around the sink.

Alternative solutions to the problem.   There are several solutions that we should discuss with the owner, ranging from installing a new top over the old one to completely replacing the countertop and back-splash with a modern type. The original countertop and back-splash are often in good but worn condition. With a small amount of sanding, a new top can be added over the old one using the piece method. (This is not a very good option for the old molded countertop.) Where there has been damage because of water and the rot has advanced, we would always recommend full replacement. This could be a new molded style or a custom-installed type.

The alternatives also include who should perform the work. If the countertop were reinstalled a piece at a time, a skilled carpenter or specialty shop employee

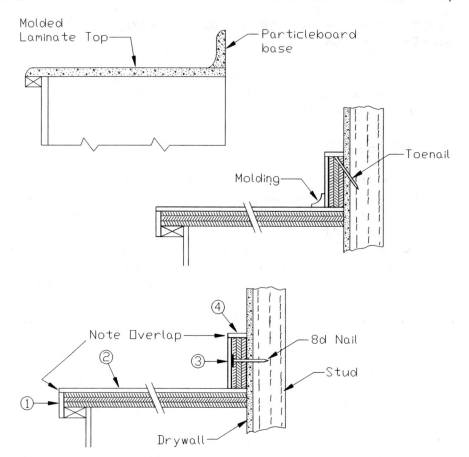

Molded Laminate Top

Particleboard base

Toenail

Molding

Note Overlap

8d Nail

Stud

Drywall

Highlighted=Laminate Top

Note: Numbers show sequence of installing plastic top

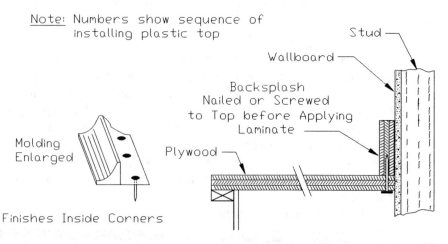

Stud

Wallboard

Backsplash Nailed or Screwed to Top before Applying Laminate

Plywood

Molding Enlarged

Finishes Inside Corners

Figure 9–7   Countertop and back-splash construction.

would be the likely person to do the work. If the best decision was to rip out the old assembly, the owner could contract for the pieces with a specialty shop and have molded countertop made to specifications. Then the owner could simply clamp the countertop in place and reinstall the sink if required. If another specialty type of countertop is selected, a specialist would bring the materials and perform the work. The work of fitting, cutting, applying cements and glues, and the like are all very critical and since the materials are very expensive, mistakes result in wasted materials and added labor costs.

Statement of work and the planning effort.   For our project we need to restore the kitchen countertop and back-splash. There is 8 ft along one wall with a sink installed and a 90-degree corner to a 4-ft section. The owner had a hand-made installation many years ago and desires to upgrade to a molded style. Our statement of work: *We will remove the old countertop and its back-splash, repair the wall behind the back-splash, have a new countertop made, and install it.* Since we also have a sink installed in the long section, *we will remove and replace the sink's rim* when we take out the sink.

Our planning effort involves the owner, a specialty shop or builder's supply that stocks molded countertops, and our company. We would plan to have the owner select the countertop color and texture for the new countertop from a wide variety of squares. By using this method we can assist the owner with matching the favorite colors and textures to their personal tastes. Then we can provide an estimate by accumulating the various costs. We also provide the specialty shop with our specifications, which include the dimensions, type, color, and even the exact placement of the sink so that they can cut out the hole. Then we plan for the installation, which can be either by our carpenter or we can have the specialty shop install the new tops.

Contract.   A fixed-price contract is very well suited to this project. The owner knows the full price and knows what he or she will receive. The contractor also knows all aspects of the job—there are no hidden problems or costs. The body of the contract would include the following:

We agree to remove the old countertop along the two walls and replace it with a modern pre-formed style. The owner agrees to make the selection of color and texture for the countertop. We also agree to make repairs to the wall behind the old back-splash and to add appropriate fillers between the wall and new countertop. At our discretion we may employ the specialty shop workers to complete installation of the new countertop and reinstall the sink.

Total labor and materials cost, including specialty shop support, is $XXX.XX.

This price is good for 30 days from the date of the contract/bid offer.

Material Assessment

Direct Materials	Use/Purpose
Countertop	To replace the old top
Clamps	To fasten the top to the base cabinet
Sink rim	To replace the old worn rim
Spackling paste	To patch behind the old back-splash

Indirect Materials	Use/Purpose
Filler pieces	1×2s of soft pine
6d finish nails	To nail filler strips in place

Support Materials	Use/Purpose
Carpentry tools	For construction
Wide putty knife	To apply spackling
Wrenches	To remove and reinstall plumbing

Outside Contractor Support	Use/Purpose
Specialty shop	To build and install the new countertop

Activities Planning Chart

Activity	Time Line (Days)
	1 2 3 4 5 6 7
1. Contract preparation	I _×_ I ___ I ___ I ___ I ___ I ___ I ___ I
2. Subcontracting and scheduling	I ___ I _×_ I ___ I ___ I ___ I ___ I ___ I
3. Removal and repairs	I ___ I _×_ I ___ I ___ I ___ I ___ I ___ I
4. Installing the new countertop	I ___ I ___ I _×_ I ___ I ___ I ___ I ___ I

Reconstruction

Contract preparation.   Our estimator would work with the owner and specialty shop in determining the materials and other requirements needed to restore the countertop completely. On the job-sheet, he or she would list the materials needed for repairing the wall behind the back-splash and obtain a bid from the subcontractor. The office personnel would prepare a contract offer to the specialty contractor that included the new requirements and call for installation as well.

The owner would be presented with a single contract/bid that he or she would either approve or ask to be modified.

Subcontracting and scheduling.   In the specialty shop the workers would cut two pieces of basic countertop with back-splash, one slightly longer than 8 ft and the other slightly longer than 4 ft. The workers would prepare the plastic top for bonding to the particleboard substratum. Both pieces are set into a mold where heat is applied that softens the plastic and permits it to fit the curves of the particleboard. The two pieces are bonded under pressure and when the time is correct, a finished surface is made. One end on each piece is mitered at 45 degrees to form a return. To each end a piece of plastic is cemented and fitted. Under the miter joint grooves are made to fit the clamps that hold the miter together. Next, the hole is marked and cut out for the sink. The shop work is done.

Now the schedule for installation can be set.

Removal and repairs.   While the subcontractor is making the new countertop, our carpenter is busy removing the old countertops and repairing the walls. We would time this work to occur the day before the new countertop is ready for installation to preclude inconveniencing the owner.

1. We would remove the sink and set it aside.
2. We remove the end from the countertop and back-splash to determine if the back-splash piece is fastened to the plywood or directly nailed into the wall's studs or both. This helps but is not vital to the removal operation.
3. We use a small 6- to 8-in. square of $\frac{1}{4}$-in.-thick plywood as a shield and pry the back away from the wall with a hammer. This minimizes damage to the wall's surface.
4. Next, we work from inside the base cabinet with cold chisel and small pry bars to free the plywood from the top of the cabinet. This eliminates any damage we might do to the facings on the cabinet if we tried to do the work from the outside. Once the top is raised slightly, we can work from the outside and free it completely.
5. Being careful not to disturb the wall above the back-splash line, we fill in holes and any hammer marks with spackling paste.
6. The base units are ready for the new top.

Installing the new countertop.   The workers from the specialty shop will arrive as scheduled and install the new countertops.

1. They will prefit the pieces to verify the angle in the corner and ensure that the base unit tops are even and level.
2. They will join the two sections together and set them in place as a unit.
3. They will custom-fit filler pieces between the back of the back-splash and wall if any are required.
4. They will fasten the top down from within the base units.
5. They will install the sink with its new rim.

Overall the installation should go very quickly. Even when filler pieces are required, the job is done in several hours.

Concluding comments.   Countertop replacement is a specialty part of carpentry, and to make the curved types and other systems available, specialty workers should be brought in to perform the work. The only time an owner should attempt the work is when recovering the old materials, and even in this case, much skill is required.

As a rule, specialty shops charge by the running foot for countertop. When the owner wishes to act in the role of contractor, he or she needs to perform all of the items indicated in the project.

PROJECT 5. REFINISH CABINET EXTERIORS

Subcategories include: removing the exterior finish by sanding, stripping, or dipping; touch staining; full staining; painting; lacquering; polyethylene finish; laminating with thin plastic; and cleaning equipment and tools.

Prliminary Discussion with the Owner

Problems facing the owner.   This is the final project in this chapter. It is last because all the work performed in the earlier projects should always be performed before refinishing the cabinets. So we shall assume that all the restoration work has been completed except refinishing the cabinets.

Wood cabinets are finished in various ways with various materials, including, stain and varnish, stain and lacquer, a water-lacquer spray and fire technique, paint, laminated plastic, and applied patterned wood grain. The problems that owners have with the finish are deteriorated surface, mars and scratches, scorching from fire, lack of proper maintenance, and cleaning.

Over time, the surfaces accumulate household films from cooking grease, smoke, nicotine, residue from cleaning agents, and buildup of waxes. All of these dull the finish and add to its darkening. The owner must recognize the problem and take specific action to restore the surfaces with detergents and natural chemicals. Stained and lacquered or varnished surfaces darken considerably with age naturally. Painted cabinets yellow with age. White, for example, turns to a dull gray or yellowish. Light blue turns pale and picks up tinges of yellow. Other more vibrant colors fade more where sunlight strikes the cabinet surface than where it does not.

The finish can crack when heat is applied over an extended period or when harsh chemicals and excessive water are applied to surfaces. As the transparent finishes age, they lose oils and become brittle. The heat and cooling expand and contract the lacquer or varnish until it cracks. Once started, there is no way to stop it, but care and application of oils can slow the action considerably. When water is able to penetrate the transparent finish, it soaks into the wood cells, which expand ever so slightly. But since the finish is so thin and dry, the result is minute cracks, which expand to larger ones over time.

Invariably, base cabinets sustain more mars and nicks than do wall cabinets. When the cabinets are finished with transparent materials, the mars and nicks that penetrated the finish can be partially hidden with application of liquid polish that contains stain. However, the finish has lost its quality and uniform appearance. Painted cabinets are even more of a problem when dealing with mars and nicks. Even when we have some paint left over from the original job, the touch-up will not exactly match, due to weathering of the paint on the cabinet.

If the cabinets were worked on to refit the doors and change the hardware and catches, we have impressions in the finish from the old hardware, and holes to fill that are not finished. These types of problems are best taken care of when the doors are off the cabinets and drawers are out. This way we can strip the trim and cabinet facings, sand the surfaces, and apply filler as needed. If we leave the doors in place, we are hampered in cleaning, stripping, and otherwise preparing the cabinet casings and trim for refinish.

Cabinets that have a painted or printed finish cannot usually be stripped and retain the original wood-grain designs. Cabinets with thin laminate plastic coverings cannot be restored by using paints or fillers because the materials do not match. Such situations present a serious problem for the owner, since the usual solution is to remove and replace the old plastic or apply a new plastic sheet over the old one. This work is very time consuming, since every piece has to be custom fit and installed. This can be very expensive.

Alternative solutions to the problem.   In every situation we have alternatives, and in restoring the finish to cabinets we also have some. In a true restoration, we would use the original materials and do whatever it took to make the cabinets look like new. In a modified restoration, we can look at alternatives that can meet architectural styles and personal tastes. Let's make a list that quickly identifies the alternatives.

Original Finish	Alternatives
Stained and varnished or lacquered	1. Strip finish, bleach wood, apply new stain, and apply polyurethane varnish or lacquer.
	2. Partially strip finish, touch stain, and apply transparent coats.
	3. Clean and repair surfaces, then paint.
	4. Severely damaged finish (scorched); repair surfaces and paint or apply plastic sheet materials.

Painted cabinets	1. Clean and sand the surfaces, fill dents, scratches, etc., then repaint.
	2. Strip paint, stain, and apply transparent coats.
	3. Clean and sand, then apply plastic sheet materials.
Plastic laminated	1. Remove loose and damaged plastic. Clean substratum and apply new plastic.
	2. Clean all plastic, rough with sandpaper, and apply a new plastic covering.
Painted or printed woodgrain finish	1. Clean surfaces and apply paint.
	2. Clean and laminate plastic materials.

Besides selecting an alternative solution, the owners can decide to do the work themselves or have it done. If they opt for self-help, they will require considerable time and a variety of tools and equipment. Except for laminating the plastic, the other solutions are well within the capability of most of homeowners. Installing plastic with contact cement and making all the required cuts and fits is much more demanding and requires skills normally beyond those of owners. Carpenters with finish skills can perform the work quite simply. Specialty shops who sell and use plastic laminates can also do the work and we can contract directly with them.

Statement of work and the planning effort.   Since we have identified so many varieties of finish for cabinets, we must select one for our project. However, later in the section on reconstruction we discuss some of the tasks required for each of the other finishes. For the project we select damaged stained and lacquered cabinets. There are approximately 12 ft of wall and ceiling cabinets plus a full-height 2 ft 2 in. oven cabinet. Our first statement is: *Restore the cabinet finish to a lighter shade of oak and apply a clear, transparent finish.* More specifically, *we shall clean the surfaces, strip only the lacquer finish, lighten the stained wood, seal, and apply new transparent finish.* To perform the work *we will remove and reinstall all doors and hardware to operate accurately.* Further, we must provide a commitment to excellence and avoidance of damage to surrounding areas and floors. *We guarantee no damage to countertops, hardware, appliances, and floors.*

The planning begins with an examination of the cabinets in the kitchen to determine the extent of restoration and a general discussion with the owner about alternatives. In this project we will satisfy the statements of work. To expedite the work, we will send two painters to the job. We might also need to have our carpenter rehang, or at the least, realign the doors removed during the job. The painters would set up a workstation which they would bring with them to keep work to a small area and easy to clean up. We would plan to install protective materials on surfaces that can be damaged by chemicals and finishes. Finally, some appliances might have to be removed and replaced to facilitate work, and these will need to be reinstalled.

Contract.   This work is time intensive. If a painting contractor has had the opportunity to refinish kitchen cabinets, bathroom cabinets, and bookcases, he or she would have either a file from which to obtain the per square foot cost of refinishing a by-system, or have a solid knowledge of the time required to perform the various tasks. If so, a fixed-price contract can be offered to the owner. All materials and labor, overhead, and allowance for profit would be determined by the number of square feet of cabinet surface to restore.

If the contractor did not have the information described above, he or she might need to offer a time-and-materials contract. The owner would need to be sure to have very specific contract requirements and would be wise to set some dollar limits for labor.

Any contract should include the following statements derived from the statements of work:

1. Remove the surface transparent finish without substantially disturbing the wood or stain.
2. Bleach the stain to lighten the wood and touch up stain to create a uniform color.
3. Apply two coats of polyurethane satin-finish transparent finish. All surfaces must be hand rubbed smooth and polished.
4. All mars and blemishes must be muted and blend with the surrounding wood.
5. All doors must fit properly when rehung.

Material Assessment

Direct Materials	Use/Purpose
Stripping chemical	To soften transparent finish
Lye soap	Substitute for chemical stripper
Mineral spirits	Cleaning agent
Detergent and water	Cleaning agent
Stain	For touch staining
Transparent coating	For the final two coats

Indirect Materials	Use/Purpose
Steel wool	To rub off the finish, smooth the final finish
Sandpaper	To smooth surfaces after removing the finish and touch sanding after staining
Plastic sheet goods	To protect floors, appliances, and countertops

Support Materials	Use/Purpose
Workbench	Surface for doing drawers and doors
Paintbrushes	To apply new products and stripping agents
Rags or towels	For cleaning and mop-up
Drop cloths	To protect surfaces as required
Power sprayers	To apply transparent finish by spray gun

Outside Contractor Support	Use/Purpose
None	

Activities Planning Chart

Activity	Time Line (Days)

Activity	1	2	3	4	5	6	7
1. Contract preparation	×						
2. Materials and scheduling	×						
3. Removing the old materials		×	×				
4. Applying the new finish			×	×	×		
5. Final finishing tasks					×	×	

Reconstruction

Contract preparation.   As we stated in the contract section, we could deal with two distinctly different situations. These would also determine how we would proceed to prepare the contract. If we already had a database with our unit costs (per square foot costs), the workup sheet would have an entry such as "300 sq. ft @ $3.00 per sq. ft; labor = $900.00—includes removal of old finish, application of new materials, and finish tasks."

In addition, the estimator would list the materials required with appropriate quantities and prices. Finally, overhead charges and allowance for profit percentages would be added to arrive at the full cost. The office person would prepare the contract/bid offer that the contractor would take to the owner.

Materials and scheduling.   By observing the materials assessment list, we see that all materials are common and readily available. This means that we can pick them up on the first day of the job.

We expect to be on the job a total of 5 days. Almost all of these will be full days. The actual calendar start date must be determined at the time of contract signing. We would expect to have someone from the family at home while the worker is there.

Removing finish and preparing the surfaces for finishing.   We need to set up a workstation that has protection and good ventilation to strip, stain, and refinish the doors and drawers. While working on the cabinets in the kitchen, we will open the windows to obtain the needed ventilation.

The series of steps for finish removal are as follows:

1. Remove the doors by taking out the screws in the cabinet frame. Then remove all hardware from the doors.
2. Clean the hardware.
3. Apply a stripping agent to the door according to directions on the can and avoid penetrating the stain and wood.
4. Wipe away the stripping agent and old transparent finish.
5. Let dry.
6. Repeat the steps above on all drawer facings.
7. Install plastic sheets in the kitchen to protect all surfaces from spray or drops of stripping agent.
8. Strip the upper cabinet first, then the base units, and finally, the floor-to-ceiling oven cabinet.

Next we prepare the surfaces for finishing as follows:

1. Lightly sand the surfaces with 150-grit open-coat sandpaper or steel wool to smooth the surface and remove scratches and nicks.
2. Apply paste wood filler to damaged spots that must be built up. Sand flush when dry.
3. Touch-stain the cabinets with wiping stain using a brush and rag. Let the stain dry.

These tasks are straightforward but require considerable time to complete. Furthermore, they are the most important since the work done at this time is crucial to a high-quality finish.

Applying the top coats of transparent finish.   In our project we are applying a polyurethane material that is manufactured by quite a few manufacturers. We would always follow their recommended application instructions. Generally, they include such recommendations as applying several thin coats versus thick coats. This is important since it is easier to control runs using thinner coats. We should also sand between coats to remove stand-up wood grain and any dust that may have settled on the wet material. The tasks are repetitive and follow this general sequence:

1. Dust off the object to be varnished. For this we use a tack rag, which is a lint-free rag lightly soaked with some varnish.

2. Apply a thin (about 1 mil thick) coat of varnish with a varnish brush. This brush has bristles that all but eliminate brush marks. Let dry.

3. Lightly sand all surfaces to a smooth-to-the-touch finish.

4. Apply the second coat of varnish. After it dries sand and remove the dust.

5. Apply the final coat of varnish.

6. *Optional:* Apply rubbing compound such as rottenstone and oil to burnish the surface and create a polished effect. It is the heating effect through rubbing that causes the polishing and increases the shine.

Final finishing tasks.   When all doors, drawer fronts, and cabinet sides and facings are refinished, we need to perform several more important tasks. First, we should remove all plastic sheet goods to avoid transporting old finish to other parts of the house and outside. Then we rehang the doors and make final adjustments to ensure that they fit accurately and are in alignment. (Refer back to Project 1 in this chapter for details.) We do the same for the drawers and their guides.

Other finishes.   As promised above, we now identify refinishing with other materials. These include stripping with lye, applying lacquer, and hand-rubbing cabinet surfaces to a finish.

Stripping with lye is a technique that uses lye soap in water or paste. The worker wears protective clothing and glasses to avoid serious burns. The soap is applied to the cabinet surface and rubbed into the finish. Then it is washed off with several applications of water and dried. This technique works very well on lacquered and some varnishes. It also works very well on hand-rubbed finishes. Once the old transparent finish has been removed, the new coats can be applied.

Applying lacquer requires a spray gun and compressor. Lacquer is made in dull, satin, and high-gloss varieties. Therefore, the owner has the choice of appearances. Lacquer is mixed with lacquer thinner and at least seven coats are applied. Since each coat dries in a few minutes, the work progresses quite rapidly. Between coats or every other coat we lightly sand to remove built-up hairs. After the final coat is applied and has dried, we can polish the surface with rottenstone or we can let the final coat be the finish. All surfaces that can be damaged from overspray from the gun need full protection. Occasional overspray can be wiped away with a rag soaked in lacquer thinner.

Hand-rubbing the cabinet is a technique where we use a mixture of tung oil and either lacquer or varnish and apply it by hand. The idea is to build up a finish by applying repeated coats of the material. This finish is well suited to bookcases, bars except for the top, and other cabinets in dens and libraries, but is a very poor choice for kitchen and bathroom cabinets. Over time, repeated applications darken the wood color and create a rich satin finish.

Painting the surfaces requires first cleaning the old finish with detergent to remove household grease and smoke buildup. Then the surfaces are sanded to remove some old finish and establish a better surface for the paint to stick to. The painter usually applies a base coat of latex primer about 1 mil thick. On top of this, he or she applies two top coats of latex semigloss or high gloss. To perform the best-quality work, all cabinet doors and hardware are removed first. This ensures a more perfect overall finish and at the same time permits easier repair for surfaces.

Concluding comments. Restoring the surfaces of cabinets is a job that the owner can do. He or she must be willing to spend the time and effort as explained in this project to accomplish the various tasks in order to have a high-quality product when done. No task can be rushed to completion, no step can be eliminated, and no fewer than two top coats can be applied. Further, a final polishing must be done to make the cabinet surface smooth and silky-feeling to the touch. Only then is the job really complete.

When the general contractor's painter or painting contractor performs the work, he or she will generally use economical techniques to minimize the number of days on the job when working with a fixed-price contract. Even in this environment, he or she cannot speed up drying of the stains and transparent coats. So the job must take several days or longer even if the painter does not work a full day.

Our example job was a small kitchen with about 300 square feet of surface area to restore. The price easily extends into several hundred dollars. In addition, we refinished only the exterior surfaces. If the job were a library with bookcases that required refinishing both inside and outside surfaces, the price would be greater. In most estimates the price is established on a "by the square foot" basis. This makes it simple to obtain costs.

Finally, we must always be concerned with health maintenance. Many of the stripping agents contain chemicals that give off slightly toxic fumes. Adequate ventilation is absolutely essential. Sometimes, we even turn on fans to clear the fumes from the room more quickly. These chemicals can also cause skin irritation or burns, so protective clothing and gloves must be used. Be safe and avoid personal injury.

CHAPTER SUMMARY

We examined a wide variety of problems associated with restoring cabinets. We examined how to restore the doors, drawers, and countertops made in different ways and using different materials, and we discussed restoring the finish to the cabinets. In all the descriptions and explanations, we identified the work as finish work, which means that considerable knowledge and skill are required for a high-quality job. We also noted that carpentry tools and machines were needed to complete much of the work and that these tools must have sharp cutting edges, whether they are saws, chisels, or scrapers. We also identified many different types of materials used in cabinets and that most of these were easily replaced. However, we did identify the problem in matching ceramic tiles. In our final project, we identified a variety of methods of restoring the surface of cabinets.

We also discussed, at some length, that quality work required workers with extensive knowledge and skills. Sometimes the best person for a job is the carpenter, at other times the tile setter was best, and at other times the painter is the best person for the job. In many situations the owner has enough knowledge and skill to perform the tasks.

We also obtained an understanding of the costs associated with each type of restoration. As a rule the costs are moderate by today's standards. Yet most jobs run into the low hundreds. We learned that contractors must account for travel time and estimating time as well as office expenses when determining the cost of a job if they expect to remain in business. Owners who must take off from work to perform restoration need to assess the economics of this action. Where the owner can make more money per day than the cost of the job, having the contractor do the work makes sense. When the owner lacks the skill and knowledge to perform the work, having a contractor do the work also makes sense.

Finally, we discussed the various safety and hazards associated with each project. In some cases hazards are from machines and tools, in other cases from physical stretching and lifting and the like, and in others from inhaling fumes or being burned by caustic materials.

All efforts taken to restore cabinets in the home must result in a high-quality finish, smooth to the touch, and free of runs; properly aligned and fitted doors and drawers; and exact workmanship in all joints, whether made of wood, plastic, or ceramic.

10

ENVIRONMENTAL SYSTEMS (AIR-CONDITIONING AND HEATING SYSTEMS)

OBJECTIVES

To understand the principles of airflow in heating and air-conditioning systems

To understand the principles of radiation in heating systems

To gain insight to sizing and selecting a replacement type of heating and air-conditioning systems

To perform rudimentary maintenance on heating and air-conditioning systems

To service the heating and air-conditioning systems

To clean filter systems

To check for heat and cooling losses and take corrective action

To improve the effectiveness of heating and air-condition systems

OPENING COMMENTS

Conditions or circumstances that necessitate corrective action.   This chapter differs from the other nine since there are usually only a small number of tasks that owners can perform. These are usually classified as preventive maintenance. They include making inspections of the heating or air-conditioning systems, exchanging filters, lubricating motors, examining wiring, listening for changes in operation, and feeling changes in operation. Several other tasks that can be performed by the homeowner fall into the troubleshooting scheme. These include checking the system for power, fan operation, and operation of the gas furnace, heat pump, and thermostat, for example. Notice that all these are safe tasks that do not involve handling high voltage or heating fuels and gases such as Freon. They do not measure fuel pressures, Btu, fuel/air ratios, and control devices attached to the environmental system. Homeowners can identify a set of conditions that make it possible to correct them. Beyond these we would call on the expertise of specialists. Let's make a list:

1. *Diminished airflow from registers and deflectors.* In order of least to most severe we have first, a clogged filter that can be exchanged quickly and easily. Next we have a clogged or partially clogged A-frame, which is the evaporator of the air conditioner and is found above or below the furnace. Last we have a defective fan motor. Most fans have multiple speeds. Heating fans operate in two speeds, while the same fan operates at high speed when cooling the home. When one speed is defective, the others may work, yet we notice when one speed is defective.

2. *Diminished cool air to very warm airflow from registers and deflectors.* This is a common condition that leads us to the air-conditioning system. Our first attempt is to restore power where the circuit breaker tripped. Sometimes a power surge trips the breaker before harming the compressor. A defective fan motor is easily detected since it usually makes wind noise.

3. *The flame in a gas unit fails to ignite when we turn on heat and raise the thermostat.* We should hear a click and within a minute or so hear the flame ignite. If the thermostat does not click, there may be a problem with the 24-volt circuit. If the gas burners and the control circuit fail to operate, the problem can be the control or wiring. In these situations we need the skills of experts.

4. Heat pumps are two-way air conditioners. In one position they create heat, and in the other they create cooling. The compressor must run in both conditions. A power outage stops the unit. Supplemental heating can be a baseboard heater coil placed in the ductwork. When temperatures fall to a point where the unit cannot deliver sufficient heat, the thermostat activates the coil and provides added heat. If the circuit fails, no heat is developed by the coil, and the house is cold or considerably cooler than expected. The circuit can be checked by the owner.

5. Drafts are either cool or hot. To make the environmental system most efficient, we must reduce drafts and reduce heat and cold penetration. We can install insulation, add storm windows, stop drafts around light switches and outlets, replace weatherstripping around doors and windows, and add insulation in the attic. Most of the work can be performed by homeowners.

Contractor's responsibility. When the environmental system is inoperative and the items on a checklist do not eliminate the problem and restore the system, we, as contractors, are called to help with the problem. Our responsibility is to restore the system quickly. We are expected to bring equipment and supplies that can restore the system, whether it is a heater or an air conditioner. This responsibility implies that we know how the system works and how to repair it.

If the problem is with the central air conditioner, it can be an electrical, mechanical, or pressure problem. We can check for shorted or open components such as switches, capacitors, relays, windings in the motors, and the like. We can connect the meters to the small ports outside at the condenser and check for proper pressures on the low and high sides. Each system is slightly different; however, the low-side pressure is around 70 psi, while the high-side pressure is around 190 psi. If the pressures are wrong or zero, there is a Freon leak or the compressor has failed. All this troubleshooting requires knowledge and proper equipment. Once located, we might be able to repair the system or we might need to obtain new parts from the shop or suppliers. In either event we would discuss the problem with the owner and advise him or her about the problem and solution and offer an estimate. We almost always charge a flat rate for a service call.

If the problem is with a gas heater, we would need to know how it works: what control devices and circuits are installed that communicate with the thermostat and activate the igniter. In older systems there is a pilot light. We would check this circuit to ensure that it stays lit. We would check the draft in the chimney. We would reset the thermostat controls or replace them if they were defective.

A defective fan could be rebuilt or replaced. Sometimes the price of a new fan is cheaper than repairing the old one. We would check prices for the customer.

Homeowner's expectations. The homeowner wants the system restored quickly and at the least cost. Most owners are accustomed to a flat rate for a service call. Many expect this charge to include parts if they are needed. Many contractors do provide a little "extra" for regular or long-time customers. They might add a little gas charge to a system, perform some rudimentary cleaning, and on occasion replace a small, inexpensive part.

Where the owner has a service contract, he or she expects the contract to cover the cost of the service call and parts. However, to minimize the contract price, most contracts do not cover every part. In situations like this, the contractor would show the owner the exception clauses where added costs must be charged for the restoration.

Scope of projects. We begin with the servicing tasks that the homeowner can perform and those best performed by experts. Then we examine the problems and solutions with various heating and air-conditioning systems.

PROJECT 1. SERVICE CENTRAL FORCED-AIR HEATING AND AIR-CONDITIONING SYSTEMS

Subcategories include: tracing down leaks and improving the effectiveness of the system; cleaning the filter system; checking and cleaning the waste systems; servicing heating and cooling components; making pressure checks; checking the electrical systems; and learning principles associated with these activities.

Preliminary Discussion with the Owner

Problems facing the owner.   Forced-air systems employ fans and filters while moving air. The fans operate at various speeds that are programmed according to need. In many systems there are two fan speeds for heating, and only high speed is used for central air conditioning. Since modern fan motors can have at least three operating speeds, any and all speeds can be selected for use. As owners of forced-air systems we have one fan in the heater inside the house, with a squirrel cage connected to the motor. Some of these motors are lubricated permanently and others are not. When the motor is operating properly, all we hear is the wind created by the squirrel cage. When bearings are dry and begin to wear, we can hear the noise created. As the problem progresses, the noise gets louder. Eventually, the motor will burn up because clearances between armature and field windings or commutator decrease. In some cases the parts touch and heat burns the components. The fan in the condenser unit outside may also require annual or more frequent servicing.

The squirrel cage draws air into its open end and forces it out through the blades. We have to keep the blades very clean to maximize the airflow. However, over time accumulations of dust particles stick to the blades and reduce the air gap between blades. Left unattended, decreased airflow increases and the efficiency of the system decreases. The result is an increase in electrical and gas or oil consumption since it takes the system much longer to reach selected heating or cooling temperatures.

In most central heating systems, the motor and squirrel cage is a unit bolted to a frame that can easily be slid out of a track. The wiring usually has connectors at each end, and each of a different color. So if we mark the wires as we take them off, we can be sure to replace them in exactly the same place. With the unit out, we can take it to the garage or shop and work comfortably while cleaning and oiling it.

Filters are used and are installed between the fan unit and return inlet in the heater closet. There are two types. One is a throw-away type. When it is clogged, we simply replace it with a new one. The other type is a reusable porous filter. This kind is held in a metal frame that has a grid to support the filter. When it is clogged, we simply remove the filter and wash it clean. After it dries, we reinstall it. Most families have two of these. So, when one is drying, the other is installed. This allows continuous use of the heating or air-conditioning system with a filtering system intact.

We also need to school ourselves to recognize audio sounds when the condenser unit outside is running. Besides the fan generating wind noise, the compressor creates noise as well. We should recognize the low-level thump, thump noise of a properly working compressor. Then when the noise increases, we have a signal that something in the system may require servicing, and the time to call the service company would be now.

We also need to pull off the covers on the condenser unit to examine the internal parts and wiring. When we discover heated wire that exhibits browning or scorching we have troubles. When parts are discolored we may have trouble starting. When we find ant beds built up over the components and wiring, we must wash out the area and wash away all the sand. Fire ants, especially, frequently build their nests here.

We also can check the air-conditioning system visually, without meters. When the compressor is operating, the large pipe should have a little condensation where it is not insulated. The small pipe is very hot, hot enough to create a burn if held for a few seconds. If these conditions, along with an apparent change in the running time of the system, are present, we have good reason to call the service company.

We can also check the airflow from the deflectors, and we can even check the temperature of the air at the deflectors as well. When the fan is operating, we must be able to feel cool or warm air by holding our hand against the deflector when it is open. More air flows from the ones that are fed from the large pipes or ducts in the attic. Less air flows from those with smaller pipes. We can also judge the airflow by the distance from the heater to a deflector. Sometimes we can also determine changes to airflow when we notice that the return air to the heater is diminished. If we use a thermometer, we can measure the air temperature at the deflectors and compare them with the approximate expected temperatures. Many systems have expected temperatures about 6 degrees below thermostat settings. The manufacturer can provide the correct expected temperature.

Alternative solutions to the problem.   There is always the obvious alternative of having a maintenance contract. When owners opt for such a contract, the workers will perform the cleaning service annually. Many owners in different parts of the country select spring or fall for this work. Where heating is much more important, owners have the work done before first frost. Where air conditioning is most important, owners have the cleaning and serving done in early spring.

We, as contractors, cannot offer many alternatives. We can meter the system for Freon levels and pressures at the compressor. We can measure airflow and locate and fix those areas that have diminished airflow. We can verify correct temperatures at the deflectors and locate the problem if the numbers are wrong.

Statement of work and the planning effort.   Let us assume that the owner wants an annual service contract. Our statement of work would be to *service the forced-air heating and air-conditioning system on an annual basis.* Specifically, we will: *clean or replace filters, clean and lubricate fans and squirrel cages, clean and service the condenser unit, make voltage, pressure, and temperature checks, as well as check airflow.* We will, as a rule, *provide the owner with a statement or checklist that shows the work done and the status of all subsystems inspected.*

For planning, we schedule the annual service call well ahead of time. In fact, when we work with established customers, we usually schedule the work order a year in advance.

Contract.   The contract used most often is a fixed-price type. Yet we can have several different styles.

Example 1.

For the service to heater and air conditioner we will replace filters, clean fans, evaporator coils, flush waste lines, oil motors as required, and generally check the operation of all subsystems.

Total cost for parts and labor is $XX.XX.

Example 2.   The form looks like a checklist. One column lists the items that can be checked, another column lists the parts replaced. A certain number of items are clustered and constitute a basic service call for annual maintenance. For this part the fee is fixed. When added work is performed, the worker simply checks off the other items and assesses the owner the amounts indicated. Using this form the owner has a year-to-year record of service and maintenance. The contractor also has a much neater database of his or her customer's system.

Material Assessment

Direct Materials	Use/Purpose
Filters	To replace old, clogged filters

Indirect Materials	**Use/Purpose**
Oil	To lubricate motors

Support Materials	**Use/Purpose**
Cleaning fluids	To clean accumulated dirt off components
Brushes and rags	Cleaning implements
Toolbox	To remove and replace parts
Short ladder	To reach higher parts, such as deflectors
Long ladder	To check the chimney
Meters	To measure voltage, pressure, etc.

Outside Contractor Support	**Use/Purpose**
None	

Activities Planning Chart

Activity	Time Line (Days)
	1 2 3 4 5 6 7
1. Annual service call	| _×_ | ___ | ___ | ___ | ___ | ___ | ___ |

Reconstruction

Annual service call.   There is no reconstruction associated with a service call for maintenance. However, there would be for an emergency service call. The service call is usually a one-person job. He or she is trained to perform all parts of the job. The time for the call ranges from about 1 to $1\frac{1}{2}$ hours. Of course, if there are two condenser units (one for upstairs and another for downstairs, for example) the job takes longer. The work is generally clean and requires no special preparation by the owner. But the owner must be at home since the worker needs to get to the heater and other inside components.

Concluding comments.   Many owners clean their heating and air-conditioning systems more frequently than annually. They change filters monthly. They lubricate motors semiannually and wash off deflectors any time there is an accumulation of dirt. Some of these ideas are appropriate and improve the operation. Some tasks need doing only annually.

We have generally described the types of work to expect from the contractor. His or her worker is trained to perform the various tasks and to spot potential troublespots. This added value may be extremely important if the detection is sound and found in the early stages of a potentially serious problem.

PROJECT 2. REMOVE AND REPLACE A WORN-OUT CENTRAL FORCED-AIR HEATING/AIR-CONDITIONING SYSTEM (GAS AND ELECTRIC)

Subcategories include: principles of gas forced-air system and electrical air-conditioning systems, components that make up a system, determining when a system is worn out, sizing the new system, testing and balancing the new system, modern electronic or computer-controlled systems, electronic ignition systems; and problems installing the replacement system.

Preliminary Discussion with the Owner

Problems facing the owner.   The life expectancy of a central gas heating system is about 15 years. The limitation is caused by the thinning of walls in the heating chamber. This iron assembly reaches temperatures above 600 degrees when the gas is fired, then cools when the flame is off. Iron filings flake off as the walls thin. At some time a hole will develop and the flames and fumes will enter the heat chamber and thus enter the house through the ducts. The air-conditioner compressor is the unit with the shortest life cycle. Although some operate for 20 years, most are warranted for only 5 years and generally operate from 8 to 12 years. Over time the control circuits can also fail, but these rarely cause a full replacement.

Alternative solutions to the problem.   When the time comes to replace the air conditioner, we must look at the heater as well. If examination shows the system to be borderline, we need to make the customer aware of the condition and recommend a full replacement. While making our inspections we need to check the energy efficiency of the house as well. We would calculate the heat loss and gain by determining the amount of glass, condition of windows and doors, amount of insulation in the walls and ceiling, and generally use our computer with its program to determine the correct size for the new heater and air conditioner.

Statement of work and the planning effort.   Our project is to *remove and replace the heating and air-conditioning system.* We also must examine the ducts and make repairs where insulation is missing and where separation has occurred.

The planning effort includes the contract preparation, negotiations with the owner on price and on the time required for installation. We must also include time to assemble the parts for the new system.

Contract.   The contract should be a fixed-price type. There should be no hidden problems and all prices should be known at the time the worksheet is prepared.

Material Assessment

Direct Materials	Use/Purpose
Air conditioner	Replacement parts
Compressor/condenser unit	
A-frame (evaporator)	
Freon lines	
Electrical service	
components	
Heater	Replacement unit
Thermostat	Control assembly
Wiring	24 volt and 120 volt
Freon gas	Coolant for air conditioner

Indirect Materials	Use/Purpose
Duct tape	To tape plenum and ducts
PVC piping	To replace the waste water line from the evaporator
Pipe cement	To seal gas pipes

Support Materials	Use/Purpose
Meters	Pressure meters and voltage meter to measure fluid, gas, and volts
Construction tools	Installation
Ladder	Working off the ground

Outside Contractor Support	Use/Purpose
None	

Activities Planning Chart

Activity	Time Line (Days)						
	1	2	3	4	5	6	7
1. Removing and replacing the system	I _×_ I	_×_ I	___ I	___ I	___ I	___ I	___ I
2. Final adjustments	I ___ I	___ I	_×_ I	___ I	___ I	___ I	___ I

Reconstruction

Removing and replacing the system.   The activity chart indicates that 2 days are needed to remove the old heating and air-conditioning system and replace it with the new one. This implies a minimum crew size of two workers. The sequence of tasks and events generally follows a set pattern:

1. Shut off the gas to the heater. If there are other appliances that use gas, these may be disabled as well.
2. Disconnect the electrical service in two places. At the outside circuit breaker, trip the 220-volt breaker marked for the air conditioner. In the inside circuit breaker, trip the one that services the heater and its controls.
3. Dismantle the heater by freeing it from the plenum, gas lines, and electrical service. Remove the heater and air conditioner A-frame (evaporator). This part of the job also requires removing the plumbing leading to the waste line for excess water and the air-conditioner lines. (Note: The Freon must be recaptured by pumping it into a tank versus letting it escape into the air.)
4. Disconnect the lines from the air conditioner at the condenser and compressor unit outside and remove it from the concrete pad it rests on. Also disconnect the electrical service. The old lines may or may not be reusable.

To install the new unit, we employ the steps listed above but in reverse order.

1. Major assemblies such as the heater and condenser unit are set in place.
2. All gas, air-conditioning, and electrical lines are connected and tested.
   a. The heater is tested for operation after the gas is turned on.
   b. The Freon is added outside and the system is tested for leaks and operation.
   c. The thermostat is readjusted as required.
3. The plumbing waste line is reestablished.
4. The plenum is refastened to the heater and all ducts are examined for fit and insulation. The chimney piping is also reset.
5. The system's airflow is examined and adjusted accordingly.

After all systems have been serviced and tested, the contractor needs to complete the paperwork, which includes the warranties and service contracts.

Concluding comments. The complexity of gas heating and air-conditioning systems precludes most homeowners from performing more than simple maintenance and troubleshooting. The remainder of the work must be done by experts who have the knowledge and skill to deal with high and low voltages, natural or bottled (propane) gas, and Freon gas.

PROJECT 3. REMOVE AND REPLACE A WORN-OUT CENTRAL HEATING/AIR-CONDITIONING SYSTEM (HEAT PUMP)

Subcategories include: expected life span of the system; determining when to replace the system; problems with removing and replacing the heater and air-conditioner components; testing the new systems; balancing the system; and the principles of a heat pump system, including auxiliary heating.

Preliminary Discussion with the Owner

Problems facing the owner.   In very basic terms, a heat pump–air conditioning system is a two-way air conditioner. When set to operate as an air conditioner, it circulates the Freon through the compressor to create a coolant. The air from the fan is forced through the evaporator coils in the house and is cooled before it moves through the ductwork. When operated as a heater, the gas in the evaporator is warmed by reversing the operation of the compressor, and as the forced air is passed through the coils, it is heated. In technical terms the heat pump draws energy from a low-temperature reservoir (sink) and transfers it to a reservoir (receiver) at a higher temperature. Figure 10–1 shows a simplified drawing. Because of the capacity limitations the heater process can produce only so much warm air. That is why the system required alternative heating sources. Most of the time this is a form of radiant heat which is produced with electrically heated coils, much like an electric stove. The forced air is passed over the coils, where it picks up the added heat called for by the control system.

The owner can do only so much maintenance and troubleshooting. The maintenance tasks include changing filters, cleaning the condenser unit, examining the wiring for problems, and oiling motors. Troubleshooting tasks include resetting tripped circuit breakers, locating inoperable fans, identifying a compressor that fails to run, the absence of electrical power to the unit, and an inoperative supplemental heating system. The owner can also detect changes in audio levels of fans, blowers, compressor unit operation, and the like. Noises always increase when bearings or other moving parts begin to wear out. Noise increases proportional to the wear.

Alternative solutions to the problem.   Because of the complexity of the heat pump system and its several subsystems, expert help is almost always required to make repairs. One alternative available to the owner is to purchase a mainte-

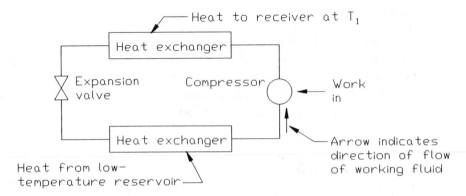

Figure 10–1   Heat pump diagram.

nance contract that includes annual maintenance of the system and a certain amount of the repairs.

A second alternative would be to replace the defective unit with an alternative heating system and air-conditioning unit. This would be drastic and probably be the solution if the heat pump system were the wrong one in the first place.

A third alternative for the owner with a heat pump system who finds the heating capacity insufficient is to supplement the system with fireplaces or electric perimeter heating.

Statement of work and the planning effort.   The contractor who would remove and replace either a subsystem or the entire heat pump system would need considerable knowledge and skill. In this project we assume that the major assemblies of the heat pump have worn out and that a newer, more efficient one needs to be installed. Our statement of work would be to *remove and replace the heating/air-conditioning system.* Further, we will *replace the system with a more efficient one.* The contractor would provide the alternative units with ratings that generally increase with increases in efficiency. The owner must make the decision regarding which to select. The judgment requires the idea of payback. The increase in efficiency of one system to another is seldom linear, although there are claims to the contrary. When a person selects a more efficient system, for example replacing one rated at 8.5 with one rated at 11, the savings in energy are relatively linear. However, selecting the one rated at 12 would not produce the same savings for the added unit; thus the payback would take longer.

The planning effort for removal and replacement would be somewhat less than that for removing and replacing a gas heater and central air conditioner. Certainly, there would be no natural or propane gas system to contend with. Since no heating gas would be employed, no special skills or problems pertaining to care and use of gas would be employed. The contractor would provide a time frame for performing the work. A team of at least two workers would usually perform the replacement.

Contract.   The type of contract well suited to this project is the fixed-price type. There should be no hidden requirements that could influence costs. The owner might need to make a down payment upon contract signing. However, many local contractors operate on the principle of a sense of understanding and trust that the owner will pay for services without fail.

Material Assessment

Direct Materials	Use/Purpose
Heat pump system	Replacement unit
Auxiliary system	Replacement unit if required

Indirect Materials	**Use/Purpose**
Duct tape	To reseal plenum and ducts
PVC piping	To divert wastewater
Assorted electrical parts	To replace connectors and circuit breakers as required

Support Materials	**Use/Purpose**
Electrical tools	For construction
Air conditioning tools	For construction
Meters	To measure voltage and pressure
Ladders	Needed if part of the unit is in the attic

Outside Contractor Support	**Use/Purpose**
None	

Activities Planning Chart

Activity	Time Line (Days)
	1 2 3 4 5 6 7
1. Removing and replacing the heat pump	I _×_ I _×_ I ___ I ___ I ___ I ___ I ___ I
2. Fine tuning the system	I ___ I ___ I _×_ I ___ I ___ I ___ I ___ I

Reconstruction

Removing and replacing the heat pump.   The workers approach the job of removing the heat pump by first removing the circuit breakers to the inside and outside units. This eliminates one potential of fatal injury. Next, they remove by the capture method the Freon from the system. After this they can break down the system into its component assemblies and begin the removal process.

1. The gas lines and electric lines are disconnected from the condenser unit outside.
2. The other ends of the gas lines are disconnected from the inside unit. Electric service is also disconnected from the 120- and 24-volt sources.
3. The plenum is freed by removing the duct tape.
4. The waste drain line is freed from the inside unit.
5. The unit is removed from the closet.
6. The lines through the attic to the outside unit are removed or cut and discarded.
7. The auxiliary heating system is removed from the duct if it needs to be replaced as well.

This list of tasks for removal is very short. The time for removing the units or assemblies is also relatively short. Two workers should have the units out in several hours.

Notice from the list that any part of the system can be removed and replaced independently. Should only one unit or assembly be defective, the workers would simply remove and replace that unit.

Installing the new unit requires placing the condenser on its concrete pad outside and placing the heater exchanger unit in the closet inside. Then either the old Freon lines are connected or a new pair of lines are placed through the attic and connected to the two units. Following this the electrical services are connected and the wastewater line is connected.

With all parts connected the workers charge the system by first evacuating the entire system. They use a pump that pulls the air out of the gas lines and other parts of the sealed subsystem. When the correct pressure is reached (about 28 to 30 psi in some units), they force the Freon gas into the system under pressure. Pressure checks, voltage checks, and other inspections are performed before applying power. Once the power is applied, further checks prescribed by the manufacturer are done.

Postinstallation checks.   Frequently, one of the workers or the contractor will make a postinstallation check. Temperatures, voltages, and pressures will be remeasured and adjusted if required. Airflow will be checked. Heating and cooling will be checked. Finally, the system will be certified as acceptable. At this time the contractor will usually provide the owner with completed warranties and service agreements.

Concluding comments.   The heat pump/air conditioning system is a complex design that produces comfort for environmental surroundings. We must recognize that most owners should perform routine maintenance to ensure proper operation and long-life operation of the system. He or she should also be able to perform the troubleshooting checks we have identified in this project. Beyond this, a defective system should be turned over to the experts. They will use their meters and make other checks to locate the problem quickly and efficiently and effect a solution. Most trouble calls include a fixed rate or approximately $50. However, the price of the call is often lumped in with the total labor bills when the workers must secure parts.

PROJECT 4. REMOVE AND REPLACE A WORN-OUT CENTRAL HEATING SYSTEM (HOT WATER AND STEAM)

Subcategories include: principles of design of the system; components of the system; task lists performed by specialists; service checks and tests of the system, and problems installing a replacement system that must be solved.

Preliminary Discussion with the Owner

Problems facing the owner.   Hot-water and steam heating systems are closed systems. This means that the water in the system recirculates and in the process is either heated (for hot water) or raised to a temperature to create steam in the furnace in a boiler. The heated water is piped to radiators that perform the job of warming the air in the room. The various units used in the system and for distribution are shown in Figure 10–2. Different units used to distribute the heat into the rooms are as follows.

1. *Forced hot water:* units may be radiant baseboard, convector baseboards, or radiant heat.
2. *Forced hot water or steam:* convector cabinets.
3. *Hot water or steam:* cast iron radiators.

Problems the owner can face range from the very simple, where the furnace shuts down and fails to heat the water, to the most severe, where the lines corrode

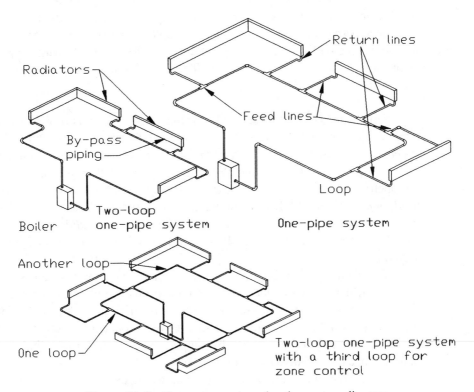

Figure 10–2   Hot-water or steam heating system diagram.

and must be replaced. Other problems include a defective control unit that monitors the water temperature, defective thermostats, inoperative radiators and convectors, and a worn-out boiler.

The furnace can be coal burning, gas fired, or one that burns home heating oil. Coal-burning furnaces must be cleaned, and over time the grates need replacing. A gas furnace needs periodic servicing by experts from a contractor or gas company. Oil-burning furnaces also require periodic servicing to ensure that burning elements are safe to continue to use.

Alternative solutions to the problem.   The owner can perform several maintenance tasks and inspections of the system. But for most owners, removing and replacing damaged or defective parts requires the skill and knowledge of an expert. He or she will have the proper tools to make safe solder joints, properly fit pipes and check for leaks, be able to remove the boiler and other parts in the furnace, and the like.

Since these systems are so integrated in the structure of the house, we seldom chose to replace them with other types, such as heat pumps and forced air. However, we can make substitutions when the price and utility of one fuel is more reasonable and cleaner to use. We might also select another fuel to reduce the work associated with firing and cleaning. For example, a coal-fired furnace requires stoking the furnace with coal and taking out the ashes. Replacing the furnace with a gas- or oil-burning unit reduces the work. The owner would select one based on the price of oil or gas.

Statement of work and the planning effort.   In this project we will just purge the system and change the type of furnace for efficiency purposes. Our first statement of work is to *remove the old furnace and boiler and replace it with either a gas-fired unit or an oil burner.* While the furnace is out of the way and the pipes are open, we will *purge the lines and radiators or convectors with appropriate fluids and pressure.* While performing these jobs, we should also *verify the control devices on radiators, air locks, and convectors, and ensure that convector fins are clean.* Over time dust and grime block the fins and thus reduce the efficiency of the system.

The planning effort begins with the estimator and contractor answering a call from the owner. They ask questions about the problem and type of heating system. With this knowledge they make an on-site inspection. For our project we discuss the options with the owner and he or she makes the decision whether to convert to gas or oil. We aid in the decision by supplying cost data for installation, maintenance, and average daily cost of operation.

Once we define the job, we prepare an estimate of the costs associated with each of the statements of work to arrive at the total cost. Due to the nature of this job, we expect to price the job using two workers. Overall this should help keep costs somewhat contained. After reaching agreement with the owner on contract specifications and price, we contact suppliers for parts and assemblies; then we schedule the workers.

The owner might need to move out of the house if the work is done in the dead of winter, since the work could take 3 to 4 days. However, if the work is done in fall, spring, or summer, there should only be minimum interference with the owner and his or her family while workers are on the job.

Contract.　If we were just removing and replacing the furnace and boiler, we could easily provide a fixed-price contract. However, we need to purge the lines and perform work on the radiators or convectors as well, and these tasks can result in added costs when problems happen. In addition, we would need to install an oil tank for oil or have the gas company install a new gas meter and pipe from the street to the house.

Therefore, we would probably offer a limited fixed-price contract with several clauses of time-and-materials type. This provides the owner with a known cost for most of the work and a variable cost with limits for the unknown work that may be encountered.

Material Assessment

Direct Materials	Use/Purpose
Furnace	To replace the old one
Boiler	To replace the old one
Oil storage tank and lines	If oil-fired furnace is installed
Gas meter and gas lines	If gas-fired furnace is installed
Water and chemicals	To replenish water and neutralize the water
Control units	Thermostats and sensors

Indirect Materials	Use/Purpose
Purging fluid	To clean lines
Convector fin cleaner	Solvent to clean fins
Solder and flux	To solder copper pipes

Support Materials	Use/Purpose
Toolbox	For installing the new system

Outside Contractor Support	Use/Purpose
Gas company	Installs the gas service if gas is used
Oil company	Delivers oil if oil is used

Activities Planning Chart

Activity	Time Line (Days)						
	1	2	3	4	5	6	7
1. Removing and replacing the furnace	| _×_ | _×_ | _×_ | ___ | ___ | ___ | ___ |
2. Servicing the radiators or convectors	| ___ | _×_ | _×_ | ___ | ___ | ___ | ___ |
3. Operating and checking the system	| ___ | ___ | _×_ | _×_ | ___ | ___ | ___ |

Reconstruction

Removing and replacing the furnace. The first of many tasks that we must perform with the removal and replacement of the furnace is to shut off the fuel, disconnect the lines, and remove the circuit breaker that supplies voltage to the controls in the furnace. When this is accomplished, we can begin the removal process. Since the boiler is customarily found inside the furnace above the burners, we would remove the boiler at the same time. This means that we must break into the closed system. Most of the systems use copper piping and sweated joints at elbows, unions, and couplings, for example. Our way of breaking into the system would be to heat a joint and separate the pipe from the elbow or coupling.

Once the system is open we would drain what water we can to eliminate puddling and flooding the basement. After this we dismantle the furnace and remove the boiler.

We replace the old unit with the new one. We install either a new boiler, or if the old one is still good, we reinstall it. We generally follow the manufacturer's recommendation for installation and connect the boiler in place. We resolder the pipes, reconnect the fuel line and electrical service to the control system, and fill the system with chemically freed water. Most of the time the water line is attached with a one-way valve that lets water in but blocks water from backing out of the system. As water is allowed into the system, air is allowed to escape until no more air is in the boiler and pipes. In steam systems regulators or expansion valves are installed to prevent excess steam pressure. New ones are installed at the same time that a new system is installed.

After all parts are installed, we test the system. We check for proper operation of the furnace. We check for water leaks and proper boiler operation. Since the system may take 4 hours or more to produce heat, we would need to make an inspection the following day.

Purging the system. When the system is open, we have the chance to purge the pipes and radiators or convectors. We can apply a cleaning solution under pressure into the pipe and back flush the old water and buildup of contaminates, rust, and the like. Several repeats of the process are usually done to clear all pipes and radiators.

Concluding comments. We have shown that considerable skill and knowledge are required to service and replace the hot-water and steam-heated system. Most owners cannot perform the various jobs, partly because they lack the skills and tools, but also because the work needs to be certified to meet insurance coverage. The job can be expensive. The work may take 3 or more days and the disruption to the household could require temporary lodging elsewhere or use of alternative heat, such as a fireplace and space heaters.

Certain maintenance tasks can and should be performed by the owner. Making checks of controls, changing filters and screens in oil lines, checking for water in the oil tank, and cleaning radiators and fins in convectors are some of the usual tasks.

CHAPTER SUMMARY

This chapter provided us with an examination of several different environmental control systems that we more commonly call heating and air conditioning. Each system is a complex assembly of subassemblies and parts that collectively create warm air or cool air in the home. Almost all systems employ some form of closed assembly. A system might contain water or steam, it might contain Freon, or it might be electric or gas. Each of these is safe as long as the system is operating as designed. But each is very dangerous when safety features are bypassed or are inoperative.

Some owners can remove and replace defective subassemblies, assemblies, and parts. Some can use the meters required to restore proper standards or measures. But owners who lack these basic understandings and skills need to use the services of a skilled worker and his or her company to maintain the unit. In this way, both correct operation and safe operation are assured.

APPENDIX:
CROSS-REFERENCE
TROUBLESHOOTING LIST

This troubleshooting reference list should make it easy to pinpoint the problems a contractor or homeowner may have with the interior of the house. First, select the major area of the problem from column 1 (these are in chapter sequence). Then search the middle column to locate the more accurate description of the problem. Then refer to the last column for the project number in the chapter where details associated with the problem are discussed. Even though the subject of the project may be different than that of the problem, the problem is a subcategory of the project, and therefore some detail is provided for understanding and solution.

Major Topic	Specific Problem	Project Number
Walls and ceilings (Chapter 1)	Cracks in plaster	7
	Damaged wainscot finish	4
	Damaged wallpaper	6
	Exposed nails	2
	Exposed seams	2
	Hole in drywall	2
	Holes in plaster	7
	Loose or torn wallpaper	6

Major Topic	**Specific Problem**	**Project Number**
	Loose plaster	7
	Loose wood paneling	3
	Loosened panel molding	3
	Painting the walls	3
	Stained walls	5
	Touching up wall paint	5
Ceilings (Chapter 2)	Drywall over plaster ceiling	2
	Replacing ceiling molding	3
	Replacing ceiling supports	4
	Replacing drop ceiling panels	4
	Replacing electrical fixtures	4
	Replacing tiles in a ceiling	3
	Stained ceiling	1
Floors (Chapter 3)	Broken asphalt tile squares	4
	Buckled vinyl flooring	3
	Cleaning brick floors	6
	Damaged carpet	5
	Damaged vinyl flooring	3
	Grouting ceramic/clay tiles	6
	Improper underlayment	3
	Loose carpet	5
	Loose ceramic/clay tiles	6
	Loose flooring over concrete	1
	Making floors even	1
	Resealing marble flooring	6
	Resealing parquet floors	2
	Resecuring parquet floors	2
	Re-tuck-pointing mortar joints	6
	Refinishing wood floors	1
	Removing stains from wood floors	1
	Replacing damaged parquet blocks	2
	Sagging floors	1
	Squeaky floors	1
	Stained marble floor	6
	Stained or marred parquet blocks	2
	Stained terrazzo floor	6
	Surface protecting brick floors	6
	Worn-out sealant on terrazzo	6
Doors and door units (Chapter 4)	Badly fitting door	1
	Bifold door knobs off	5

Major Topic	Specific Problem	Project Number
	Bifold door off track and hinges	5
	Bifold doors do not fit	5
	Damaged interior door unit	3
	Door badly stained	2
	Door delaminated or separates	2
	Door needs refinishing	2
	Door won't close	1
	Door won't lock	1
	Loose door stops	4
	Loose door trim	4
	Loose hinges	1
	Pocket door does not close	6
	Pocket door jamb damaged	6
	Pocket door off track	6
	Split frame and poor fit	3
	Split jamb	4
Interior trim (Chapter 5)	Damaged baseboard molding	1
	Damaged or loose ceiling molding	3
	Damaged shoe molding	1
	Damaged window sills	2
	Loose window trim	2
	Repainting molding and trim	3
	Taking play out of window sash	2
Electric service and lighting (Chapter 6)	Defective circuit breaker	1
	Defective entry bell or chime	3
	Defective outlets	1
	Inoperable range hood	2
	Inoperative switches	1
Plumbing (Chapter 7)	Blocked commode	1
	Broken commode	1
	Corroded waste lines	2
	Damaged water faucet	2
	Gas won't light in heater	3
	Inoperable dishwasher	4
	Inoperable garbage disposal	4
	Inoperable ice maker	4
	Leaking faucet	2
	Leaking waste lines	2
	Leaking water lines	2
	Leaking water tank	1

Major Topic	Specific Problem	Project Number
	Leaky hot water heater	3
	No hot water from water heater	3
	Problem with dishwasher lines	2
Staircases (Chapter 8)	Broken or cracked stringer	1
	Damaged moldings	1
	Damaged riser boards	1
	Damaged stair treads	1
	Loose and dangerous carpet	3
	Loose banister	1
	Loose newel post and spindles	1
	Marred staircase wood parts	2
	Refinishing staircases	2
	Squeaky stairs	1
	Stained staircase wood	2
	Worn-out carpet on stairs	3
Wood cabinets and counters (Chapter 9)	Adjustable shelves are broken	2
	Back-splash is damaged	4
	Badly fitting cabinet doors	1
	Cabinet exterior damaged and scarred	5
	Cabinet exterior faded and dull	5
	Ceramic tiles are loose or cracked	3
	Door catches are broken	1
	Doors on cabinet will not close	1
	Doors stick and won't open	1
	Drawers and roll-out shelves don't work right	2
	Grout is missing or stained	3
	Handles and pulls are broken	1
	Loose cabinet door hinges	1
	Old countertop is marred or burned	4
	Paint on cabinets is stained	5
	Plastic laminate is loose	5
	Plastic top needs replacing	4
	Rot and decay under ceramic tiles	3
	Rotating corner unit is inoperable	2
	Seal is worn off ceramic tile grout	3
	Sink rim needs replacing	4
Environmental systems (Chapter 10)	Air conditioner blows hot air	2
	Baseboard convectors do not radiate	4
	Boiler will not heat	4

Major Topic	Specific Problem	Project Number
	Checking airflow	1
	Checking compressor operation	1
	Checking for a worn-out gas heater	2
	Checking waste lines	1
	Cleaning filters	1
	Compressor won't operate	3
	Convectors are clogged with dirt	4
	Corrosion in heating system	4
	Forced-air fan motor inoperative	3
	Furnace does not work	4
	Gas furnace won't ignite	2
	Heat pump won't cool	3
	Hot-water heater does not heat	4
	Inoperative air-conditioning system	2
	Inoperative auxiliary heat system	3
	Inoperative gas furnace	2
	Inoperative heat pump	3
	Lubricating fan motors	1
	No steam for heating	4
	Poor operation of a gas furnace	2
	Radiators knock	4
	Servicing forced-air system	1
	Tracing leaks	1

INDEX